MW00697883

Cities at the End of the World

Cities at the End of the World

Using Utopian and Dystopian Stories to Reflect Critically on our Political Beliefs, Communities, and Ways of Life

David J. Lorenzo

Bloomsbury Academic
An imprint of Bloomsbury Publishing Inc

BLOOMSBURY
NEW YORK • LONDON • OXFORD • NEW DELHI • SYDNEY

Bloomsbury Academic

An imprint of Bloomsbury Publishing Inc

1385 Broadway   50 Bedford Square
New York   London
NY 10018   WC1B 3DP
USA   UK

www.bloomsbury.com

BLOOMSBURY and the Diana logo are trademarks of Bloomsbury Publishing Plc

First published 2014
Paperback edition first published 2016

© David J. Lorenzo, 2014

All rights reserved. No part of this publication may be reproduced or transmitted in any
form or by any means, electronic or mechanical, including photocopying, recording, or
any information storage or retrieval system, without prior permission in writing from the
publishers.

No responsibility for loss caused to any individual or organization acting on or refraining
from action as a result of the material in this publication can be accepted by Bloomsbury or
the author.

Library of Congress Cataloging-in-Publication Data
Lorenzo, David J., 1961–
Cities at the end of the world : using utopian and dystopian stories to reflect critically
on our political beliefs, communities, and ways of life / David J. Lorenzo.
pages cm
ISBN 978-1-4411-4155-2 (hardback)
1. Utopias.   2. Dystopias.   3. World politics–21st century.
4. Political science–Philosophy.   I. Title.
HX806.L67   2014
321'.07—dc23
2013042964

ISBN: HB: 978-1-4411-4155-2
PB: 978-1-5013-1770-5
ePub: 978-1-4411-4256-6
ePDF: 978-1-4411-4423-2

Typeset by Newgen Knowledge Works (P) Ltd., Chennai, India

Contents

Acknowledgments

My interest in the subject of utopias and dystopias was originally piqued in the early 1980s by a class at the University of Arkansas taught by the late Diane Blair, titled "Politics and Literature." The required reading list included *Utopia*, *Brave New World* and *Nineteen Eighty-Four*, three works that immediately caught my attention. I fortunately received the opportunity to pursue this interest at Arkansas when Conrad Waligorski, assisted by Robert Savage, agreed to direct my honors project on George Orwell. At Yale, David Apter looked kindly upon my interest in utopias and encouraged me to write my dissertation on the Aurobindo movement. Consequently, I spent five months in India living in a utopian community, which eventually resulted in a book on Auroville. My deepest thanks to all these scholars for sharing their hard-earned knowledge and passion for these subjects.

My thanks also to the students in my Politics and Literature classes at Virginia Wesleyan College, the syllabus for which informs this book. Additional thanks go to fellow faculty members who provided useful feedback on my talk "Rethinking Politics through Utopian and Dystopian Stories," sponsored by the Faculty Forum at Virginia Wesleyan. My gratitude as well to Sarah Tytler of Virginia Wesleyan for reading and providing comments on an early draft of the book, and to Shannon Seylor for doing the same with the final version. I would also like to acknowledge the Batten Endowed Teaching Fund at Virginia Wesleyan College for research funding, and the National Science Council of the Republic of China (Taiwan) for providing the resources for a visiting appointment in the Department of Diplomacy at the National Chengchi University. My thanks also to Dean Chung-chian Teng of the College of International Affairs and Chair Ren-rang Chyou of the Department of Diplomacy at the National Chengchi University for their support and encouragement.

Notes on Reading the Text

While located in separate chapters and capable of standing alone, the discussions of these stories are meant to be read in pairs: *Utopia* with *Isle of Pines*, *Looking Backward* with *News from Nowhere*, and *We* with *Nineteen Eighty-Four*.

Introduction

Cities at the end of the world

Thinking through the fundamental elements of politics is always timely, but it is especially so now. Every 30 to 40 years nations rethink themselves. Understandings based on new experiences and events overthrow the prior cluster of views, which were themselves generated and shaped by the experiences of previous generations. The West in general and the United States in particular is now at one of these points. The rethinking generated in the 1960s, which itself replaced the views of the generation that experienced the Depression and World War II, is outmoded. The same is true of the variety of criticisms of this view. We no longer need to come to grips with the Cold War and Vietnam. We are dealing with the triumph of both sides of the culture wars—the right has prevailed in outlawing the consumption of most intoxicating substances, resulting in a high rate of incarceration and the perpetuation of drug wars. The left has triumphed in terms of redefining privacy and expression, ironically resulting in a reinforcement of capitalism's privileging of individualism, a deterioration of public and social solidarity, and a fierce conflict with the government over security requirements in an age of possible terrorist threats.

Consequently, the dichotomies that generated political debates over the past several decades do not necessarily make sense of our political and social environments. Debates over foreign policy take place in the context of American unipolar dominance rather than a bipolar world. Rather than arguing over whether big government or the private sector can deal more effectively with the problems of generating economic growth, eliminating poverty, providing health care, and educating our children, we are faced with the failure of both to perform these tasks and the need to redefine economic well-being and the good life. The science fiction fantasies of computers and technology are now real, as are the economic possibilities of everyone living a relatively affluent life. We inhabit a more economically integrated and culturally pluralistic world than 40 years ago, all the while facing important problems involving pollution, the depletion of global resources, and probable climate change.

I propose that part of our confrontation with these problems be a reading and consideration of the utopian and dystopian stories that previously played important roles in fundamental political debates. The title of this book refers to the idea that utopian and dystopian stories often describe endings. "The ends of the world" refers importantly to frontiers, in that these stories exist at the limits of our imagination. Ends can also signify the completion of historical journeys, trips that can conclude badly or well. In yet another sense, endings can be the termination of things. Poverty, war, or alienation may cease to exist. But it could be that it is freedom, civilization, or the essential nature of humans that expires. Endings can be good or bad, the result of much hard work and planning, the culmination of a large process, or the outcome of a fortuitous or unfortunate accident. All are relevant to thinking about politics.

As exercises of imagination, accounts of completed journeys or processes and descriptions of how some things may cease to be, utopian and dystopian stories in particular address fundamental questions and dilemmas of life that are important to consideration of the issues and problems we now face. Most importantly, they address the problems of life lived collectively. They are concerned with the dilemmas of the city rather than of a scattered existence, of politics rather than just of individuals. In discussing cities at the end of the world, we engage in a conversation about fundamental political understandings and assumptions. What works and what doesn't work economically, politically, and socially? What is relevant about human nature in the context of community life? What does it mean to live a good life in a polity? What problems of our shared existence can be solved and which must we live with or work around? How do we avoid tyranny, disorder, and terror? How might we live in peace, prosperity, and freedom?

Utopian and dystopian stories are therefore useful because in focusing on ends, they explore fundamental propositions and assumptions and raise these types of important questions in interesting and accessible ways. They also provide a foundational set of dichotomies that allows us to sharpen our vision and develop our critical capacities. On the one side are narratives that describe how we can provide ourselves with radically better lives. They portray societies in which people are secure, happy, and often (though not always) free. These stories allow us to contemplate whether problems and conditions we consider unsolvable might be subject to resolution. On the other side are stories that alert us to the fact that even the ordinary quest for a good life contains trends that can overwhelm us. They depict societies that allegedly provide justice, security, and freedom, but deliver instead a radically unsatisfying and usually terrifying existence.

Given the need to rethink our understanding of politics, a case could be made for only reading utopias. We wish, after all, to make politics and society better. Utopias provide models of the good state, a good economy, and more generally the good life. But one should not consider one set of stories without the other. Dystopias remind us that utopias can be cloaks for all sorts of political treachery. More's Utopia may turn out like Zamyatin's One State; Bellamy's creation may lead us to the uncivilized conditions Neville describes. Rethinking requires not only models of what we desire and how to attain it, but also explorations of what we don't want and how such undesirable situations may arise, given existing contexts.

As indicated above, these stories pose a plethora of useful, indeed crucial questions: What tasks should government perform? What do we fear most? Now that we have the technical means to live well physically, what constitutes the good life and how is that life related to our political and economic systems? Is the quest for a perfect place dangerous? What, at bottom, is human nature? Is it preset, formable, programmable? Is it good to be socially constructed, or should we somehow strive to preserve some sort of natural existence? Is the provision of material security conducive to order and the good life, or does it spur degeneration, a lack of discipline, and the loss of productivity? What accounts for disorder and are there ways of dramatically reducing the amount of disorder we experience? Is civilization something we should strive to maintain and push forward, or is it a dangerously artificial existence that empowers states and ultimately robs us of our humanity? Each of these questions in turn raises other questions and issues. What kind of government do we want? What type of economy? What type of good life? Can we eliminate parties, factions, and politics as usual? How should we deal with disorderly people? How do we motivate people to work, and do we need to do so? At what point do collective arrangements endanger the level of individual identity and freedom necessary to live a good and truly human life? What roles do justice, equality, and freedom play in our understanding of the good life?

There is no universally accepted set of answers to any of these questions. While I have my own favored positions, the intention of this book is not to persuade readers to adopt them. It would be a simpler and less contentious world if everyone did gravitate to the same answers. But that is not the world we live in. Rather, my purpose is to encourage readers to think about these questions anew as they pursue formal and informal educational endeavors. Being aware of where we stand, what assumptions we hold, what analyses we accept, what we fear most and desire most keenly is valuable knowledge to possess in a world of inescapable pluralism and inevitably knotty problems.

Discussing utopias and dystopias

Given these aims, this discussion has particular characteristics that differentiate it from other treatments of utopias and dystopias. It analyzes these stories as political literature; that is, it discusses them as examples of political philosophy. Unlike most brief academic studies, it addresses several stories rather than one; however, it does not seek to provide an encyclopedic overview of either genre.[1] It provides far more discussion of each story than is possible with such an approach. It is not a reader of these stories, nor does it contain long passages from them. It likewise does not set out to explore in depth the utopian or dystopian temperament or philosophical stance, but to grapple with the message of each story. In doing so, it covers stories that are written and set in a large variety of contexts, contain very different messages, and spin out disparate philosophies; it also addresses stories that are famous and lesser known. Set in chronological order, the stories discussed are Thomas More's *Utopia*, Henry Neville's *Isle of Pines*, Edward Bellamy's *Looking Backward*, William Morris's *News from Nowhere*, Evgenie Zamyatin's *We*, and George Orwell's *Nineteen Eighty-Four*.

This approach allows us room to investigate, compare, contrast, think about, and generally explore the questions these stories generate. Given that focus, we see that there are interesting similarities and differences among the stories. Both *Utopia* and *News from Nowhere*, for example, think that greed can be mastered. Likewise *We* and *Nineteen Eighty-Four* are concerned with outside interference in humans' abilities to process information. But there is also a great deal of variety both within and across the genres. Neville is concerned by the potential loss of civilization, while Zamyatin fears that civilization may proceed too far. More and Bellamy argue that leisure is what allows humans to fulfill their potential, while Morris argues that it is labor that allows humans to construct themselves and Neville sees too much leisure as the enemy of civilization. Orwell fears the loss of rationality and the impact of that loss on individual autonomy, while Zamyatin depicts mathematical logic as potentially hegemonic and dangerous to such autonomy. More sees important improvements coming about through the training of people in morality, while Zamyatin and Orwell dread what might be done to the insides of people through attempts at programming them.

It is up to us to decide which of these positions to accept. Are institutional changes or attempts at programming and thereby socially constructing citizens the most important for positive change or the most important thing to fear? Is civilization good or bad for us as humans? Should we go forward or backward in our search for a better way of life? Does the provision of material security allow us to remove most problems and conflicts and set the stage for better, more cultured citizens, or does ease breed intractable problems of its own, including the loss of science and civilization and the dangerous empowerment of the state? Is it possible to have a collective economy and significant negative individual freedoms? One cannot have an informed view of politics without coming to grips with questions of this type and confronting the arguments and assumptions that underpin them.

The literature on utopias and dystopias

While I do not provide an exhaustive discussion of the literature on these genres, nor of the literature on the particular stories treated here, it is necessary to touch on some important questions regarding the nature of utopias and dystopias.

It is important to note that the very vocabulary by which utopian and dystopian stories are described is contested, as Levitas and Claeys among others have documented.[2] I provide a set of definitions to settle terms. As used here, *utopian stories* are tales told about imagined communities that provide through their organization of political, economic, and social matters a superior way of living when compared to contemporary communities. As Frye among others notes, the message of the utopian story is two-fold.[3] First, in revealing the better community, such stories seek to delegitimize through comparison and often blunt condemnation the organization and living conditions of contemporary society. Second, these stories support fundamental alterations to society in the direction of the institutions and practices described in the utopian community.

To reveal a utopian community as promising a better life is to attempt to persuade people to think about how the problems that community is said to resolve can be addressed concretely. Most famously, Bellamy's *Looking Backward* became the catalyst for the formation of political clubs meant to initiate change.

Several related types of stories are loosely associated with the utopian genre. As defined here, *dystopian stories* are stories that serve as warnings regarding the future of contemporary society. They take what their authors perceive as problematic trends and by projecting those trends into the future (or onto another location) lay out their consequences in the form of societies that produce highly undesirable ways of life. *Anti-utopias* are a type of dystopian story whose warnings serve to oppose utopianism in both its literary and philosophical forms.[4] That is, they oppose the projects of searching for and devising radically different and more perfect social, political, and economic institutions and of advocating fundamental changes in the ways we understand and organize our lives. Anti-utopian stories make good this opposition by depicting the unforeseen and perverse results of radical reform and by generally illustrating the futility of fundamental changes, thus employing important elements of conservative rhetoric.[5] Dystopias, in general, warn us against what is already present in our society and deliver the message that the deepening of problematic trends must be resisted, possibly through radical reform. Anti-utopias identify radical change and the striving for perfection as one of the problematic trends. So where *Nineteen Eighty-Four* is a generic dystopia, Zamyatin's *We* and Neville's *Isle of Pines* are dystopias that take an anti-utopian form.

A final alternative form is a *satirical utopia*. This is a story of a community whose substance mirrors and distorts the institutions and practices of contemporary society for the purposes of ridicule. It does not, however, provide explicit ways of dealing with the absurdity of those institutions and practices. Such stories, therefore, perform the first function of utopian stories, but only implicitly perform the second and do so not by depicting a perfect society, but by painting a community that is manifestly undesirable. Its orientation toward change is more ambiguous than is the case with most utopian stories. Though not addressed at length here, I do on occasion reference *Erewhon*, which is a good example of a satirical utopia.

We can usefully generalize about these genres by observing that utopias emphasize the proposition that existing institutions are dysfunctional and the current understanding of the good life wrong, incomplete, or harmful. They reject the usual charge that to be utopian is to be impractical and usually criticize existing political, economic, and social institutions as unreasonable and contrary to common sense. Their authors claim to be the true realists and hold that conventional society is founded upon grave mistakes.[6] They argue that the prevailing wisdom erroneously takes central problems and harmful conditions as natural or intractable, then point the way toward resolving or transcending those problems or conditions. Far from only engaging in wistful dreaming, utopian stories often emphasize knowledge, understanding, and insight, as well as hope and reform.

Dystopian stories, meanwhile, are often set closer in space and time to their author's home. They point to trends that will lead to severe problems in the future. They stress that the good life, as we know it, is in danger because the future will see a vast deterioration of current conditions. In the case of dystopias that function as satires of utopias, they also argue that influential understandings of the good life are flawed and will eventually lead to disaster. Such stories underline the existence of contradictions between values and practices and emphasize the importance of irony and tragedy in human affairs. So where utopias point to the future as potentially providing a better way of life, dystopias argue that we may face a future in which life is much worse than is currently the case.

Given this discussion, it is important to keep in mind that utopias are not just about distant and perfect societies, nor are dystopias only about future hellholes. Both have strong roots in their author's contemporary society. Both act as critiques of existing institutions and generally call for changes in social relations, economics, and politics. The difference is first that utopias emphasize the point that problems can be overcome by common sense, while dystopias argue for the application of an often ironic sensibility to undermine the complacent acceptance of dangerous trends; second, utopias provide possible answers to their criticisms while dystopias concentrate on spinning out current undesirable trends to illustrate their malign potential. One must infer solutions from the latter rather than reading about such solution in action. For example, Neville implies that we require challenges and virtues to remain civilized while Zamyatin appears to argue that we should reconsider civilization as a human project. But neither puts forward those explicit solutions to the problems they identify, nor demonstrates how those solutions would work in practice.

Despite some readings of them as such, neither utopians nor dystopias are automatically progressive or conservative in character, nor can we always infer quickly the politics of the authors from their work. Thomas More, the father of modern utopias and an apparent proponent of change, proposes conservative solutions to problems as he looks back fondly to the closely integrated communities of the Middle Ages that he saw under attack by new economic forms. Morris, while a socialist, attempts to recapture the ethos and much of the structure of an earlier age in his utopian romance. Orwell was a socialist who wrote dystopias as warnings against an unreformed present and advocated many progressive policies that latter-day readers mistakenly think he rejected. Zamyatin embraced Bolshevism even while he wrote a book critical of technology, progress, and civilization.

Understandings of human nature

inherently selfish, greedy, power hungry

modern society has molded human nature

The most important element of any philosophical story, whether utopian, dystopian, or other, is its understanding of human nature. As I discuss each story, I emphasize the understanding of humans found within it. Is human nature depicted as fixed or fluid? Are humans portrayed as reacting differently under different circumstances or do they always act in the same way no matter their environment? Can individuals change the way they react to particular circumstances? Can actors outside them change how people react to particular circumstances? What are the causes of crime and other forms of disorder? What are humans' orientations toward work? How do they fulfill themselves? Can and should they be socially constructed?

Adopting the terminology used by some who discuss this question, I refer to humans as depicted in these stories as being in varying measures *hardwired* or *programmable*. We can think about these in terms of the continuum provided below. To be hardwired means that human reactions are immutable. At the extreme (symbolized by the left terminal point of the continuum), this would mean that humans will always operate in the same fashion no matter their circumstances. Put them in any environment, in any economic system, in any stage of civilization, and they will be greedy, or altruistic, or violent. Such traits are naturally and ineradicably part of being human. To be programmable, on the other hand, at the extreme means that there is no inherent human nature. Humans are completely mutable, either because they adapt themselves to their environments or because they are completely molded or constructed by their environment or other outside actors. This latter description of humans is not meant to sever the connection between environment, stimuli, or circumstances on the one hand and human behavior on the other; it is rather meant to convey the notion that there may be many different connections between human behavior and a particular type of environment, and that these connections can be created by humans.

No story considered here understands humans in either of these extremes. As we see below, they fall into two groups along the spectrum:

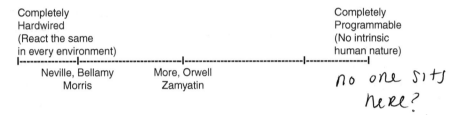

Completely Hardwired (React the same in every environment)

Completely Programmable (No intrinsic human nature)

|------------------|---------------------------|--------------------------------|-------------------|

Neville, Bellamy   More, Orwell
Morris   Zamyatin

no one sits here?

The first group asserts that humans are mainly hardwired. In many cases, the way humans react to particular kinds of environments cannot be changed, and they are moldable only on the margins. But in this humans are importantly not impervious to *changes* in their environments. Change environments and human behavior will correspondingly change even if they have not been molded differently in many significant ways. The trick therefore is to find and create the environment that corresponds to the behavior that one wishes to elicit, or conversely to identify what it is about current or emerging environments that will lead to disaster and eliminate those unhelpful elements. Bellamy puts this most clearly in his story of the rosebush, but the same understanding can be seen in Neville's discussion of environmental challenges and Morris's arguments regarding climates created by civilization and industrialization.

This position on human nature is sometimes attributed to all utopian stories. But as we see, it is not associated purely with utopians, as dystopians can also adopt it. Nor do all utopians adhere to this position. Thomas More is sometimes associated with it, but that is an error, as we shall see. It is also important to note that members of this group attribute some behavior to culture and general training. But this factor is subordinated to hardwiring and its relationships with particular environments.

For the second group, training and programming are much more important. More trains his Utopians to disdain gold and jewels. Orwell and Zamyatin point to problematic attempts to program humans so that they become obedient servants of the state. Yet hardwiring is still important for these authors. More's Utopia is successful due in large part to society's careful understanding of the hardwired desires for material security and leisure, as well as to environmental reinforcements of morality. Zamyatin identifies inbred and conflicting desires for freedom and security as important for understanding the human condition, while Orwell argues that humans at bottom will always be processors of information and locates in humans problematic desires for certainty.

These differences in how human nature is characterized are important to the messages contained in the stories. The more hardwired humans are said to be, the simpler the prescriptions for the good life that are to be found. But to say that hardwiring is more important than programming also narrows options and places a premium on getting the environment exactly right. Likewise the more amenable humans are to programming, the more they are able artificially to construct themselves to adapt to different environments, holding open the potential for eliminating environment and circumstances as obstacles to their happiness. But such mutability equally makes possible the distortion of humans and opens humans' interior life to the manipulation of states and leaders, as Zamyatin and Orwell note. Completely programmable humans potentially have no privacy, no thoughts, no autonomy, no dreams of their own, and can be constructed to the order of outside actors.

Of equal significance are the types of hardwiring and potential for programming to which these authors point. Can we trust outside programming of any kind, even if it does not rise to the level that Orwell and Zamyatin caution against? How much should we allow government agencies, society, culture or civilization to program us? Do they program us, and if they do, do they make us more or less human and create for us a better or worse life? Likewise, the identification of our irreversible and innate attributes is important for these stories and for our rethinking of politics in terms of particular environments. Do we innately and inevitably crave material security? Do we find fulfillment in leisure or in work? Do we require challenges to live a good life? Will we be happy only if we are allowed to choose our work? Only if we can choose what we consume? Only if we can choose our lifeplans? What part of ourselves poses the greatest danger? Is it our desire for certainty? Our quest for security? Or is it our greed, or our lack of self-motivation? Are we inherently disorderly or does disorder arise from environmental causes?

While each story lays out a series of questions to ponder, each also has what I argue is a core problem that I discuss at greater length than others. This is both because these questions are inherently interesting and because they are particularly relevant to thinking through contemporary issues and examining relevant contemporary assumptions. For *Utopia*, the question is the morality and utility of providing material security to all citizens. More holds that such security is everyone's due and the most important factor in the attainment and maintenance of stability and order in a community. For *Isle of Pines*, the issue is the human response to a lack of environment challenges and the allegations that material security leads to a deterioration of civilization and the need for a government that promotes virtues. For *Looking Backward*, the most important theme is the morality and practicality of maintaining both a collective economy that guarantees everyone an equal share of the nation's income and a very significant degree of individual freedoms. *News from Nowhere* is about free and easy wandering in the context of constructing ourselves through work, as well as how we can attain a green existence by rolling back the economy and state some 400 years. Finally, *We* is about the dangers of social construction of humans brought about by civilization and the desire for security and *Nineteen Eight-Four* is a warning regarding the dangers of fanaticism and the underlying desire for certainty that allows leaders to gather and exercise power in an unaccountable fashion.

Contemporary problems

Still better than socialism!

Before engaging with these stories, it is useful to rehearse the types of problems we now face and which we wish to rethink and grapple.

Looking around us, we see that we are faced with an economy that features gross inequalities of wealth and income, including a significant number of people living in poverty due to unemployment or underemployment, with increasing numbers of those being below 30. Monopolies and near monopolies continue to exist and grow, with financial institutions increasingly important, beyond the control of governments, and prone to breakdown. Equally important are the onset of de-industrialization, uneven development, boom and bust cycles, depressions and recessions, and the increasing scarcity of natural resources.

In the social realm we are experiencing sharp cultural cleavages and clashes of traditions and civilizations, the beginnings of overpopulation, increasing levels of disorder, and an unprecedented percentage of the population in the United States incarcerated. There are also increasing intolerant radical movements from across the political spectrum, the manipulation of popular culture and breakdowns in marketplace of ideas, and a suspicion of science and empirical evidence. Also important are the aging of the population in many developed states, increases in obesity and related diseases, and rapidly escalating health care costs.

In terms of politics, we are again faced with sharp political cleavages and the unwillingness to compromise, a growing suspicion of empirical evidence, dysfunctional institutions, and the breakdown of checks and balances. Voters and others exhibit increasing suspicion of the state in the face of escalating costs associated with policing the world, growing sovereign debt, and the invincible position money occupies in politics. We also face increasingly intrusive security measures, a lack of governmental transparency, and the general perception that government is unaccountable, out of touch with the ordinary citizen, a playground for elites, and generally ineffective.

Plan and layout of the book

The book proceeds in roughly chronological fashion. Each chapter discusses a separate story, but chapters are paired for comparative discussion. I explore these stories by addressing the following topics:

Story—I do not assume that readers have had exposure to any or all of these stories. In order to understand the particulars of the story, we need to have an overview of the story itself, which these sections provide.

Contexts and Problems—Each story is written in a particular context in response to particular conditions. Understanding each story both as a reflection on the politics of the human condition and as a political act in itself requires that a consideration of those conditions. Each story is also written in reaction to a set of problems the author detects in ordinary society. This section outlines these problems and discusses how an understanding of these problems informs the substance of the story.

Themes—Each story has particular recurring arguments that come through in various ways: in the portrayal of characters, in descriptions of physical layouts, in the unfolding of the plot. These reveal the understanding of the world the author employs and the methodology used to reveal problems and construct solutions. By paying close attention to these themes we can understand why the author selects particular problems as those most in need of redress and why the author believes that solutions will in fact do the redressing.

The Good Life/Life in Dystopia and Solutions—Each utopia outlines an understanding of the good life. Each dystopia, in turn, provides an understanding of how the good life is turned upside down and for some, how people are progressively dehumanized. Each utopia also by its very purpose provides solutions to the problems identified in ordinary society.

Human Nature and *Applications*—Both genres make important assumptions about humans: what motivates them, what completes them, what accounts for disorder among them. In light of these understandings as well as the understandings of political, social, and economic life contained in the story, the text reconsiders contemporary problems, rehearsing what the author of the story would have to say with regard to those problems and tests the plausibility of that response, as well as exploring the nature of those problems in the context of the story's assumptions and analyses of human nature and the human condition.

Notes

1 For example, Frank Manual and Fritzie Manual, *Utopian Thought in the Western World* (New York: Belknap Press, 1979).

2 "Utopian" stories and philosophy have been understood various to include socialist tracts, Land of Cockaigne stories, Arcadian tales and millennial accounts. Dystopias and anti-utopias have likewise been defined variously. For discussions of this variety as well as different definitions and uses of these labels, see G. Claeys, "News from Somewhere: Enhanced Sociability and the Composite Definition of Utopia and Dystopia," *History*, Vol. 98 (2013); Ruth Levitas, *The Concept of Utopia* (Oxford and New York: Peter Lang, 2010); Krishan Kumar, *Utopia and Anti-Utopia in Modern Times* (Oxford and New York: Oxford University Press, 1987); J. C. Davis, *Utopia and the Ideal Society: A Study of English Utopian Writing 1516–1700* (New York: Cambridge University Press, 1983); George Kateb, *Utopia and Its Enemies* (New York: Schocken, 1972); and Manuel and Manuel, *Utopian Thought in the Western World*.

3 Northrop Frye, *Anatomy of Criticism: Four Essays* (New York: Atheneum, 1966).

4 For these differences, see Kumar, *Utopia and Anti-Utopia* and Frye, *Anatomy of Criticism*.

5 Albert Hirschmann, *The Rhetoric of Reaction: Perversity, Futility, Jeopardy* (Cambridge, MA: The Belknap Press of Harvard University Press, 1991).

6 A point emphasized by Manuel and Manuel, *Utopian Thought in the Western World*.

2

Utopia

The first two stories considered in this book contrast sharply. In *Utopia*, Thomas More (1478–1535) ostensibly describes a more perfect society. If we assign to More the admiring views of the traveler Hythloday, More is interested in improving the human lot by a combination of environmental changes and social programming. He proposes to eliminate greed, share goods equally, provide material security to all, hold rulers accountable, supply everyone leisure for self-improvement, and closely regulate the lives of citizens. Everyone is to enjoy a sufficient, equal, safe, and pleasant standard of living within the confines of a closely knit community. In *Isle of Pines*, Henry Neville (1620–1694) rejects the environmental changes More proposes. While he is not averse to people living a better life in general, Neville is not sanguine about the ways in which people such as More would go about helping them do so. His understanding of the role of environments in the shaping of human lives is quite different. He sees a good environment as one that challenges people, forcing them to use their abilities and advance civilization rather than one that provides material security. He implies that rather than providing material security and solidarity, governments should promote virtues. In all, Neville suggests that the Utopian way of life may be detrimental to civilization, progress, and general human happiness.

The story and interpretations

The story

Utopia, written ca. 1515, is ostensibly a transcription of conversations between Thomas More and his friends with a traveler, Raphael Hythloday, during one of More's trips to Antwerp on diplomatic business. The book begins with a discussion of England and its troubles, in which Hythloday surveys the contrast between England and other nations and criticizes English economics, society, and politics in the face of More's half-hearted defense. This discussion sets the stage for the "utopian" part of the book, for it lays out the problems that Utopia as a society is said to resolve. These problems are familiar, being located in well-known territory and widely experienced by everyone who would read the book.

The heart of the story is Hythloday's description of Utopia. That description takes the form of a travel document. Utopia is in the New World; its physical remoteness signals its normative distance from England, and the difficulty in traveling to it signifies the effort needed to achieve the change it exemplifies. Utopia itself is an island, the physical and human structure of which was created by a founder; thus, it is importantly artificial. It has an economy based on handicrafts and agriculture that has abolished private property and money. People are assigned houses and must rotate them every ten years. Most take their meals communally, and everyone obtains their everyday goods at bazaars at which no money is exchanged. Utopia has no professional military force; instead, it relies on its citizens, hires outsiders to do its fighting, or preferably uses its financial resources to buy off enemies. Utopia has accumulated gold, silver, and jewels, but internally places no value on them. It punishes its few criminals by making them work for the good of society rather than executing them. Its inhabitants are content, generally orderly, healthy, comely, physically secure, and intellectually stimulated.

Hythloday recounts his experiences in Utopia with enthusiasm. He is quite taken with the way Utopians arrange their affairs and considers their way of life to be materially and morally superior to that of Europe. In relating his story, he becomes a kind of missionary in reverse, in that he sees himself as someone who spreads the word about Utopia in Europe. His eagerness to return, along with the positive gloss he lends to almost all his discussion of Utopia, illustrates that he has been converted to the Utopian way of life.

Interpretations

The literature on *Utopia* and More is vast and complex, reflecting ongoing debates and disagreements regarding the nature and intent of the work. There is widespread disagreement regarding a host of questions: What genre does *Utopia* inhabit? Was it meant seriously? Is it a work depicting a perfect society or one of political imagination alone? How do we go about digging out its meaning? What is its relationship to Plato's *Republic*? What relationship does it have to More's contemporary and later thought and actions? What is its place in Western philosophy in general and utopian discussions in particular? How does it fit with the general intellectual community of Renaissance thinkers with which More is associated? What is its connection with Christianity and Catholic doctrine?

The Cambridge Companion to Thomas More presents an essential, up-to-date, and immensely informative introduction to the context of *Utopia* in terms of More's life, work, and environment, as well as an overview of contemporary scholarship on More.[1] Bradshaw's "More on Utopia" is also useful in presenting an important overview of the host of large questions of interpretation, both in terms of content and method.[2] Trevor-Roper's valuable "The Intellectual World of Sir Thomas More" provides an important discussion of More's context, as well as an insightful discussion of the origins of the twentieth-century fascination with More and *Utopia* and the modern struggles to appropriate More and his work.[3]

Accounts of the debates surrounding More's and *Utopia*'s relationship with the various strains of Renaissance civic humanism and republicanism can be found in Bradshaw, "More on Utopia" and Nelson, "Utopia through Italian Eyes."[4] An important intervention in the debate on whether More was an "ancient" or a "modern" is found in Engerman, "Hythloday's Utopia and More's England."[5] Likewise, Baker-Smith's "Reading Utopia" furnishes additional discussions of the background of the piece, important reflections on cultural values and customs, and a useful select bibliography of recent work.[6]

An important aspect of the literature takes on the question of intentions. Is *Utopia* a satire (and thus *anti*-utopian), a literary joke, or a serious piece of normative political philosophy? A recent practical discussion in this line, which addresses the economics of Utopia is found in Bostaph, "Deepening the Irony of *Utopia*."[7] Likewise, Nendza in "Political Idealism in More's Utopia" creates a skeptical argument regarding human nature and Utopia's radical politics.[8] Important defenses of *Utopia* as serious political philosophy include Logan's *The Meaning of More's "Utopia"*[9] and Skinner's "Thomas More's Utopia and the Virtue of True Nobility."[10] The latter provides an important justification for engaging with *Utopia* philosophically even while acknowledging More's ambivalence, jokes, and contradictions, arguing that More's "principal aim was to challenge his readers at least to consider seriously whether Utopia may not represent the best state of a commonwealth." This is the view largely adopted here.

Contexts and problems

The outer structure of the story of Utopia, which tells of the encounter of More and his friends with Hythloday, mirrors the real situation of the book itself. It was not meant for the masses. Originally published in Latin, audiences for both the original and the later English translation were restricted because the capacity to read English, much less Latin, was confined to the educated few. Therefore as a political act, it is not democratic in content or intent, though the description of Utopia itself gestures toward the importance of popular accountability.[11] Given the speech the character More delivers to Hythloday regarding the duty and necessity of subtly introducing wisdom to rulers, one can see the book as an attempt not to persuade the masses, but to "wittily" discharge the duty of counseling kings and their advisors. Thus it can be seen as a counterpart to the volumes of political wisdom addressed to rulers that were popular at the time (the most famous of which was Machiavelli's *The Prince*) in addition to being taken as a contribution to discussions within the humanist circles More frequented.

In its description of a seemingly better world set at a distance from the familiar, *Utopia* sets the tone and character for much of the modern Western utopian literature that follows. But its ambivalence also differentiates it from many subsequent works. We never quite know where Thomas More stands.[12] He is both author and a character, the outside creator of the world of Utopia and a critic of that world inside the story. The terminology itself throws doubt on many aspects of the story. It is set in "nowhere" and described by a "spouter of nonsense."[13] Thus, *Utopia* is what I call a weak theoretical story, a narrative that serves more to raise questions than to answer them.

More explores the roots of English problems and their solutions by criticizing English conditions and conjecturing how social, economic, and political matters may be differently and more perfectly arranged. More engages in this project by imagining a place where life is radically better than in England in economic, social, and political terms. This place is different enough in both practice and result for the contrasts to be real, but not so alien to English geography and cultural heritage to be fantastic. In the course of this endeavor, he raises questions of both contemporary and current interest. If greed and its attendant social evils really are the products of scarcity and inequality, can they be overcome with the kind of collective and planned security that Utopia provides? Given that the

English countryside is being transformed willy-nilly for the worse by the wool industry, can a government overcome this problem through planning? The poor in England starve while the upper classes live abundantly; can this situation be changed by abolishing money and property? If people are too caught up with accumulating wealth and not interested enough in developing their intellects and character, is it possible to train them to reverse this attitude?

From references in the text, it is clear that More in part sees his book as a response to (and a critique of) Plato's *Republic* in its attempt to grapple with the human foundations of political communities, the structure and purpose of government, the character of the good life, and the responsibilities of rulers. The exchanges in Book One take the place of the opening dialogues of *The Republic*, with More himself acting the part of a skeptical audience. There is also conjecture that Europe takes the place of Plato's cave, with Utopia as the sun of reason.[14] The differences, though, are clear. Not only is *Utopia* a different type of story from Plato's work; it is also premised in part on a different understanding of knowledge than *The Republic*. In contrast to Plato's emphasis on the superiority of abstract conceptions, More argues for the importance of experience. Indeed, the story of Utopia acts as a kind of surrogate experience rather than an abstract Platonic form. Utopia is said to work, in practice. But here More's readers confront the dilemma that will present itself with all utopian stories (and which Plato escapes by locating his city in the realm of the forms)—the ultimate appeal of Utopia is that it works. Observers report that it does. Yet it only works *on paper*. Do we really know it works? Can we trust the author in the same way we trust our own experience? Does the story convince us that it works? Can we translate the operations of "nowhere" to a concrete here and now?

Added to these levels of uncertainty is the fact that More is writing at the cusp of the early modern era and thus in quite different times than our own. It is a time in which great transformations economically, socially, and politically were beginning to take place.[15] More decried the effects of these economic changes and dislocations, as the handicrafts and village system of the Middle Ages gave way to the first in a series of economic consolidations that would bring about the modern industrial age. The old commons system in the countryside was being discarded in favor of enclosure by big landowners. Greater wealth was being created and more people were becoming wealthy, pursuing wealth, and displaying wealth. Simultaneously, more people were being deprived of communal safety nets and experiencing extreme poverty. Previously independent peasants were being pushed either into paid service to the wealthy or dispossessed altogether to wander in search of work or charity. This surplus labor had yet to be fully absorbed by the towns. More saw the growth of the wool industry in particular as a disaster rather than a harbinger of a different kind of economy. He saw no way for those displaced by pasturage to make their way in the world.[16]

Changes were also taking place politically. The old feudal system was giving way to the creation of modern nation states. This meant that power, both political and economic, was flowing away from local gentry, guilds, and other medieval centers and into the clutches of the monarch and London. Henry VIII was at the center of such changes, and his later actions would spur a variety of incidents that mixed religious beliefs with political anxieties. Henry's break with Rome would be as much a new-fangled crisis of his early modern state in reaction to the universal pretensions of the Church as it was an old-fashioned affair of dynastic anxieties. The tensions created by this mix would be relevant for the next 300 years. While probably no more amoral than the political structure they replaced, these early attempts at consolidating power across traditional internal political boundaries and at the expense of Rome appeared to disconcert More, and he viewed them as creating an abusive system of politics.

More does not connect these problems with larger economic or political forces. He appears unaware of their scale and direction. He sees them instead as signs of moral and social degeneration. Morality was in decline in tandem with the deterioration of the medieval sense of community. He takes for granted the old style handicrafts and commons economy that had prevailed for the past 500 years. Thus, there is something profoundly conservative in More's understanding of and response to the problems he perceived. Rather than tackling the larger trends that were driving the changes he decried, More wished to create through government agency a social, political, and economic environment that would allow humans once again to act morally. Thus, he did not wish just to push forward, but also to look backward to an idealized Christian community, the departure from which he suggests abandons a true understanding of human nature. As other commentators have noted,[17] Utopia brings to mind an enlarged and idealized monastic community with a reformed leadership at its head, the entire citizenry as its faculty, and rational mores instead of traditions as its norms.

More's criticism is therefore mainly leveled at the government, which he believes should be responsible for social and economic affairs. He appears unhappy that both Henry VII and Henry VIII and their courts had not done more to care for the people of England, particularly the poor, and is equally concerned with the general decline of morality he sees in government circles. Contemporary princes, More argues through Hythloday, are interested only in war, power, chivalry, and entertainment, while their counselors seek favor. He suggests that these characteristics make those figures unfit to hold government power. Moreover, he argues that both rulers and counselors wrongly eschew experience and rationality; rather than knowledge of the world, they find in their own personal goals and desires, or in tradition, all the understanding they require. He decries the incapacity of rulers to educate themselves by consulting men of experience or philosophers. Rather than guaranteeing government by the wise, he argues that political structures in Europe create situations in which even the best men degenerate into fools.

This is because political structures are such that rulers and their associates are allowed to pursue their personal interests rather than govern in the interest of the commonwealth. They are responsible to no one but themselves or the selfish monarch. Consequently, magistrates focus on expanding the boundaries and power of the state relative to those outside and gathering power and money into their own hands at the expense of citizens. It is both the neglect of the citizenry and the accompanying attempt to centralize power that More bemoans. The first problem has obvious ramifications for the public good and the well-being of citizens. That farmers are being turned off the communal land to wander about in poverty, he believes, is the result of scandalous neglect on the part of the government. The second problem he sees as a distortion of good governance because increases in power were not accompanied by increases in responsibility and knowledge. To centralize power excessively is to take decisionmaking power away from local officials who are better placed to make policy. It is also to stimulate rulers' appetites for power. As with all other goods, excessive power leads to the desire for more, ultimately to the destruction of the community itself. So while he argues for expanding the responsibilities of government in some areas, he wishes to see the functions of government dispersed geographically, government power held by many hands, and government officials held responsible by the community as a whole.

Through Hythloday, More also criticizes the economic conditions the government tolerates, denouncing the large disparities of wealth found in England and the resulting large numbers of rootless, impoverished people roaming the towns and countryside. He argues that England's economics are wrongly organized on moral grounds. Existence is predicated on the possession of money and private property. The result is poverty and crime. There are too many people who are unable to take care of themselves and are not provided for by the community. This situation is most immediately symbolized by the impact of the growth of the wool trade. That trade has stimulated the keeping of sheep in the countryside, with the attending enclosure of the commons and the dispossession of villagers and cottagers who have no way of making a living. This condition is exacerbated by the keeping of soldiers who, in their idleness during times of peace or as a result of their wounds and lack of transferable skills, are unable to do anything but starve, beg, or steal. Beggars multiply, as do criminals. The state's response, which More also appears to condemn, is to treat even minor crimes severely, routinely handing out the death penalty. Such policies, More argues, are both functionally inadequate (in that they treat symptoms rather than causes) and morally reprehensible. The government at the least should regulate the wool trade, curb enclosures, and make provisions for those who have been pushed out of work rather than harshly treating the symptoms and victims of economic dysfunction.

More appears equally disturbed by the growing wealth of the few. The stipulations he places on everyone to work, to have the same kind of houses, to wear the same types of clothing, and generally to share the results of work in the context of a static standard of living are transparently attempts to level living conditions. His emphasis on training people not to esteem such holders of value as gold also indicates distaste for the transformations wrought by the pursuit and acquisition of wealth. If no one is to go about hungry or homeless in Utopia, it is equally the case that no one will traipse about in rich clothing, waste resources on extravagant banquets, or build a life materially superior to others.

Finally, More condemns the growth and spread of the smaller vices associated with a burgeoning money economy. The tightly controlled small towns and villages of England were being prized open by people of independent means who bought their pleasures, stimulating in turn a market in gaming, prostitution, drinking, and other forms of entertainment, all of which More bans in Utopia. More no doubt understood that these vices existed before his time, but he appears nevertheless discouraged by what he portrays as a rapid expansion in their indulgence.

Solutions, themes, and conceptions of the good life

Solutions

More sees the communal organization of life as the solution to many of the problems he identified. Rather than allowing tradition, individuals, capital, or markets control the flow of goods, labor, energy, and other elements of life, and place responsibilities on individuals alone to secure their living, it is the community as a whole that makes these decisions and assumes those responsibilities. People work for the community and receive their sustenance from it. The community decides holidays and the timing of planting and harvesting. It builds and repairs houses. It creates and supplies communal kitchens. It operates a community church (though it claims no monopoly on religion) and keeps an eye on the moral conduct of its citizens. It also takes surplus population from Utopia and places it in a foreign country, to be recalled if the Utopian population declines. Given that it makes these decisions and shoulders all burdens, the needs and organization of the community as a whole take precedence over the preferences of individuals and the ties of blood.

More, in turn, argues that good government flows from the placement of power with people who are accountable to the community as a whole. While such rulers as Henry VIII were free to pursue their dynastic ambitions with scant attention to the welfare of common people, officials in Utopia are constrained. Lower level magistrates (eligible due to their learning) are selected by families; higher level magistrates are chosen by the lower, while princes are elected from among higher magistrates, subject to recall. Thus a limited form of democratic practice, in the guise of elections from a particular pool of candidates, is seen as part of the solution. However, the limitation on democracy in this selection process is also part of the solution. It is knowledge, not heredity, patronage, or money that gives one potential access to decisionmaking power. All elected magistrates come from the class of those excused from manual labor so that they might dedicate themselves to the generation of abstract knowledge and the exploration of accumulated experience. With the abolition of hereditary office and nobility in favor of election among the educated, what results is a kind of meritocracy.

Decentralization of power is also important. While the community makes all important decisions, not all decisions are made in the capital, or by the prince. Rather, significant policymaking power resides with local and regional magistrates. Being closer to the people, these magistrates have greater knowledge of local conditions and are subject to their own recall if they neglect their duties. All magistrates up to the level of prince also share significant experiences with ordinary people. While it is true that they do not routinely pursue manual trades, they are allocated no superior share of material goods. Magistrates do not live in palaces, surrounded by servants, choice foods, and lavish furnishings. They cannot lord their power over ordinary citizens; they feel with their own lifestyles the fullness or scarcity of the nation's common larder.

Another part of More's substantive reformation of government, made possible by the abolition of private property, is a reduction in the number of laws. There being few laws, More excludes lawyers and policemen from Utopia. There are courts, but (as with Bellamy's legal system) citizens represent themselves. More has Hythloday argue that the presence of officers of the court does nothing but complicate public affairs, putting both morals and the administration of justice beyond the reach of ordinary persons. He particularly sees the exclusion of lawyers as a bonus. It is better, he argues, to have a system that dispenses contextual and rough justice than to create a complex system that would dispense a more sophisticated and strictly fair brand.

These structures as a whole perform several tasks. They help spread power beyond the hands of the prince and the influence of the capital. They take the focus of policymaking away from the welfare of the prince and ostensibly place it on the welfare of the community as a whole. They simplify the administration of the nation. As with Plato's republic, these measures also elevate knowledge (though not only abstract knowledge) as a prerequisite for holding power. They make the prince and the entire executive structure accountable to and representative of the population as a whole. They place responsibility for order with the community itself. But this does not mean that government is limited. As noted above, government in More's understanding is probably more powerful and has a longer reach than that under which he lived. It is true that there is more religious liberty in Utopia than England at that time, but in other matters government is more prescriptive and much less liberal than many modern governments.

Another important part of the solution to the problems More addresses is the abolition of private property and of a money economy. No one in Utopia owns land or houses, nor do they have money, gold, or jewels (the latter by custom rather than by law). Here, More extends what Plato reserved for the Guardians alone to the entire community largely because the entire community will be involved, to some degree, in civic affairs. As with Plato's Guardians, Utopians at most possess such personal items as clothes and furniture, but even this assertion must be qualified because Hythloday asserts that no locks are on doors, allowing anyone to help oneself from any house. That people do not and will not do this is put down importantly to the fact that it is not necessary—any desired article can be had for the asking from a free bazaar. Everyone works for the community and is, in turn, supported by the community by means of in-kind provisions. Given that there is no need to exchange holders of value for goods, there is no money economy. There is no market in the modern sense of an economic system that determines the price of things through individual decisionmaking and regulates the kinds and supplies of goods that are produced. How the information that would otherwise be created and distributed by market mechanisms makes itself into the hands of communal decisionmakers is not well described. More probably assumes that this information will be easily available by means of historical data and rudimentary accounting systems.

One byproduct of this system is the harnessing of most able-bodied citizens into productive labor. There are few free riders. While educated people are exempted (and they are to work in the realm of ideas and policy), everyone else but the very old and very young must work at a craft. This arrangement, More argues, puts at the community's disposal many more sets of hands than was then the case. Those who in England remained idle or labored unproductively (e.g., as servants of the rich and noble) or who have no work are instead producers of valuable, usable goods. With those who were formerly rich or noble, merchants or vagrants equally put to work under the paternal eyes of the local magistrates, the productive power of the community is significantly increased.

However, the major benefit of this economic system, in More's mind, is the efficient and moral, because equitable, distribution of goods. The burgeoning market economy of his times left More cold on several counts. First, it was focused foremost on the accumulation of wealth in private hands rather than on the sustenance of all members of the community. Second, it allowed some to accumulate many more goods than others, to the detriment of themselves and those who must do without. More saw economic production in zero-sum terms. He did not see new-fangled economic activities as expanding the economic pie, but merely redistributing it in objectionable ways. The takeover of the distribution of goods by the government through moneyless markets allows for their equitable distribution (on the basis of equality and need) at the same time it also avoids activating the survival instinct or stimulating human desires. While goods are free for the taking in Utopia, More did not see people taking more than they really needed, with need defined in terms of relatively simple and equal living standards rather than display, status-seeking, or generally high living standards.

More relies primarily on social pressure to mold citizens and their behavior as ways of keeping order and harnessing the labor necessary for the community's survival rather than laws and the individual incentives of a market economy. He continually refers to the opprobrium or praise that is heaped on particular actions, objects, and attitudes. It is through the material environment as well as this social tool rather than the blunt instrument of punishment and laws that order in Utopia is routinely maintained and the community held together as an organic whole. For example, people are not forbidden to keep gold and value it; rather, they are trained and conditioned, mainly by their families, to hold it in low esteem. Once trained, people will keep such valuations no matter where they go, thus the impeccable conduct of Utopians when employed in responsible positions outside of Utopia, where gold, silver, jewelry, power, and social status are valued.

More was also particularly concerned with the creation and maintenance of a full-time soldiery and moves to abolish them in Utopia. With the emergence of the modern nation-state, military establishments expanded, making even more burdensome the support of troops. More addresses this problem in a variety of ways. He does not argue that Utopia will not need a military. Indeed, he argues that it is justified to take unused land from neighbors to plant surplus populations even if those neighbors object. But he argues that Utopians will deal with conflicts more astutely than nations in Europe. They would rather use money than citizens as weapons by hiring mercenaries, buying off foes, bribing key officials in enemy countries, and placing bounties on the heads of enemy commanders. Only as a last resort are citizens used, but these are citizen-soldiers who occupy the majority of their time with nonmartial pursuits.

Finally, it is not merely the presence of a particular environment, or training, customs, and morals that accomplish the goals of order and solidarity in Utopia. Other social pressures are also present, most notably the constant presence of other eyes. More refers throughout his description to the presence of watchers: magistrates see that no one is idle; old people keep an eye on the younger at communal dining facilities; workers watch each other to see that all are doing their share; the council watches the prince and the prince the council, and both are watched by lower level magistrates brought up to the capital for short periods of time. Utopian society works importantly by everyone ensuring that everyone else is doing his or her part.

Themes

In proposing these solutions, More paints Utopia as, above all, the product of a founder's vision rather than evolution, revolution, or war and as possessing a purpose beyond the ordinary. As such, it intentionally creates a special set of social, political, and economic environments. Utopia is not just a place to work and live, but a place to work humanely and live morally and well in accordance with that vision. The routine extension of this purposeful implementation of vision is planning. Because Utopia is not an ordinary place, life is consciously organized on a day-to-day basis to reach the higher goals of universal material security, leisure for intellectual inquiry, and moral living. The assumption is that these communal goals must be consciously and collectively pursued. They will not arise spontaneously out of the autonomous actions of individuals. There is no assumption that an invisible hand will convert the pursuit of private goals into a larger public good. Thus, the community controls the location of towns, the working of the crafts, the planting of crops, and the allocation of labor.

In suggesting that communal planning is superior to relying upon natural rhythms, tradition, or the market, More assumes that to plan is to act in a rational manner, that is, to utilize systematically and communally our understanding of the world. What sets off Utopia from England is this use of knowledge (as planning) in the policymaking process. Such use, More holds, allows the community to impose order on the randomness of individual actions and to counteract whatever evil that fate might happen to hand the commonwealth. As a result, Utopia's government is said to conduct its policymaking on the basis of a realist understanding of Utopia's interests, not on whim or dynastic pretensions. Utopia also takes advantage of knowledge as planning's companion in intentionality. Planning allows officials to consult experience and other forms of knowledge to use their resources wisely, to keep order, and to conquer the challenges presented by human nature, empowering Utopians to create the environment most conducive to human flourishing. Planning is, therefore, More's key to a real, albeit limited, kind of human transcendence. If *fortuna* is a woman, as Machiavelli would have it, More argues that Utopia has mastered her insofar as it is possible to do so.

Another theme is sharing, in the form of the detachment of benefits and burdens from particular persons or classes. The products of the island are shared, with goods available for free in markets and food provided by communal kitchens. Work is also shared. No one is allowed to live in idleness because they own sufficient property to support themselves or decide to live on the margins of society. Conversely, if productivity is sufficiently high that production can be slowed, universal holidays are declared, and everyone partakes of the resulting extra leisure. This concept of sharing is ultimately rooted in the understanding that Utopia's inhabitants exist not as individuals, but as part of a community. Inhabitants share a common identity, common goals, and a common destiny as well as work and leisure. Thus, they also share a common responsibility to one another. To be a member of Utopia is first and foremost to be a citizen of the community rather than a member of a family or a private individual. The concept of sharing, therefore, is underpinned by the understanding that the good of the individual should be subordinated to the needs of the community. However, it is also bolstered by More's assumption that both individual and communal goods coincide when sharing is organized by the wise, well-trained, and environmentally constrained officials in Utopia.

The final theme is embedded in More's argument that Utopians live well in part because they live simply, thriftily, and plainly. They do not, for example, expend effort in creating great varieties of clothing. Housing is uniform and of simple design. Most people eat in communal kitchens, where economies of scale lead to the most efficient use of material resources and labor. Thrift and economy are connected here with uniformity and plainness and therefore, as we shall see, with the attempt to deactivate the human circuitry that produces greed. It is not, however, associated with deprivation. Life is said to be good, food plentiful and housing pleasant and airy, but none is overtly fancy. There is none of the ostentation that one can find in *Looking Backward*, but also none of the forced austerity of Airstrip One. Utopians appear to feel no need to put on displays to differentiate or call attention to themselves. Nor do they require choices to constitute their own particular ways of life. Thus, More argues that Utopian cities are pleasant—possessing wide streets, gardens, rivers, and good sanitation—but neither they nor their inhabitants are as colorful as cities and citizens in Bellamy's vision of the future.

The good life in Utopia

More's argument that people can and ought to be (to some degree) socially constructed in a conscious fashion, along with his assumptions regarding the correct environment, ultimately allows him to assign a perfectionist goal to Utopia's government when it comes to the good life. That is, he argues that the state should teach and inculcate particular moral values that constrain people to follow a particular plan of life. Thus, More is not a pluralist when it comes to definitions of the good life within a community. He does not see humans as fulfilling themselves through the choice of lifeplans, or fundamentally through choice at all. He believes that beyond simple types of choices, the freedom to choose is harmful to the community in that it is likely to breed disorder, immorality, and abuses of power. His is a moral and unitary community. While people are differentiated into various occupations and divided between intellectuals and craftsmen, fulfillment does not follow this differentiation, as is the case with Plato. The good life the community promotes is one that everyone is to enjoy: it must be the *same* kind of life, one that everyone *can* enjoy in terms of shared wealth and leisure, and one to which *everyone* must contribute. As noted above, this life resembles much more that provided to Plato's Guardians than the freer and more pluralistic life ordinary citizens enjoy in the latter's republic.

What are the implications of this lack of pluralism? Not only can people not choose to live a different kind of life; it is also the case that both through the construction of particular environments and through programming and training, Utopia seeks to heavily influence who people are in terms of self-definitions and self-fulfillment. They are all to self-identify fundamentally as Utopians. Humans in this understanding are not meant to be autonomous social individuals—they can be happy, satisfied, peaceful, and content without deeply exercising power over their own lives. There is, to be sure, some scope for individual decisionmaking. One may choose an occupation different than that of one's family and can decide to reside permanently in the countryside if agriculture is an appealing way of life. There is no single prescribed religion. But in the vast majority of instances, choice does not exist. One cannot choose to live a free and easy life of a wanderer. One cannot choose to remain permanently in a city and not to go to the countryside for a stint of pastoral labor. One cannot attempt to amass wealth. One cannot be different by dressing in a new or unorthodox manner. One cannot indulge in the types of pastimes many in contemporary England took for granted, including sports and gaming. One can choose not to believe in an afterlife, but only at the price of being excluded from public office. People are not that innately different when it comes to what they want in terms of a good life, More implies. They can be satisfied with a lifeplan that features the enjoyment of material security, the leisure to develop themselves intellectually and social solidarity, evidently because they naturally are passionate about little else.

More's Utopians therefore experience an interesting mix of collective regimentation and autonomy when compared with the life most Englishmen lived during his time. In contrast with ordinary society, More wishes to reinstitute many of the social controls that were being unwound with the demise of Middle Ages. Yet he also wants to spread power beyond those hands into which sixteenth-century political structures had placed it. The prince is not the king, having none of Henry's absolutist character. Order is kept by persons who differ from England's traditional political elite in large part because they are chosen by families rather than being appointed by the king, inheriting their power, or buying office. There is, in this sense, a greater degree of communal and decentralized political autonomy collectively exercised by the people of Utopia as compared to the inhabitants of More's England. More also points to freedom from work in which people are able to indulge (though they have little freedom in terms of using that leisure in general), while the provision of food, clothing, and shelter also means that people are free from the economic insecurities that preyed on many people in sixteenth-century England.

At the same time, the extension of the communal exercise of power into almost all areas of life, as well as the emphasis on equality of consumption and on thrift and plainness, leads to a Utopian culture that was at odds with contemporary England and Europe as well as the modern world. There can be no exotic lifestyles; few eccentricities are indulged. Solidarity is prized more than individuality. The community and the common good come first. The purpose of this set of priorities is to root out the harmful conditions that More sees developing in England. To put the individual above the community is not in his mind an admirable thing, while uniformity and plainness are required by morality as well as utility. In return, citizens are provided with the important goods humans have always sought. Utopian satisfaction comes from the contentment derived for a belly filled with plain and wholesome food, a solid house for oneself and family and the leisure to develop one's mind rather than choices and indulgence of the senses.

Materially, More foresees the continuation of an agricultural and crafts-based economy in his good society. He does not anticipate larger-scale industrial activities nor does he prophesize technological change that will greatly enhance productivity, at least in part because he does not see Utopian society as primarily a consumerist society even if economic security is an important social goal. Universal sufficiency is the aim, and it is achieved through the input of new labor sources rather than technological advances. The system is also importantly streamlined by the fact that the nature and kinds of goods created and consumed are limited. Given that the accumulation of goods is not socially approved or a sign of status, given the fact that everyone has access to the same set of goods, and given that no perception of shortages will create the desire to hoard goods in anticipation of future need, More argues that this system will be sufficient.

The good life in Utopia is, therefore, primarily one of material and physical security that supports feelings of social solidarity, moral development, and the leisure required for "the free liberty of the mind and garnishing of the same."[18] One need not worry about finding work or obtaining food and shelter. Medical facilities have been developed to the fullest extent possible for the times and are available freely to all without distinction. Everyone shares in society's wealth, and so no one (allegedly) experiences the pangs of jealousy, the baleful effects of envy, or the angry nip of hunger. Everyone enjoys the comforts of an orderly society in which crime is minimal. Everyone is sheltered as far as is technologically possible from the forces of nature and disease. Yet More concedes the possibility of epidemics and natural disasters that exceed the powers of the state to prevent. Crime even raises its head occasionally. One cannot enjoy complete physical security. Utopia is not perfect, just more perfectly organized.

Human nature and applications

Human nature

As noted in Chapter 1, More's understanding of human nature is a mixed bag that includes references to important types of hardwiring and the possibility of programming that constructs citizens in particular ways. Utopia is a place that both provides a particular environment conducive to moral living and molds citizens into particular types of beings.

More's understanding of hardwiring and subsequently of the environmental influences on humans is best illustrated by his views on greed. He argues that people are not inevitably greedy even though humans possess hardwiring associated with greed. He holds that humans accumulate goods and strive to maximize their share in two circumstances: when they perceive that the future is uncertain, or when they already have a surfeit of goods and use them as tokens of social standing. In the first instance, humans' survival instincts lead them to hoard goods. He assumes that people are hardwired to obtain goods for survival, a hardwiring that is satisfied by a guaranteed sufficiency. In the second instance, when many goods are present, humans' desires not only for goods but also for esteem and power are stimulated and they crave ostentation. Here, he assumes that people are hardwired (through pride) to accumulate and display wealth and power should they gain access to surplus goods. This hardwiring can also be avoided: if citizens' rights to possessions are limited to everyday necessities, the hardwiring associated with pride and status seeking will remain inert. Because this hardwiring can be circumvented, resulting in an absence of individual material desires for more, better, and different goods, More believes that people will be content with uniform clothing, solid food, and rotating houses. Rival understandings of human psychology might argue that this view strips humans of any innate sense of ambition. More would probably respond that ambition is separate from greed, though it must be environmentally controlled lest it lead to greed. Individual ambition can be channeled into service for the community. But it is true that he would reject the notion that people would innately desire a constantly rising standard of living and would hold that people are not materially ambitious if they have confidence that their material needs will be met.

Along with the manipulation of environments meant to elicit particular responses from hardwiring or to avoid its activation, citizens are also programmed (and thus socially constructed in a direct fashion) in Utopia. The view that people can be trained tells us that More presumes that not all human behavior can be changed or controlled by directly interacting with hardwiring. Something in addition is necessary in the form of customs, practices, norms, and values. These appear to have permanent effects on people, shaping them as persons in ways that manipulations of environments cannot. Training is most prominently displayed in Hythloday's discussion of the Utopian treatment of gold and jewels, but it takes place in other venues as well, including those associated with communal solidarity and patriotism. The assumption that citizens can and should be programmed gives the collective an important opening into the lives of individual citizens, in that it is not up to families alone to train their children however they see fit; rather, training is undertaken collectively as well as in the family to ensure uniformity. All Utopians are programmed similarly so that there is minimal chance that Utopia will contain social dissidents.

Informing this nonpluralist understanding of the role of programming in the social construction of humans is More's underlying assumption that objects of desire and admiration, models of aspiration, and other important attributes of culture are on the collective level relative and pluralistic. Because they are also the products of programming rather than only the expression of hardwiring or dictated by natural necessity, they vary across communities, making them the objects of social criticism and choice. To elaborate, More's understanding is that social customs and mores are flexible and ultimately artificial. There is nothing natural in differentiating sharply between men and women, or living in single-generation households. Likewise, he rejects the argument that economic rationality inevitably leads to the creation of a monetized market economy. People can be trained to operate in different systems. Customs and systems can be changed consciously by society as a whole in pursuit of larger goals, such as making life more comfortable for the majority of people. Or, as with England, they might be mistakenly adopted, preserved through tradition, and require rational criticism. As such, he would hold that criticism of a community's program of social construction is the job of a civically active philosopher. He would also hold that the collective's social conditioning of people is not inherently immoral or inhumane, as will some later liberal and libertarian individualists. All societies consist of citizens who possess hardwiring that both incompletely accounts for their behavior and which can be manipulated. To socially construct citizens in a particular way, so long as the goal is morally defensible, does not impinge upon a natural right to autonomously control one's construction or warp humans by removing their inherent nature. When it comes to social environments and types of citizens, there are only artificial models from which to choose, and in this argument More holds that it is the right of the community, not the individual, to do the choosing, and that it should choose on the basis of both morality and utility.

In sum, while More assumes that humans are hardwired in particular ways, he also believes that the behavior that stems from this hardwiring is amenable to significant influence. Particular characteristics can be encouraged, satisfied, muted, or shut off by the workings of environments which, in turn, are intentionally and collectively constructed. But not all behavior is connected with hardwiring. Some types are created through programming. Thus, as with Bellamy, More believes that a better way of life comes from the realization that the hardwired aspects of human nature do not dictate a single way of being or behaving. Change the environment and hardwired responses will change in tandem. Program people and they will also behave differently than if they are not programmed or if they are programmed in alternative ways. The acknowledgment that there are limits to training and the capacity of the state to cause people to act in particular ways by means of social construction is also important to his position. While people may be morally trained and influenced by their environment, such influence does not result in the erasure of free will such that people cannot choose to act immorally, or will automatically act morally. The presence of crime in Utopia shows that people can still choose to act in a disordered way even if the community is constructed in the best possible fashion. So while More (most probably) considers Utopia to be a good place and much better than contemporary England, it is by no means perfect. And even though he argues that Utopia extensively influences human behavior, he rejects the notion that humans are puppets of, or purely the creations of, their environments. If environments are subject to manipulation, humans are not completely governed by such manipulations.

In terms of the substance of hardwiring, both More's understanding of Utopia and the knowledge he expects Utopia's magistrates to possess importantly implicate a belief that people will be satisfied with uniform clothing, public housing of standard form, and the generalized servings of communal kitchens. More's most basic assumption therefore holds that people prefer material security over choice and self-expression. This may have been an easier assumption for More to accept than for us. He was familiar with sumptuary laws that forbade the lower classes from aping their betters in clothing, the uniform style of clothing that guilds prescribed for their members, and the clothes that set apart priests and monks. But he also generalizes this attitude, assuming that people will not rebel against this state of affairs by demanding the freedom to choose to differentiate themselves from others in their clothing, housing, and foodstuffs, or a higher standard of living in general. Here, More contrasts most strongly with Bellamy.

More also holds that people are better served, more content, and generally better persons by trading greater wealth and a higher standard of living for more leisure. More has Utopia institute a regulation six-hour day and to permit periodic holidays rather than to have the population work harder to sustain a higher standard of living. The reason why More argues that this prioritization of leisure is humanly desirable and practically acceptable has to do with his understanding of human development. For More, humans find, fulfill, and complete themselves most importantly in their leisure rather than in labor. He assumes that people become fully human, and thus civilized, only after necessary tasks are accomplished and when such tasks do not monopolize citizens' time. Development requires a kind of freedom from necessity that allows the intellectual and emotional self to engage in activities that are superfluous to the direct support of life, a freedom that both necessitates material security and the absence of work for significant periods of time. However, More bounds this negative freedom by dictating that it be used for more than frivolous purposes, though he assumes that people will naturally gravitate toward activities that will improve their minds and general well-being.

More is also importantly concerned with the origins of evil and disorder. He suggests that though they are responsible for their choices, humans usually engage in harmful actions because they inhabit uncongenial environments. People who are starving steal to survive. People who are taught to kill in war and have no other skill will also kill in times of peace. People unanchored by firm rules and dislocated from their communities will fall into the ways of vice. Humans will discard rules, mores, and customs if they are faced with uncertainty, need, or danger. An orderly people must be one that is well cared for, materially and physically secure, and firmly ruled. There is nothing inherently depraved or nasty in humans in Utopia's philosophy. The types of disorder with which governments are concerned (theft, assault, rape, etc.) are assumed to arise mainly as a result of the interaction among environments, hardwiring, and negative freedoms.

Put succinctly, More holds that evil is generally a matter of becoming disordered through the influence of a disordered or threatening environment, the absence of training and weakness of will. People will choose to act in ways that are not in conformity with the hierarchy of values they should hold as moral beings importantly due to the effects of outside forces. More reflects this attitude by attributing to Utopians a middle way between a lenient and a harsh view of criminal activity. They do not think that criminals are merely misguided or ill. There are criminals in Utopia; as such, they are not responding to uncongenial environments. Lawbreakers can and do bear responsibility for their actions, and potential criminals can be deterred by witnessing the community's punishment of crime. But given the different environment that Utopia provides, More argues that there will be much less disorder in Utopia than in England. Lower levels of disorder are due to four important factors. First is material security. People will no longer need to steal to live. Second, there will be no private property or any emphasis placed on the possession of holders of value or the accumulation of possessions that lead people to act in a disordered fashion through the force of envy or pride. Third, there will be no professional soldiers, who, with no practical skills or employment between wars, turn to violence to survive. Fourth, power will be rationally distributed. With no nobility, cadet royal lines or others to fight over offices and the throne, civic peace will reign. Utopia, therefore, will not contain the most important elements that breed disorder.

Applications

We should approach Utopia with some ambivalence, as it appears More did himself. Questions regarding his commitment to this alternative should give us pause, but his seriousness in attempting to flesh out an alternative that reflects critically upon contemporary practice should not be in doubt.

While More's actual context is quite different than ours, we are also facing many of the same problems. Economic dislocations, even if they are resolved in the next 10 to 20 years, promise to put many people out of employment for the rest of their working lives. Economic inequality is on the rise. While levels of violent disorderliness fluctuate, a disturbingly high percentage of people transgress existing laws and are incarcerated. People feel themselves politically helpless, believing that a professional political elite monopolizes policymaking totally and that elites of all partisan persuasions have little in common with nonprofessional politicians.

In More's alternative society in contrast, the addition of economic security, the abolition of money and of private property, equalization of material provisions, planning, increased surveillance, a perfectionist role for government, greater accountability for officials and a decentralization of policymaking, a particular and conscious social construction of citizens and a collective identity are said to bring drastically reduced levels of disorder, dramatically simplified and better government and administration of justice, the elimination of inequality and poverty, a universally sufficient standard of living, and justice.

Putting aside the question of full implementation of More's scheme, let us grapple with the fundamental and timely questions that *Utopia* raises. One set of problems has to do with the growing disparities of wealth that the United

States in particular is experiencing and the growing percentage of people who are incarcerated. More (or at least Hythloday) would argue that those two trends are related. Unequal distributions of wealth and the lack of security that people feel with regard to their material welfare leads to both greed and disorder. Rather than allowing the rich to gather in an ever-increasing share of national wealth and fill an ever-expanding prison system with those who are left out, he would argue that we should guarantee everyone material sufficiency, make sure that everyone is employed in productive labor, and do away with the possibility of accumulating wealth individually. It is mainly because people are not able to make a living in the legal realm that they turn to illegal activities.

This position is a blunt repudiation of capitalist assumptions, which hold that it is only the prospect of unequal rewards and economic autonomy that allows for a prosperous and orderly society. In the capitalist perspective, take away unequal rewards and economic autonomy and the result will be a significant enlargement of black markets and other forms of activity that are contrary to official policy, as well as a lack of productivity in the official sphere. People are materially ambitious, and no amount of environmental tinkering can change this hardwired characteristic. If society removes the legitimate possibility of getting ahead, people will either vegetate or forge ahead illegally. Rather than eliminating criminality, such a regime would make even more ordinary people who are pursuing quintessentially human aims into criminals. Which is the case? Is the current situation the United States faces the result of the inadequacies of our current system and a failure to change environments to deactivate or circumvent greed (through an equitable distribution of goods and the abolition of money and markets), or is it the best that can be had and thus, its problems more a reflection of human failings than problems with the system?

More would also point to the political corruption among American political officials and the polarized positions taken by US citizens in their lack of engagement with political matters or extreme partisanship as ripe for systemic criticism. While not a strong democrat, he would argue that the American government has lost touch with ordinary citizens not only in terms of substantive policy, but also in its ability to gauge and act on citizens' preferences. The culprit in his mind would be large, centralized government as well as rich political actors. Putting more power in the hands of local and regional government, he would argue, would lead to greater satisfaction among citizens as well as functionally superior policies.

In addition, if decisions are to be made by an elite (and he would agree it should be), More would argue that this elite should be identified by educational credentials (in the form of educational requirements to hold office) and strict moral standards. More would point to Utopia's attempt to sever the connection between wealth and political power as an argument in favor of stricter eligibility standards for office and generally eliminating wealth as a factor in choosing candidates for office. In taking this stance, he rejects the historical defenses for allowing wealth into the political system: wealth is a sign of God's blessing; wealth is a marker of good judgment and knowledge; wealth provides decisionmakers with an important stake in society that will guide them to the best policies, and the use of wealth to advance one's preferred political agenda is an important political freedom. Instead, More appears to accept contrary arguments: wealth is not connected with knowledge and judgment, and the possession of private wealth by policymakers will lead them to distort policies to further their interests. Thus, Utopia prizes demonstrated learning over wealth as a marker of policy competence. Recent court rulings in the United States in contrast have privileged the liberal position over democratic and civic republican objections as well as More's, arguing that the individual freedom of the wealthy to use their large resources to influence the political process must trump concerns that would privilege equality of influence, the importance of participation and civic republican concerns over the quality of participation. Are we convinced by More that this decision is harmful to the community? Would we agree with him that, as in England, political problems and dysfunctions in the United States are in part the result of a political mistake in allowing wealth equal footing with knowledge, virtue, and political equality?[19]

A third set of problems has to do with happiness and freedom. Modern capitalist systems bring enormous amounts of pressure and stress on citizens as well as providing large amounts of goods and room for extensive negative freedoms. More would argue that what modern citizens deem happiness, wound up as it is in the possession of technology and material goods and the pursuit of individual lifeplans, is not true happiness, and that they would be more content and more orderly, and more people would be happy, if they were to trade in some negative freedoms (and stress) for more economic security. More paints Utopians as well-contented and Hythloday is so taken with their way of life that he yearns to return. Would this be the case now? Even contemporary European mixed economies, held up as providing more security than do Anglo-Saxon neoliberal systems, provide much less economic security and equality than does Utopia and many more negative freedoms. Is the modern understanding a more natural conception of happiness? Or is it a matter of modern programming, as More would probably argue? If More is right, then another, moral, question arises: ought we to continue pursuing a market-oriented system stressing negative freedoms when such systems have tended to mold citizens to equate happiness with the possession of ever larger amounts of material goods? Is our toleration of such programming in the context of a world of diminishing resources morally defensible?

It would perhaps be best to separate out different types of freedom here and look at the question from both sides. First, is our conception of economic freedom worth sacrificing the general distribution of happiness that More argues we give up? Is preserving the possibility of some gaining more material goods worth the very real chance that many will be impoverished? Does the pursuit of an ever-rising standard of living justify highly unequal standards of living, high levels of stress, and the loss of security and leisure for many people? Modern liberal, capitalist societies at the very least make the latter bargain (or possibly that contained in Rawls's Difference Principle),[20] and one virtue of reading *Utopia* is that we can see that bargain clearly. More would doubt that the terms of that bargain can be met and point out the negative effects on society (as filtered through human nature) of such inequalities.

The other proposition has to do with the freedom to devise our own lifeplans. Is it worth discarding the pluralism we now have for the security More proposes we gain, and do we agree that we must sacrifice plural lifeplans for material security and diminished disorder? More thinks we must, and here modern liberal theory and important strains of dystopian thought generally converge in opposing his views, though only partly for the same reasons. Liberal theory holds that large measures of conscious social control require a strong state that cannot be trusted with power, and that being human requires the type of general autonomy that allows for choices of lifeplans and the greater likelihood of disorder; thus, it rejects the trade. It is better to be free and have a choice of lifeplans than to strive for less disorder and more security in general and not have that choice. More's position is largely based on his understanding of the importance of environments and the ways in which everyone in society is complicit in maintaining the correct types of environment. In his mind, environments must meet exacting standards for reasons of avoiding the activation of uncongenial human hardwiring. Give people choices regarding their lifeplans, and some will choose in ways that will destroy the environment necessary for all to prosper, as well as risk activating their own harmful hardwiring and encouraging disorder. Environments are important precisely because people (both citizens and rulers alike) do not have total control over the process by which they make choices, cannot choose rightly on their own, and can only choose rightly in the most limited of circumstances. In other words, he does not think that humans can ever truly be autonomous. Moreover, the influence of the environment he constructs in Utopia, along with the checks he outlines, provides More with reasons to believe that rulers could be trusted with power and to believe one cannot trust citizens outside that environment. He would also argue that we already posses a distant and powerful state that citizens can do little to control or hold accountable. At least in his state, power is more greatly dispersed even if it does intrude more directly into individuals' lives.

To push this debate further, we see that *Utopia* raises the question of the desired role of the community in shaping the lives of its citizens. Should the community create an environment in which people are guided in their (assumed) attempts to live morally upright lives, or should it leave citizens (outside the minimal laws necessary to keeping order) to find morality and a conception of the good life on their own, or to allow society randomly to construct humans and their morality? More puts forward the proposition that we are not morally responsible if we embrace the second or third propositions; moreover, he would probably argue that modern society already does construct humans, just not in a morally defensible or pragmatically desirable fashion. Modern liberal philosophy, influenced by individualistic conceptions of the person and pluralism in general, tends to reject that position in favor of various justifications of individual autonomy as normatively desirable, pragmatically valuable, and empirically possible. Which is the better and more defensible position? Is there something morally askew with consciously molding citizens in the ways Utopia attempts? Is there something morally wrong with allowing private agents, such as the producers of cultural artifacts, to do so with only minimal social control, as is the case in the modern West? Is there something practically wrongheaded with Utopia's substitution of material incentives to work with surveillance? To what degree is society morally justified in consciously manipulating environments and in attempting to train and program citizens? Many of these answers will be derived from positions on whether there is a natural core to humans that relates to their responses to the environment, choices over lifeplans and other areas that Utopia consciously targets. If there is substance inherent in humans that values autonomy, Utopia's citizens are no longer recognizably human. More might reply that such thinking is insupportably essentialist, taking for granted a human individualism that is as much a conscious, modern social construct as is Utopia's social conformity.

What about More's proposition that greed really is the root of many of our problems? If we take it seriously, we should reexamine a whole variety of economic and political institutions. Of course, the soundness of More's understanding of human nature is open to question. If greed is not connected with the types of hardwiring he assumes, then his environmental solution will be stillborn. If we do accept More's views, what are the consequences? If people can act and do act in the ways More depicts, if they would be satisfied with the same, rather plain menu of clothing, housing, and food as everyone else so long as they are sure they will have sufficient goods, would it be best to provide ourselves with such in the attempt to eliminate greed and to discharge our responsibilities to future generations to conserve our resources? Or are there other goods and values that would make us hesitate to accept such a proposition even if it were possible? What should we put in the balance when making such a judgment? Should it be the case, for example, that we ought to place a value on colorfulness and variety? Could we argue that the life More sets out lacks a necessary human texture, a position Orwell would appear to take? Or are we reaching a point in the life of human civilization and the planet that such considerations may need to be subordinated to a more sober evaluation of the stock of resources now available to us and our descendants?

While More would have the community shape the moral lives of its citizens, he would also have it control their economic lives. Economic planning is the counterpart to the collective control of lifeplans. In More's argument, planning is superior to market forces because the former represents the collective and conscious use of rationality and information. Again, modern liberal economic theory differs, preferring to rely importantly upon markets and the diffusion of rational decisions among many people for reasons of efficiency, productivity, flexibility, and individual autonomy. There is no room to delve deeply into discussions of the problems with either planning or free markets, but it is necessary to bring up central questions involved in those debates: to what extent are we willing to sacrifice the common good that may be protected by planning in exchange for negative freedoms accompanied by market distortions and inefficiencies and the burdening of those who fair worst in a competitive atmosphere? And to what degree are we willing to sacrifice the prospect of economic growth, flexibility, and individual freedoms that are part of a market economy in exchange for an economic security that is marred by the rigidities, inefficiencies, and lack of negative freedoms that accompany planning? While probably not entirely aware of all these questions, More comes down on the side of planning. Are his reasons for favoring planning—efficiency, equity, the conscious use of rationality, decisionmaking by those who are best educated— convincing in a modern setting?

Finally, we should confront the fundamental proposition More sets forth— that by changing political, social, and economic environments in particular ways, along with specific kinds of training, we can comprehensively change the way people act, and that in failing to do so, we live in a less equal, more disorderly, and less morally defensible society. Are we hardwired in the ways he holds? Can that hardwiring be turned off or otherwise neutralized? Could citizens be trained to accept the community as the ultimate holder of value and eschew all others? Or is there a different kind of hardwiring in us that impels us to attempt to outstrip our fellows citizens and continually to improve our standard of living, hardwiring that is active despite everything a society may do to deactivate it? We assume now that greed and ambition are so deeply engrained in us that we must allow them a legitimate outlet, in the form of rewards for hard work and ingenuity, differential wages, the possibility for bigger and better houses, and for greater social esteem. *Utopia* fundamentally challenges us through its assertions that communities can do much more than they now accomplish to create the material and psychological conditions necessary for everyone to live the good life. If it is possible to change behavior communally in the way he describes, might it not only be reasonable, but necessary to empower our communal institutions to do much more than they do now? Given that we agree that institutions are to make people orderly, how much further should they go in the direction of molding the lives of citizens?

Many of these questions arise because of the large differences we find between Utopia and contemporary society. We have different expectations of individuals and families, different understandings of economics and politics, and indeed different types of problems and needs. More might argue we have been molded differently and that we should pose hard questions of ourselves that challenge that molding. Shouldn't we be willing to accept the provisions of Utopia even though they infringe upon our autonomy as individuals because they spread security and happiness more broadly? If More is correct that disorder and crime are the result greed and pride, shouldn't we be willing to adopt his scheme for those functional reasons? If not, why? Is it because we do not think that these proposals will work? Because we refuse to relinquish our moral autonomy? Or is it because we are unwilling to accept the constricted outlook and vanilla life those proposals would appear to bring?

Notes

1 George Logan, ed., *The Cambridge Companion to Thomas More* (Cambridge: Cambridge University Press, 2011).

2 Brendan Bradshaw, "More on Utopia," *The Historical Journal*, Vol. 24, no. 1 (1981).

3 Hugh Trevor-Roper, "The Intellectual World of Sir Thomas More," *The American Scholar*, Vol. 48, no. 1 (1979).

4 Eric Nelson, "Utopia through Italian Eyes: Thomas More and the Critics of Civic Humanism," *Renaissance Quarterly*, Vol. 59, no. 4 (2006).

5 Thomas Engeman, "Hythloday's Utopia and More's England: An Interpretation of Thomas More's Utopia," *The Journal of Politics*, Vol. 44, no. 1 (1982): 131–149.

6 Dominic Baker-Smith, "Reading Utopia," in G. M. Logan (ed.), *The Cambridge Companion to Thomas More* (Cambridge: University of Cambridge Press, 2011).

7 Samuel Bostaph, "Deepening the Irony of Utopia: An Economic Perspective," *History of Political Economy*, Vol. 42, no. 2 (2010).

8 James Nendza, "Political Idealism in More's Utopia," *The Review of Politics*, Vol. 46, no. 3 (1984).

9 George Logan, *The Meaning of More's Utopia* (Princeton: Princeton University Press, 1983).

10 Quentin Skinner, "Thomas More's Utopia and the Virtue of True Nobility," in Skinner, *Visions of Politics*, Vol. 2 (New York: Cambridge University Press, 2002).

11 William Cotton, "Five-fold Crisis in Utopia: A Foreshadow of Major Modern Utopian Narrative Strategies," *Utopian Studies*, Vol. 14, no. 2 (2003), provides a useful discussion of the scholarship on the production and publication of *Utopia*.

12 For an overview of the problems and debates surrounding *Utopia* in this regard, see Susan Bruce's *Introduction* to *Three Early Modern Utopias* (New York: Oxford University Press, 1999) as well as David Bevington, "The Dialogue in 'Utopia': Two Sides to the Question," *Studies in Philology*, Vol. 58, no. 3 (July 1961).

13 For these and other translations of the names More coins, see Bruce, *Introduction*.

14 Eric Nelson, "Greek Nonsense in More's Utopia," *Historical Journal*, Vol. 44, No. 4 (December 2001): 889–917.

15 For a discussion of *Utopia* with regard to change in More's life in Europe in the imagined context of Utopia itself, see Cotton, "Five-fold Crisis in Utopia."

16   Scholars have noted that More exaggerated the effects of economic transformations
     in his time; this observation, however, merely underlines the power of More's
     understanding of the nature of those changes and, in part, their future effects. See
     G. R. Elton, *England under the Tudors* (New York: Routledge, 1991).
17   For example, Baker-Smith, "Reading Utopia," 150.
18   This interpretation agrees that More was putting forth a "Erasmian humanist"
     vision of the good life. See Bradshaw, "More on Utopia," 3–4.
19   For an illuminating discussion of this issue in More's context, see Skinner, "Thomas
     More's Utopia and the Virtue of True Nobility," 230–236.
20   Which holds that unequal distributions of income and material goods can only be
     justified if they result in raising the standard of everyone, and particularly that of
     the poorest members of society. See Rawls, *A Theory of Justice* (Cambridge, MA:
     Belknap Press, 2nd edn, 1999).

3

Isle of Pines

Henry Neville's *Isle of Pines* (ca.1668), as with *Utopia*, is something of an enigma. I think it is importantly a response to such works as *Utopia* and Francis Bacon's *New Atlantis* rather than a companion to them or merely a send-up of travel narratives. Neville's main philosophical point, I argue, is the peril associated with the quest for perfection and in particular the dream of an easy material life. He poses serious questions: If humans attained utopia, what would happen to them? If there was no work to be done, no obstacles to face, no Nature to conquer, what would we do? What would come of our intellect, our culture, our science, our civilization, our ability to order ourselves if life was easy and completely enjoyable? Neville suggests that we would lose them all, leaving us eventually to live on par with animals.

This interpretation construes *Isle of Pines* as the prototype of an important type of dystopian novel, the kind that criticizes the urge to obtain perfection. As with some later dystopian pieces, Neville's work depicts the acquisition of an idyllic environment as ironic; that is, it shows that the attainment or discovery of paradise produces different results than intended. Rather than security and leisure providing the good life that More describes, the tropical paradise Pines inhabits leads eventually to debauchery, ignorance, tyranny, and violence. The difference between this story and later dystopian works is that Neville concentrates on the desire for ease and pleasure, encapsulated in the banal male dream of a life with no work and a variety of willing sexual partners rather than on the more complex problems associated with the power of the state and the price to be paid for technological advancement. He does not anticipate the labor-saving devices of the industrial age, nor does he focus on the paternalism that is the subject of twentieth-century dystopias. His primitive dystopian paradise is natural rather than man-made and thus has broader targets.

The story and interpretations

The story

The two narratives of *The Isle of Pines* constitute two travelogues. The inner narrative chronicles the experiences of George Pines, an English bookkeeper who while on his way to India with his merchant employer is shipwrecked on an island. He is accompanied in his escape from the wreck by four young women: two servant girls along with his employer's daughter and an African slave. This beginning of Pines's adventure is marked by a lapse of European morality, for Pines and his companions survive because they are forced to stay with the ship as it foundered, the ship's captain and the merchant having selfishly abandoned them by taking the only lifeboat. The latter pay for their immorality with their lives and the subsequent narrative reinforces the message that insurmountable problems eventually arise when people desert conventional norms.

The bulk of Pines's narrative details Pines's sexual relations with his female companions, complete with detailed discussions of their attributes, the number of progeny that each produce and the extraordinary expansion of the island's population by the time of his dotage. In turn, Pines relates his efforts as patriarch of the island to organize these progeny in ways that will minimize the chances of genetic damage to resulting offspring and bring him some peace and quiet. Pines creates a primitive society among his children and their descendants, dividing them into tribes, each of which is initially filled with the children of one of his female companions. This structuring provides some initial order, as each tribe goes to a separate part of the island to live.

Accompanying this discussion of social organization is an extended description of the conditions that Pines and his companions enjoy on the island. These provide a far easier life than available in England. For those people who wish to experience life as a vacation, the islanders' lot is certainly enviable. There is no poverty, hunger, or illness, though conditions are primitive. People perform almost no labor and no one must sell his soul and body to a master because everything is freely available, courtesy of Nature itself and the absence of private property. No one works with noxious substances, or freezes or burns because the environment is benign and manufacturing, even of the primitive kind then found in Europe, is absent. There is plenty of free time to do what one wishes. In sum, there is no manufacturing or trade, no markets, no money, no private property, no scarcity, and plentiful leisure.

The outer narrative is provided by Henry Van Sloetten, a Dutch captain who re-discovers the South Pacific island upon which the descendants of George Pines live. This narrative serves several purposes. Most mundanely, it explains how the manuscript written by Pines is transported to Europe. But more importantly, it reinforces and underlines the themes of degeneration implicit in Pines's manuscript. Whereas in Pines's reminiscences one sees life in the island from the view of someone who has spent decades there and exudes some pride in his residence, with Van Sloettern's narrative we get the views of an outsider who visits the island several decades after Pines's death. Where Pines is prideful, Van Sloettern merely observes the life of the islanders. He not only describes the fruitfulness of the land (in both vegetation and people), he also notes the nakedness of most inhabitants, the lack of tools, the dawning of an age of violence, the ferociousness of the set of rules instituted by Pines's patriarchal successors and the general cowardice of the inhabitants. Van Sloettern is not so blunt as to condemn openly the inhabitants of the island or to point a finger at the island as a contributing factor to their degeneration. But the evidence for such an explanation as well as the conclusion that something is seriously wrong with the Pineans is available in both narratives for the reader to find. The story ends with Van Sloetten leaving the island after using his weapons to help the current ruler put down a violent uprising perpetrated by one of the tribes. Unlike Hythloday, he does not act as a promoter of Pines's island in publishing his description. He displays no desire to return to the place and would probably find it very strange if anyone would be tempted to join its community.

Interpretations

Many have interpreted this story as a kind of utopian work, or even as a "Land of Cockaygne" story, that is, a rural tale that portrays a perfect place where no work needs to be done.[1] Several commentators see it as a story of colonialism and a description of the impact of Western power and culture on the non-Western world.[2] Others identify it as a farce and hoax, a discussion of patriarchy, an Arcadian story, a retelling of the Garden of Eden story, and even as an example of pornotopia (i.e., a sexual utopia). These and other discussions are addressed in Mahlberg's treatments of the story. Mahlberg's own considered view is that while its meaning was the subject of great debate at the time and since, it was a hoax that nonetheless was meant to have a local and political focus. Substantively, it was a criticism of the rule of the Stuarts, a warning to Charles II regarding continued strife and factionalism, and a lament about the unexploited potential, both commercial and military, of contemporary Englishmen when compared with the endeavors of their ancestors and the energy of their Dutch competitors. In terms of the story's republican message, Mahlberg sums it up by commenting that "By depicting the patriarchal ruler of a remote island who preferred sexual relations with women to looking after his political affairs, [the story] ridiculed both the depraved morals of the Stuart court and the patriarchal political theory used by Charles II to defend his authority by divine right."[3]

Perhaps the interpretation that presents the greatest contrast to the one presented here (and which is representative of the important line of interpretation emphasizing race, gender, and colonialism) is Boesky's.[4] She construes the story as a version of the Noah tale. That narrative type was important for the period because it was seen as the original legitimator of patriarchic power (Noah rules because he is the literal father of the community) and of racial differentiation. As such, it is a story that construes national identity through themes of interracial relations, political insurrection, and sexual desire. Patriarchy is depicted as desirable yet "explosive" because it creates identity through the subordination of a racialized and sexualized other that cannot be completely contained. Subordination takes the form of social and political hierarchies, thus addressing difference and slavery in both the utopian and contemporary political contexts. As such, the story in this interpretation questions the utility of racial miscegenation and rules of racially marked sexual conduct in the context of creating a nation of homogenous and strong citizens and a pervasive fear of slave insurrections. In this understanding, the disorder that is alluded to in Van Sloetten's narrative should not be construed as attributable to humans in general, but to the effects of the system of slavery and racial subordination; it is not the physical environment that is the problem, but rather the dynamics of a socially constructed system of colonial racism that inevitably results in the mixture of different races.

While this interpretation is intriguing, the discussion here does not follow its reasoning. It does hold that the story is a dystopia and one that has a larger target in addition to the perverse politics and life of the Restoration court, but that it also embraces a partially Machiavellian analysis of the impact of physical environments on humans and takes civilization itself as the entity that is endangered by a life of ease and plenty. Thus the interpretation used here pushes further the understanding of the story as an exploration of civic republican political analysis.[5]

Contexts and problems

Neville was an important figure in republican circles in mid-seventeenth-century England. A companion of James Harrington (himself the author of a work detailing an ideal state, *The Commonwealth of Oceania*), a onetime supporter of Cromwell, possibly a combatant on the Parliamentary side of the Civil War, a member of Parliament during the 1640s and 1650s, and a skilled controversialist who published a number of critical and satirical pamphlets, Neville was deeply involved in the political and intellectual questions of the day. Later, in exile after the Restoration, he moved to Italy and was exposed to the writings of another important civic republican, Nicolo Machiavelli.[6]

By the 1660s, the changes that More foresaw transforming Medieval life had begun working their way through English society. It was now a nation of towns, discrete country holdings, and commercial activities rather than communal, agricultural villages. Political institutions were congealing in the aftermath of dynastic struggles and the Civil War, though social structures were still in flux. Neville was also writing in the aftermath of a half-century of intense speculation. Politics, society, and economics had been laid bare by immense numbers of books, pamphlets, sermons, and broadsheets.[7] People were no longer content to take inherited ways of living for granted. The educated classes wished to understand and improve life, while the uneducated had shown themselves willing to follow leaders who promised them heaven on earth. As with his contemporaries Thomas Hobbes and John Locke, Neville was influenced by the events surrounding the Civil War, which not only produced upheaval, violence, destruction, chronic disorder, and the spectacle of Parliament and King locked in mortal combat, but also the creation of social movements and the sprouting of perfectionist doctrines. Quakers and Shakers preached the possibility of the spirit of God dwelling within oneself, making external doctrines and institutions superfluous. Fifth Monarchy men hailed the approaching Second Coming and a new kingdom with Christ at its head. Levelers promoted a radically expanded political franchise, while Diggers proclaimed the merits of primitive communism. Even the Puritans, more thoroughly indoctrinated as they were in the concept of Original Sin than their enthusiastic rivals, looked forward to building and inhabiting a City on a Hill that would serve as a shining example to all others. Less outlandish but nevertheless perfectionist in their tendencies were the writings of such people as More, Bacon, and Campanella.[8] These works depended more on political and economic doctrine than the spirit of God and the efficacy of scripture. That Neville was addressing these perfectionist ideas as well as the bucolic "Land of Cockaygne" stories and the spiritualist utopias is seen in the depiction of Pines as more than just a fortunate stranded traveler. Though he builds little in comparison with ordinary society, Pines does create his own doctrine, organizing his descendants in a particular fashion and acting as a founder.[9]

Coupled with these perfectionist tendencies were a variety of experiments in new social mores as well as conscious attempts to discard old virtues. Neville was, of course, well acquainted with the antinomian tenets of the perfectionists that were often expressed in consciously brazen violations of traditional sexual and social arrangements.[10] Just as importantly, he would be equally aware of the growing tendency towards libertinism found in the upper ranks of English society. Neville invites a comparison of Henry Pines and his descendants with the smart social set under Charles II. The latter also lived as if on permanent vacation, free from practical worries. They, too, appeared to care little for industriousness and to confuse licentiousness with culture. Given this background, I think we should take into account Neville's political views even more than do many of other interpreters of this story. As Mahlberg underlines in her work, we should appreciate the fact that Neville was a civic republican—someone who believes that republics are the best form of government and can only be maintained by the exercise of virtue and self-restraint on the part of ordinary citizens.[11] This political orientation not only helps account for the fact that in his story Pines and his descendants ineffectively rule as monarchs over the island, alternately abetting and feebly responding to outbreaks of immorality and disorder. It also informs the larger point of the story in this interpretation—that without the strengthening of individual and social discipline, conceptualized as the development and exercise of virtues, the good life is unattainable. For monarchs and nobility, such discipline is not necessary because, as the court of Charles II illustrates, all their needs are met. The political virtues of ordinary citizens, meanwhile, atrophy for lack of use and encouragement.

Neville published the materials we now take as the story of Pines in several pieces. First was the narrative of Pines himself. Shortly afterward, Van Sloetten's narrative was added to sandwich Pines's story.[12] The story was published in a popular form—the pamphlet. Here Neville was able to take advantage of advances in literacy and publication technology that had taken place over the past 150 years to reach a wider and more humble constituency. Thanks to the

Reformation, the general population was now more literate and due to the religious and political controversies of the past half-century it was accustomed to the circulation of written polemics. Neville sought to influence a greatly enlarged group of educated people who formed the bedrock of republican politics. He was cautioning those who may still be excited by radical religious or political doctrines to rethink their basic assumptions. Republicanism is good; excessive enthusiasm that results in turning the world upside down is bad. In this sense, he is putting forward a conservative cultural message. That is not to say that he supports the old society that propped up an absolute monarchy. In reality, he steered a middle course between the strictly hierarchical society that supported absolutist kings and the cultural and political anarchists who wanted to reinvent everything. It is just that the larger targets of his satire here are the radicals who wish to provide themselves with the perfect life.

In discussing Pines's island, Neville projects onto it a series of problems he sees afflicting contemporary England that are associated with the breakdown of social and individual virtues. He connects these problems with utopianism and other factors. The first of these problems is the institution of monarchy. In drawing Pines and his successors as monarchs and implicitly equating Pines with Charles II, he points to the danger of that mode of government. While possessing most power (by virtue of his maleness), Pines loses his moral compass. He lapses into a state of idleness. His policies are meant primarily to benefit himself and only secondarily to benefit those over whom he rules. He initiates only minimal social or political structuring, and does not encourage science, commerce, or general education. He does nothing in terms of moral education but mouth pious platitudes that his own behavior undermines. As a patriarch and father figure, concepts with which seventeenth-century apologists defended absolute power of monarchies, Pines is not immune to the degenerative forces on the island and does little to help his subjects resist them.[13] As people with little constraints on their power and desires, monarchs are prone to corruption.

Connected with the conduct of Pines is the more general problem constituted by the neglect of morals and social order. The Restoration period was notorious for its open flaunting of traditional sexual morality. As any reader of Pepys diaries can attest, libertinism was around during Cromwell's Protectorate but kept discreet. This was not the case after Charles II was invited back to the throne. It at least appeared that social discipline was deteriorating quickly at the time, with sexual indiscretions being the marker of that degeneration.[14] In the story, this degeneration starts with Pines's relationship with the four women and the revival of incestuous practices in latter generations when they are no longer dictated by a limited number of possible sexual partners. This move, in turn, generates further problems in terms of general disorder, violence, rape, and murder. As Neville develops the point, deviating from accepted mores in any way is so dangerous that all other social and cultural goods crumble in the wake of such actions.

It is unclear, however, whether Neville wishes to portray sexual degeneration on the island solely in terms of a lack of self-discipline and deviation from conventional morality that are essential for inculcating civic virtues in citizens, or if he also sees Pines's behavior in particular as abusive in gendered terms. Pines's treatment of the women on the island certainly lacks an appreciation of their humanity. He appears to consider them as only so much breeding stock. He professes some attachment to his employer's daughter (because she is the youngest and probably because she comes from the higher class), but he conveys no such sentiments toward others. Indeed he seems to think the African slave girl repulsive, yet continues to sleep with her out of a desire to maximize the number of his progeny. If Neville does wish us to condemn Pines for these attitudes, he would be adding an important modern element of equal respect to his list of necessary virtues.

Neville is not concerned with the breakdown of sexual mores alone, however. He is also worried about the general destruction of social structures that are part of the bedrock of any stable society. This is in keeping with his general orientation as a civic republican. Civic republicans are not democrats per se. They do not see people as completely equal, nor do they see the attempt to equalize people socially as desirable. Drawing upon Aristotle's and Machiavelli's arguments that mixed regime types are the most stable, they are sympathetic to the retention of classes and the distinctions that serve to mark particular classes. Social discipline entails everyone knowing their place. Thus in one reading, Pines's indiscretion is not just that he is sexually promiscuous, but that he is promiscuous with a wide variety of people. He literally ranges the whole scale, from his master's daughter at the top, to the serving girls in the middle, to the African slave at the bottom. Having instituted a sort of sexual democracy with his women, Pines is thereafter unable to institute a suitable class system for his progeny. A variant of this argument would include race as well as class in the dangerous boundaries that Pines transgresses. While Pines does separate the tribes racially, there is necessary racial crossing of boundaries by his descendants.

Yet, while the rejection of mores is depicted as the gateway to further social problems, the root causes of social degeneracy in general, including the erosion of mores, appear to lie elsewhere in this narrative. The primary problem that Neville identifies is not lust or a democratic spirit; rather, it is the desire to live a life of comfort and ease without work and the effects of attaining such a dream. The aristocracy enjoys such a life in England; in Neville's view, this atmosphere explains their morally squalid lives. But Neville detects in the popularity of utopias and perfectionist schemes a more widespread longing for an easy life that infects the population as a whole. Given the choice between working for a living and not, people would invariably choose the latter, preferring to live at ease on a tropical island. Neville wishes to educate people to the dangers of such a life.

Themes in dystopia and dystopian life

Themes

The most important theme of the story is that of degeneration. Pines's narrative is a different kind of travel story than Robinson Crusoe's even though it appears to be a similar story of shipwreck, survival, and seeming prosperity. The overt message of Pines's own reminiscences is the happy, long, and idyllic life he has lived despite his exile from his homeland. Pines's shipwreck is on the surface a blessing, or at least a story of how an initial calamity turned into a lifelong vacation. He never works hard, is blessed with a beautiful environment, and looks back at the end of his life at an enjoyable existence crowned with the presence of a veritable horde of offspring. Superficially therefore, Pines *is* a kind of Robinson Crusoe figure, albeit one with a much more satisfying sex life. Yet if we read between the lines, we see that not all is well. Pines and his companions do nothing but procreate and recreate. Even their enjoyment appears to be more sloth than fulfillment. Nothing really happens on Pines's island except for the expansion of its population. Nothing more is constructed in terms of organization or civilization other than the creation of the most basic and primitive of social structures and cultural artifacts. Blessed with leisure and a salubrious climate, Pineans do not ape Crusoe in his desire to recreate and uphold European culture, industriousness, and inventiveness; instead, they vegetate and decline.

To underscore this point, the degenerative effects of such a life are signaled in Pines and Van Sloetten's narratives in ways that echo observations made at the time with regard to the wealthy. Pines argues that it was the condition of "idleness and fullness of everything that begot in me a desire for enjoying the women." Here Pines's sexual desire is not initially produced by natural impulses (that of procreation), but artificially stimulated by his release from labor. His time, energy, and inclination to engage in sexual relations are the surplus created by the sparse effort needed to support himself, just as the libertine activities of the Court were put down to their life of idleness. Another clue is in his treatment of the resulting children. Pines notes that they were fed but otherwise not cared for; the women being pregnant every year, children could easily be replaced. Here the ease of producing and supporting children results in a cavalier attitude toward them as humans, just as the availability of the women resulted in his treating them as merely breeding animals, and just as the rich and noble of the time regarded their servants as subhumans. Given that he need not struggle to provide for those he impregnates or brings into the world, Pines places no value on them and instead concentrates on his own pleasure and fulfillment. Though he sets himself up as the originator and enforcer of morality, Pines demonstrates nothing more than a keen self-interest and does little but indulge his own desires. Under his tutelage the whole island is arranged for his comfort and satisfaction (being someone who prizes his privacy) rather than the greater good of the population as a whole.

The further effects of this environment are seen in the cultural and technological spheres. While there are religious ceremonies held in Van Sloetten's presence, customs appear to be primitive and generally scarce. Those customs, in turn, are merely diluted and bastardized holdovers of what Pines brought with him from Europe. Nothing new has been invented; nothing indigenous of value has been created, and even what has been brought over has not been well preserved. Likewise, the only technology available when Van Sloetten arrives is those items that had been salvaged from the storm so long ago, and those (like an ax) are now so worn as to be useless. Indeed the ax is a metaphor for most things inherited by the group of castaways. They are the only products of an advanced civilization in view. Useful once, they are now decayed. They cannot be replaced because the group has not the ambition, the knowledge or the pressing need to invent ways of creating duplicates, much less improved successors. In general, the civilization of the Land of Pines is a watered down, stagnant, and more disordered version of what the original castaways left when they sailed from Europe because the discipline necessary to maintaining that civilization is absent. Neither Pines nor his descendants have enough virtue to counteract this environment.

The second major theme is the failure of Pines and his descendants to act as good rulers and founders given their environment. If one part of Neville's ironic understanding of the quest for an easier life is his argument that pleasant environments tend to breed nasty because undisciplined people, the other part is his understanding of the need for external political and social structures to offset the human incapacity for self-discipline. Here he partially recapitulates Machiavelli's analysis of physical environments and their connection with governments. The easier the life, the more active the government must be in instilling and enforcing the use of virtues. Pines and his successors are clueless with regard to their responsibilities and do nothing of substance to instill virtues. The necessity of doing so is mandated by the environment, which saps the inhabitants of their ambition. Despite the storms that wreck Pine and his companions and beset Van Sloetten on his voyage, Pines's island appears blessed with nearly perfect weather. There is no excessive cold to require elaborate clothing or extensive shelter. There are no ferocious creatures or other humans to endanger the castaways and force them to exercise bravery and fortitude. The island is inhabited by singularly tame animals, namely a goat-like creature that fears no one and a tasty bird whose stupidity allows easy hunting. Other foodstuffs and water are likewise procured without difficulty, thus short-circuiting the need for ingenuity and hard work. When tools are lost, break, or wear out, the inhabitants feel no desire to replace them because they are not needed. Prey can be clubbed, nuts and other fruits effortlessly harvested, and grass, flowers, and bark serve for what little clothing and shelter is required. Pines and his descendants do not recognize the danger of the situation, taking for granted instead the general assumption of the time that an easy physical life with no private property or shortages allows a community to dispense with discipline, particularly social discipline. Yet this is to get it exactly wrong, Neville argues.

This story therefore provides much the same moral as the tale of Robinson Crusoe and his successors in the early spirit of the Protestant ethic, but it comes from the other direction. Pines's story is not a tale documenting dogged determination, ingenuity, morality, or cultural conservancy. These virtues are not necessary in this environment (in contrast to Crusoe's), and Pines himself fails to provide them when he slides away from the original values and discipline he possessed; consequently, his descendants follow him in this descent. In the face of plenty and ease he takes for granted the rightness of his relations with his women. He is unconcerned in general about his progeny and arranges his life to suit his own desires. If Crusoe must work doggedly to survive in his island exile and fears losing his European identity and cultural bearings in his isolation and interactions with Friday, and as such represents a model of an outstanding civic republican Founder, Pines has few such anxieties. Rather than preserving civilization and culture, and retaining, strengthening, spreading, and renewing the discipline and order that his European upbringing provided him, Pines does the minimal amount of organizing and encourages by example and deed the lazy life the island promotes.

Life in dystopia

Life on Pines's island is schizophrenic. The purely physical part of life on the island is generally idyllic. The weather is fine, the people beautiful, food abundant and easily procured, and leisure time abounds. One need work hardly at all to live well. Sex is plentiful and varied. For the first few generations, physical security is also absolute. Even for latter generations, none starve to death, disease is unheard of, and people routinely live to very advanced ages.

Yet from the beginning and increasingly as time goes on, this physical ideal is matched with a moral, social, and cultural decline. If life is physically good, there is increasingly nothing else that advances humans as good persons and citizens. There is no literature or other manifestations of higher culture. There is no science; no attempt to map, explain, and otherwise understand the physical spaces people inhabit is in evidence. No one tries to build a ship, explore the environs, or contemplate leaving the island in search of knowledge and adventure. There is no endeavor to establish beautiful, human-created spaces, or stately buildings. There are few social rituals, dances, or other organized manifestations of communal solidarity. There appears to be no educational system or other pillars of an intellectual life. Besides the infrequent and minimal tasks one must discharge to eat, clothe oneself, and keep primitive housing in repair, everyone is content to loaf about.

The question is whether this lack of social and cultural activity is relevant. Neville suggests that it is. His attitude is in closer sympathy with that of the restless Van Sloetten than with the sensibilities of the sluttish islanders. Neville wishes the reader to sympathize with rather than envy the plight of Pines's descendants, stuck as they are on their island and their downward cultural spiral. Incapable of progressing, they are unable to attain full humanity. They are increasingly beast-like, akin to the dodo birds they prey upon. Their potential for human advancement has been rendered inoperable by the sapping of their moral and cultural strength. Lacking discipline and character, they occupy a libertine limbo.

An indication that this is Neville's attitude is signaled by the description of the disorder that comes to mar this seeming tropical idyll. Not only are there no intellectual or cultural stimuli; the exhaustion of moral values and social structures, Neville implies, comes to threaten the ease and beauty people enjoy. In particular, the seeming paradise is slowly but surely beset by jealousy, violence, rape, and murder. From a situation in which physical security is taken for granted with little effort, the island has descended into a situation in which one's life may be threatened even if everything that anyone could possibly want—shelter, food, and a mate—are readily and universally available. This last observation is crucial for the meaning of the story. Both the tragedy of the situation and its roots come from the absence of scarcity. People are not violent and rapacious because they are in need, but because the very abundance of all they need means they are not required to develop the virtues that allow them to control their appetites and desires. In reaction, a government has been created and it strives to create order. But it has little moral authority. Pines as the founder of the island's order has lost his moral and cultural background by the time political and social norms are instituted. The Old Testament rules he and his descendants grasp for as an easy and work-free solution are primitive and brutal rather than inspiring and generative of discipline and virtue. Significant and growing numbers of islanders ignore these rules and defy attempts at punishment, ultimately forcing Pines's grandson to appeal to Van Sloetten and his weapons to put down a rebellion that threatens to tear his community apart. One can see that in the future such developments will be all too common, with the community eventually descending into chaos and widespread violence.

Human nature and applications

Human nature

Where More attributes much human evil to environments, Neville initially appears to suggest that evil comes largely from internal sources, in the form of sexual appetites, jealousy, and the desire for ease and comfort. These are inherent in people. Neville does little to develop this understanding explicitly and though he has Pines's grandson hold that human nature is "depraved," the pattern of the story suggests he may in fact hold that these causes of evil are not totally to blame, for they are useful in other ways. Sexual appetites are not inherently evil; it is their abuse that creates evil. Jealousy comes from the necessary drive to survive. The desire to live an easy life likewise stems from an instinct to preserve one's strength and energy. Instead, Neville appears to argue that there is something else that is also to blame. To prevent these innate desires and instincts from straying into harmful practices, Neville suggests throughout his story that humans require either environmental adversity to force them to develop discipline or social reinforcement, that is, social programming in the form of culture and government rules, in order to live orderly lives. Humans, Neville argues, always need some external source of discipline, whether it be Nature or human institutions, for it is not the absence of useful things that breed disorder, nor is it pride or desire alone, but the congenital lack of human self-restraint. The more benign the environment, the more people need external, human-created props to provide restraints. Paradise, it appears, brings out the worst in humans because it indulges rather than disciplines them.

Thus, as with More, Neville's model of human contains hardwiring that is ambiguous when it comes to desirable behavior. Put humans in a desert, for example, where they must work hard to survive, and you will find humans who are disciplined and cultured. They will still have appetites, but these will be disciplined by the environment. Where Neville differs appears to be in the degree to which innate human traits are productive of undesirable behavior. Where More would agree that human desires are themselves good, yet can be stimulated by the presence of many material goods and thus can lead to disorder, he also thinks people would be content with a sufficiency and generally remain orderly. Hardwiring can be circumvented or turned off because desires are easily satisfied and humans posses some innate measure of self-control. Neville appears to reject the notion that hardwiring can be circumvented or turned off. He also appears to reject the notion that greed importantly comes from scarcity or anticipation of want, and that desires are easily satisfied. He implies instead that people will always want more and better things, or the things that others possess, if those things can be obtained with a minimum of effort. Desires cannot be deactivated in the way More argues they can, nor are they easily satisfied in terms of quantity, or satisfied through the provision of choice (as

Bellamy will maintain). Nor do humans innately possess self-restraint. That is why they must depend on virtues and culture (which is really the externalization of virtues) to discipline desires. Take people out of a desert and their discipline may disappear. Likewise, a situation in which there is no money, no markets, and complete equality will not lead to the elimination of greed in this scenario. Such arrangements are not relevant to the expression of innate desires, nor do they provide discipline. While Pines does not pursue wealth, he is greedy in many other aspects; the presence of food and companionship does not easily slake his appetites. He is not happy with sleeping with one or two women—he must have all four. He is not content with a few children; he must generate 47. He and his companions are not content with living a healthy life. They instead indulge themselves and become fat.

Thus, while Neville places more emphasis on programming than does More, that does not mean that hardwiring is not important to him. It is not programming or the impact of environments on programming that is the primary factor in his understanding of human problems. It is, rather, environmental impacts on hardwiring. Put humans in benign circumstances and they will respond automatically by ceasing to work hard, though they will still lust after more things. Programming only mitigates these tendencies if it is of the correct kind—that which generates and preserves virtues. In making this argument, Neville moves in a different direction from More and most utopian authors. Material security in his mind does not make people better; it makes them worse. Neville sees such security as removing the need for the self-discipline central to controlling greed and other vices. Such discipline does not eliminate desire, much less satiate it; rather, it allows people to resist and to curb the ever-present impulse to act excessively on desires. Individually, they do so by developing such virtues as abstinence, diligence, and fortitude. Collectively, they do so by creating traditional rules and mores they take for granted as behavioral guides. The fewer the environmental challenges that force people to discipline themselves or die, the greater the need for an effective republican government.

The conclusion to draw from this picture is that humans require discipline to reach their full potential, and that environments lacking challenges make the development and exercise of discipline more problematic than difficult environments. The best environments are those that force people to either develop and employ the virtues, morality, and culture that allows them to exercise self-discipline, or to die. Such an environment also spurs people to develop themselves intellectually, socially, culturally, and spiritually. Without challenges, the intervention of a Founder who creates a republican government and a list of public virtues is necessary, and in the absence of both, human potential lies dormant. This argument parallels, but does not duplicate, the proposition that humans find meaning and fulfillment in labor. Here, Neville depicts leisure as the enemy of development—the inhabitants of the island have plenty of it, but engage in none of the self-improving activities that More's utopians enjoy. Where Neville's understanding differs from the labor theory of human fulfillment is in its broadness. It is not just physical or mental labor that people require to fulfill themselves. Rather, it is also the challenge of overcoming major obstacles and building a higher form of life, spurring both individuals and communities to marshal their resources, sharpen their wits, strain their sinews, and test their fortitude.

Van Sloetten's observations regarding the empty and undeveloped nature of the island also suggests more broadly that a sign of progress and human fulfillment for Neville is the transformation of Nature. Not having to do much in order to win a living from their surroundings, people on the island do not do much to alter their physical environment. This position again will find both echoes and dissonance in later stories we will discuss. Some later sensibilities might praise the lack of activity on the island as a virtue; after all, if the environment does not require transformation, it is better that it be left intact than wantonly rearranged. But Van Sloetten can only see the potential for wealth and a higher level of social and material prosperity and is puzzled and scandalized that it has not been exploited. Neville appears to agree; a civilized and moral community demonstrates its mastery over Nature, not its dependence upon it.

Applications

Neville questions the heart of the original utopian project and of some later progressive understandings: if people succeed in eliminating all human and natural obstacles to the good life, will they become better, fully human creatures, or will they come to regret that condition? Given his understanding of humans, he does not expect the quest for a completely benign environment to turn out as people believe it will. Neville suggests that eventually such an environment produces a life that is not worth living. It not only lacks external sources of discipline; it might also eventually undermine the contributions of a solidly republican government. Neville seeks to discourage people from seeking outsized goals, or even to create or tolerate conditions in which the drive and discipline derived by a struggle with nature are absent. The quest to attain a secure environment only serves to distract us from what may be accomplished through hard work and ends up plunging us into a far worse condition than where we started. Place humans in either a man-made or natural setting in which they no longer need to struggle to survive and rather than a race of energetic, orderly, and inventive humans striving to improve their minds, what you eventually generate is a breed of savages whose intellectual dullness matches their moral turpitude. In short, humans are not built to enjoy paradise.

The problems Neville addresses are therefore quite different from those More wishes us to contemplate. Where More produces a plan for a more perfect place, given the problems of poverty, unemployment, irresponsible government, and crime he sees afflicting England, Neville questions the rationality of producing such a plan by connecting the quest for radical improvement with the gluttony of the aristocracy and the vicious anarchism and antinomianism of millennial religious sects. To seek perfection is, at best, to greatly complicate the foundations for making life civilized and orderly, and therefore enjoyable and pleasant. To seek perfection is a fool's errand, particularly when it entails attempts to provide economic security. As such, Neville can be read as gesturing toward a minimal state when it comes to policies not directly related to order, discipline, and virtues. He would not be a fan of the welfare state or any attempts to shield individuals or groups from the bracing effects of working to survive, nor of efforts to bolster the economy to produce a high standard of living. Yet he differs from libertarians in pointing to the problems of developing and maintaining civilization rather than concentrating on questions surrounding the autonomous self-construction of the individual. Having little faith in the capacity of individuals to discipline and develop themselves by drawing upon innate resources, he is inclined to favor strong cultural, moral, and regulatory structures that empower the community as a whole at the expense of the individual. Thus, contrary to the libertarian position, he appears to argue that the more prosperous a state and the easier the life within it, the more important it is that the state's coercive organs be strengthened, that the community consciously encourage or impose virtues, culture, and science on citizens, and that citizens be active in the community to strengthen their virtues and ensure collective autonomy.

Is Neville right? Do humans need challenges or a strong state in order to thrive? Do we lack that internal ability to produce self-discipline and the inward desire to remain civilized under any circumstances? If left with abundant leisure, would we vegetate? If life were a permanent vacation, would we tend to slip backward into a beastlike state? One thought experiment is to put ourselves in Pines's place. If marooned in an environment in which we need do little work to survive, would we work anyway to create a more sophisticated material and cultural life? Would we engage in the types of intellectual and scientific projects we have said we would pursue if we only had the time and resources? This is a difficult question to answer, and people will probably answer it differently depending on their fundamental assumptions. One might argue that boredom would inevitably arise, and start us down the path of arguing that humans are innately ambitious. Humans will develop themselves intellectually, culturally, and materially because they are restless and hungry for new accomplishments. Or one may hold that there is an inborn survival instinct in humans that makes them suspicious of their surroundings and driven to create a society and culture that will allow them to survive if natural conditions turn against them. Humans will always pursue science and civilization as a hedge against disaster. Each of these answers would turn us in a different direction than the one Neville takes, at least in part because they locate in humans resources that Neville does not find.

Another way of approaching these questions is to ask if a different version of the story would be plausible. If Neville had written of such an island, blessed with a temperate climate and abundant, easily gathered sources of food, would we be surprised if he allowed that the inhabitants had built towns, developed an economy, created a sophisticated culture, and lived happily ever after? Our temptation would be to say yes, such a story is plausible. But to be fair to Neville, such a response would be influenced by what we consider normal (a sophisticated economy and culture) in circumstances that are quite different from those he describes. And perhaps the fact that disorderly behavior has consistently arisen in our own time among those who are wealthy and leisured (as it did during Neville's time) may also give us pause. We might find the story plausible only if it contained a description of some cultural and political means of enforcing discipline—cultural injunctions to work hard, say, or religious precepts that condemn laziness and promiscuity as sinful. Neville, as we see, would argue that such cultural props, while necessary, would eventually be undermined by the environment, necessitating a strong, forceful, and republican state to intervene to impose discipline, civilization, and civic virtue on the inhabitants.

This brings us to questions of disorder in our own society. Might high levels of incarceration, periodic massacres in settled communities, domestic terrorism, and puzzlingly high levels of crime be due to our unwillingness to emphasize virtues, particularly given the high standard of living enjoyed in industrialized nations, particularly the United States? Might social conservatives be correct that citizens require outside sources of discipline to make up for the easy environment and lack of inherent resources that could provide discipline?

If so, the direct policy implications of the story are important. Neville suggests the opposite of More's prescription when it comes to economic security. Government should not promote endless economic growth that will raise standards of living or that make living itself too easy. The focus should be on maintaining civilization, not in elevating the Gross Domestic Product (GDP). Moreover, the community in this understanding should not provide citizens with a safety net. Doing so only leads to laziness and disorder. Taken to its extreme, to follow Neville would not only mean ending state policies that provide material support to individuals who are down on their luck, but also terminating private charitable endeavors as well. The source of support is not important; it is, rather, its effect on both individuals and humans in general. This position appears to replicate the philosophical position taken by the most fundamentalist of capitalist theorists in terms of exalting the virtues of competition, but with a twist: it is not narrow market competition that Neville favors, but competition with Nature itself, and the good that comes from that competition is not economic growth, but cultural, moral, and scientific advancement.

Would we agree? Should governments not focus on endlessly expanding the economy and encouraging technological, labor-saving innovations if the result is that making a living becomes too easy and life itself becomes cushioned by creature comforts? Do we agree with this position? Does the welfare state contribute to disorder and cultural decline? Does capitalism itself, with its drive to increase human wealth, do so as well? Or would the refusal to create a safety net when possible represent the real rollback of civilization and moral understanding, and the rejection of economic progress (whether based on a capitalist foundation or otherwise) embody a needlessly austere understanding of the human potential to remain orderly and civilized?

What of Neville's apparent adaptation of a Machiavellian understanding of the relationship between states and physical environments?[15] Would we agree that the richer the economy, the stronger and more active the state must become to preserve order and civilization in general? More would probably concur in the prediction that the presence of more than sufficiency as a standard of living would activate greed and pride, triggering the need for a stronger state. Of course, he is also a proponent of thinking of morality on a communal scale. But Neville appears to be saying something more. It is not just the plethora of goods, but also the ease of life that is the problem, and such ease does more than activate greed and pride; it sets in motion a general decline that makes state activity (albeit in the limited set of areas outlined earlier) and citizen involvement increasingly important because such ease removes a crucial disciplinary element that individuals by themselves cannot replace. Does this make sense? Must the strength of the state and the scope of civic involvement be responsive to environments? The literature on the state does point to the different functions states play in different times and places, how functions might be differently performed given different types of social environments, and how the presence of abundant natural resources may retard such modern goods as democratization.[16] Should the type of environment that Neville identified be included as well? Was Neville correct in his analysis, meaning that we are condemned to live under an increasingly strong state if we choose to continually improve our standard of living and wish to remain civilized and conversely, that the only way of scaling back the state is to cut back on our standard of living? And if it is true, what choice would one make: to enjoy a high standard of living under a state that heavy-handedly imposes disciplines and virtues, or to live with a much more moderate standard of living and a less intrusive state?

One might also go in another, completely different direction in evaluating this story and argue that the situation on the island is in some ways defensible. This judgment is not in reference to the growing levels of violence and disorder on the island, but to the simplicity of life the islanders enjoy. To refuse to change an idyllic natural environment by not building large structures, mining the ground and cutting the forests may be the more responsible and ethical course of action. Indeed, sophisticated cultures have often been associated with highly stratified societies and ruling elites harnessing the labor of their inferiors to build monuments to themselves. Aside from the evidence of disorder, one could argue on those grounds that the Pinean lifestyle is a morally superior choice when compared with the type civilized social existence that Neville appears to accept, with all the implications such a judgment generates with regard to the human reshaping of natural landscapes, whether it be urbanization, the construction of dams, or other similar projects.[17]

Such a position would posit that the conquest of Nature is only one way of living a civilized existence. Indeed, that position may also question whether or not civilization itself is necessary for the good life. What should we expect in terms of a good life given a benign physical environment? Is a sophisticated social structure necessary in the absence of want? Do we need science if we have all that we materially desire? Do we need culture if we are surrounded by physical beauty? Neville argues that while it would be difficult to do so, we do need to construct these things, not just to fulfill ourselves but more importantly to develop and sustain the disciplined existence that marks us off from animals. The sign of a human existence for him is life in a society surrounded by culture, stimulated by education and science, living apart from and above Nature. Even if these were not important to order, they would still be necessary as a way of exercising and developing our skills and virtues. In some ways, to build and enjoy society and culture culminating in civilization necessarily constitutes part of the good life for Neville. Without them we not only eventually become less than human, but also do not lead the full life of which we are capable.

We may want to question this position. Do society and civilization make us human? Might not a good and recognizably human life be found collectively in surroundings that we consider socially and culturally simple? Might not such a life consist primarily of little work, much leisure, and the enjoyment of a beautiful and undisturbed natural environment? If so, we again would have to consider the policy implications. Do we spend too much time and effort as a society attempting to build things, whether tangibly or culturally, when a better life might entail less activity, or at least less materially disruptive activity? Might our lives be more sustainable, less stressful, less disharmonious, violent, and disorderly if we were to adopt a more minimalist life?

Even if Neville were to grant that such an existence would constitute a good life, he appears to reject the proposition that it could last. Here we confront his basic assumptions about human nature. He argues the human impulses that manifest themselves in greed, violence, and jealousy are so strong and innate human inhibitors so weak that we would expect fatal problems to emerge in a physical paradise. We should not be surprised that Pines sleeps with all the women, or that standards of civility degenerate and increasingly stern measures are called for to keep order despite the easy availability of the economic, physical, and emotional items humans desire. Do we accept this judgment? Or are there other defensible ways of understanding the relationships among the good life, virtues, the state, the ease of life, standards of living, and undisturbed Nature?

Notes

1   See Susan Bruce, "Introduction," *Three Early Modern Utopias* (New York: Oxford
    University Press, 1996), xxxiv. Bruce suggests a nationalist reading in which the
    story is said to decry the failings of the English versus their rivals, the Dutch.

2   For example John Scheckter, *The Isle of Pines, 1668: Henry Neville's Uncertain
    Utopia* (Farnham, Surrey, England, and Burlington, VT: Ashgate, 2011).

3   Gaby Mahlberg, "Authors Losing Control: The European Transformations of Henry
    Neville's *The Isle of Pines* (1668)," *Book History*, Vol. 15 (2012), and "An Island with
    Potential: Henry Neville's *The Isle of Pines* (1668)," in J. C. Davis and Miguel A.
    Ramiro (eds), *Utopian Moments: Micro-Historical Approaches to Modern Literary
    Utopias* (London: Bloomsbury Academic, 2012). See also Gaby Mahlberg, "The
    Publishing History of the *Isle of Pines*," "The Critical Reception of the *Isle of Pines*,"
    "The Historical and Political Context of the *Isle of Pines*," all in *Utopian Studies* Vol.
    17, no. 1 (2006); *Henry Neville and English Republican Culture in the Seventeenth
    Century: Dreaming of Another Game* (Manchester and New York: Manchester
    University Press, 2009).

4   Amy Boesky, "Nation, Miscegenation: Membering Utopia in Henry Neville's *The
    Isle of Pines*," *Texas Studies in Literature*, Vol. 37, no. 2 (1995).

5   Mahlberg provides in passing a similar reading in "An Island with Potential."

6   For an overview of Neville's life and political adventures, see Mahlberg, "Historical
    and Political Contexts of *The Isle of Pines*."

7   S. J. Wiseman, "Pamphlet Plays in the Civil War News Market: Genre, Politics, and
    Context," *Prose Studies*, Vol. 21, no. 2 (1998).

8   See Francis Bacon, *The New Atlantis* and Tommaso Campanella, *City of the Sun*
    in *The New Atlantis and City of the Sun: Two Classic Utopias* (Mineola, NY: Dover
    Publications, 2003).

9   Peter Stillmann, "Monarchy, Disorder, and Politics in Isle of Pines," *Utopian Studies*,
    Vol. 17, no. 1 (2006) argues to the contrary that the problem is that Pines does not
    act as a political founder.

10 Antinomians argued that having attained a perfect conscience, one no longer need
    to abide by ordinary codes of conduct. Quoting the New Testament, such persons
    would hold that "everything is pure to the pure." For an informative discussion of
    these, see Christopher Hill, *The World Turned upside Down: Radical Ideas during
    the English Revolution* (London: Penguin, 1984). With regard to the broader social
    scene, which often was in reaction to the narrow strictures of English reformation,
    a review of the social history of the period including the diaries of Henry Pepys
    would provide the reader with useful background to Neville's counter-reaction. For
    a discussion of this and related topics, see Harold Weber, "Charles II, George Pines,

and Mr. Dorimant: The Politics of Sexual Power in Restoration England," *Criticism*, Vol. 32, no. 2 (Spring 1990) and Stillmann, "Monarchy, Disorder, and Politics in Isle of Pines."

11   This would account for his interest in Machiavelli, as discussed by Bruce and other commentators. For Machiavelli's discussion of the role played by physical environments in shaping the moral character of citizens, see Niccolò Machiavelli, *Discourses on the Histories of Livy* (New York: Oxford University Press, 1997), bk 1, ch. 1.

12   For the story's publication history, see Bruce, "Introduction" and Mahlberg, "The Publication History of *The Isle of Pines*."

13   See Mahlberg, "The Critical Reception of *The Isle of Pines*."

14   For a discussion of the parallel between the community on the island and the smart set around Charles II, see Stillmann, "Monarchy, Disorder, and Politics in Isle of Pines."

15   Where Machiavelli does argue that a rich environment necessitates a strong republican government, he does not necessarily agree that a severe physical environment would help inculcate discipline and virtue.

16   See for example Francis Fukuyama, *The Origins of Political Order: From Prehuman Times to the French Revolution* (New York: Farrar, Straus and Giroux, 2012).

17   This would make the tale into an Arcadian story which, as Mahlberg succinctly puts it in "An Island with Potential," advocates the understanding that "humans are at one with nature, and civilization and domination of the country are implicitly rejected."

4

Looking Backward

The following two utopias, *Looking Backward* and *News from Nowhere*, are broadly representative of nineteenth-century Anglo-American utopian writing. Both are influenced by Marxist thought, though neither adopts an orthodox Marxist position. Both foresee societies in which economic class has been eliminated, but not necessarily all differential measures of social esteem. Both depict a good life characterized by a relatively high degree of individual freedom, choice, and material security. Both are reactions against what were perceived as the failure of capitalist industrialization to improve the lives of everyone. Of the two, *Looking Backward* was the more successful, spurring the development of a movement to implement its vision. This is in part because Edward Bellamy (1850–1898) created a utopia that does not appear far-fetched. The kind of life one lives in his depiction of the future is not dramatically different from the life lived in the late nineteenth century in terms of technology and industrialization. In contrast, William Morris's (1834–1896) utopia, written partly in response to what Morris believed was Bellamy's misguided understanding of the good life, appears to assume stupendous changes, including the elimination of mass industrialization, urban life, much technology, and most conventional governing structures.

This contrast leads us to other differences between these two versions of utopia. Bellamy's future appears attainable not only because he embraces industrialization and technology, but also because he accepts wholeheartedly what was becoming the modern understanding of the good life—choice and consumption. His aim was to allow everyone to enjoy a consumerist lifestyle, first by leveling and guaranteeing income, and second by ensuring that everyone in fact did contribute to the community. In these attributes there are also important echoes of More, who also thought economic security and the mobilization of productive citizens to be essential to improving society. Bellamy, however, adds opportunities for choice in the realms of work, culture, and consumption. Morris, meanwhile, has a heightened concern for nature, beauty, the freedom to wander, and the fulfilling character of labor. Consumption is measured qualitatively rather quantitatively and subordinated to the fulfillment of humans as creative beings in his utopia. His vision of the good society, while prizing the medieval economic and social contexts More inhabited, is quite different from Utopia in this regard as well as in its even more radical decentralization of power and heightened emphasis on individual freedom.

The story and interpretations

Story

Looking Backward (1888) is one of several utopian stories that gain a necessary distance from ordinary society by moving the action to the future rather than displacing it to a different location. This technique has the virtue of providing a closer connection between the audience and the realization of utopia. Rather than reading of far-away places and people with different traditions, the story gave its American readers a set of familiar signposts, allowing them more easily to accept that a radically better society was attainable from where they stood. The story opens with its protagonist, Julian West, arriving in the utopian future accidentally—he oversleeps by well over a hundred years. Waking in the year 2000 after bedding down in 1887 allows him the luxury of instant comparison. He is physically in the same place he has known all his life (Boston) and he has intimate knowledge of utopia's political, economic, and cultural history.

The book constructs a series of comparisons between the old and the new, between a capitalist existence and a socialist life within this familiar cultural and experiential landscape. The most important difference between the past and future is that *everybody*, not just the Julian Wests of the world, are able to live a moderately affluent lifestyle. The plot of the book is transparently structured around introducing the reader to this new world and the democratic implications of a transformed economy and society. West's hosts, the Leetes, either take Julian on tours of the city or discuss various social, political, and economic practices. As with the future society (which does not foresee future improvement), the book itself is static in the sense that there are no discussions of long journeys.

The only movements are West's translation into the future and his psychological integration into his new environment.

The latter development is of some interest. Bellamy insists on afflicting West with cognitive confusion despite his arguments that this new society is not practically alien from that of the nineteenth century. This may merely be a plot device to provide the author the excuse for making characters explain everything to West in great detail. Yet it also suggests the mental transition that has occurred since West went to bed in nineteenth-century Boston and with which he now struggles, in the form of shedding taken-for-granted assumptions regarding class, worth, work, leisure, education, civic property, economics, and life in general. While Bellamy argues that the movement from capitalism to the future society was clear at the time of the change, it was not so clear beforehand for West or for nineteenth-century readers in general. If those readers initially found the book fantastic, then they are not alone. But more importantly, the book implies that their confusion is not a barrier to change. Nor, in fact, is culture or other sources of diversity because the entire world has embraced these changes. If West can overcome his disorientation and come to accept the future as both possible and radically better than what he left behind, so can the reader, whether she lives the 1880s or in the 2010s, and whether she lives in Boston or in Bombay.[1]

Bellamy lays out his utopian vision from the viewpoint of the prosperous portions of the middle and upper classes. West had been firmly rooted in the upper reaches of society during his previous life. Having access to inherited wealth sufficient to keep him in moneyed leisure, he is aware of lower class discontent through the inconveniences labor strife brings to his life rather than direct experience of the hardships of labor. This sets an important part of the tone of the book. In Bellamy's understanding, the conflicts that arise as a result of a competitive economic system are dysfunctional and illogical. Also in his view, everyone should be able to grasp this, even the rather self-absorbed West. Thus for Bellamy, the way out of the conflicts, crises, and general disorders that afflicted Gilded-Age America is not through more conflict, nor in the triumph of industrialists in breaking labor unions. Rather, both the transition out of the old and the character of the new society will be based on an intellectually self-aware organization of people and resources that emphasizes coordination and cooperation in the context of a nationalization of both capital and labor, a common sense solution in Bellamy's eyes in that it merely extends further the existing logic of economic development.

Bellamy's future world is at once familiar and different both to us and its original audience. Life there is importantly pluralistic, marked by choices of lifestyle and the existence of multiple media outlets. Independent religious organizations exist. There are primitive debit cards and electronic entertainment. There are still families and traditional sex roles. Bellamy does not propose radical changes in the way affluent people live, but in how the economic and political systems are organized that allow everyone to live affluently. There is no circulation of money or economic markets. The state owns all houses and means of production. People are not motivated to work by means of material incentives, but through appeals to their patriotism, pride, and competitive desire for social approval. Everyone gets an equal share of the nation's production and is educated at the expense of the state up to the postsecondary level. All males work in labor armies from the ages of 20 to 45, when they retire to private pursuits (women appear to work in the labor armies until they have children). There are no military establishments or wars, nor are there prisons, though those who refuse to work are shut away. Those who otherwise are unruly are treated in hospitals. Thus in many ways, Bellamy's future is an updated, industrialized, pluralistic, consumeristic, and looser version of More's utopia.

Interpretations

There is some controversy regarding Bellamy's general intent in writing *Looking Backward* and the actual nature of the utopian society that he formulated. These discussions differ with regard to whether the intent of the novel is economic, social, or psychological, and whether or not the changes it proposes are revolutionary. For example, Prettyman argues that *Looking Backward* was a pragmatic utopia that attempted to use contemporary business practices for new purposes, in the course of which the individualistic foundations of capitalism are subverted and the collective potential of the capitalist inventions of incorporation, trusts, and monopolies is realized.[2] In contrast, Beilharz argues that the basis for the story is a description of the project of solidarity, expressed in terms of the direct connection between individuals and large organizations, actualized by the absence of intermediary organizations and the reduction of politics to rule by experts. As such, the story itself looks backward in its attempt to locate a type of small town pastoral America within the industrialized milieu of the late nineteenth century.[3]

For Auerbach, the story is less prophetic or utopian than therapeutic in the sense that it acts as a coming to terms with modern economic, capitalist developments; insofar as it is prophetic, it anticipates developments in capitalism in terms of centralization and professionalism rather than a turn to socialism.[4] Finally for Davis, the ultimate purpose of the story is not to encourage political or economic change, but to perform a social function, in that it is a story of healing in the aftermath of the Civil War that develops and promotes the concept of universal brotherhood.[5]

For the most part, these various readings are peripheral to the current project. We are more interested in the understandings of human nature and the depictions of social, economic, and political institutions and organizations on display in the book. Here the literature is somewhat thinner, with some practical critiques in evidence, but not much in terms of attempts to come to grips with the type of life portrayed in this utopian story. Such attempts were more the grist of contemporary efforts to respond to, criticize, and extend the story than of later discussions that attempted to assess the desirability and practicality of Bellamy's vision.[6]

Contexts and problems

Bellamy was writing at the end of an initial phase of the American industrial revolution. Industrialization came with a set of promises that appeared likely to change society for the better. It would provide cheap goods that would improve everyone's standard of living. Its use of labor-saving devices promised that the necessities of life could easily be provided with a shorter work day and less stressful labor. Everyone could enjoy the consumption patterns and the leisure of the upper classes. The reality, however, was much different. As Bellamy notes within the story, the gap between those who lived well and most ordinary people widened with the coming of industrialization (even if more people lived better than before). Poverty stubbornly persisted and there was more and more overt class strife, as ordinary workers refused to accept the unequal distribution of the benefits industrialization brought. Most people worked harder and faster than in the previous rhythms of life, particularly those found in the countryside. The cities became dirtier thanks to industrialization's unique contributions of air pollution, industrial waste, and noise. The ultimate outcome was violent

confrontations between an increasingly desperate and organized labor force and
a progressively monopolistic set of industrialists.

These contexts had spawned a series of attempts to rethink social arrangements.
Some of these followed in the footsteps of European-style socialism, advocating
the elimination of capitalism through the forcible appropriation of the means of
production by a state controlled by the working class. Such socialists, including
those who drew consciously upon Marxist theory, saw the new and better world
arising out of sharp conflict between classes. Others followed in the European
and American utopian tradition, arguing that a better world could be created by
conscious, nonviolent change. The power of persuasion or (in the case of small-
scale utopias) example would be sufficient for the transition.

Bellamy importantly paints nineteenth-century industrial society as defined
by class conflict, which he seeks to eliminate. These conflicts, he notes, are
not only economic, but social, educational, and cultural. Society is divided in
ways that make people of different classes like people of different races and
nationalities. But it is class differences that are at the bottom of all conflict for
Bellamy. Differences of culture and experience ultimately turn on differences of
material interests. These differences are created and cultivated by the competitive
economic system in place. While people are not always negatively motivated
by material interests, they are so in environments which force them to be. As
Bellamy's metaphor of the coach (in which some people ride a coach, others
fall off it, while still others push and pull it) illustrates, the capitalist, class-based
economic system as a competitive economic model produces a zero-sum game
in which some benefit enormously though precariously, and the many must pay
for those privileges through a life of misery and drudgery.

Bellamy points to class as the unjust product of competition in part through
his discussion of the unproductive lives of the rich in nineteenth-century
America. West's family is well-off; for generations none have had to labor to live,
yet they have managed to live quite well. This situation, like all other examples
of the accumulation of wealth in a capitalist system, Bellamy holds, was not
the product of superior intelligence, organizational ability, or hard work, as
the classical liberal theorists would have it, but instead the result of a violent
and ruthless expropriation of socially produced value. To live off interest in
investments or to keep the profits of products workers have made, he holds, is
to tax workers' labor without their consent; thus, it is to be expected that the
working class would struggle against capitalists because capitalists steal the
fruits of their labor. Throughout the story, West expresses sympathy for the

laboring classes even though he is not at ease with strikes and other labor action. From his place in the future, West begins to see that the demands of the lower classes are completely understandable and human, but cannot be satisfied in a competitive market system. It is only natural that people should want to escape poverty and to gain shorter working hours, better working conditions and access to educational opportunities while resisting those who would prevent them from attaining those goods, a situation that a capitalist system inevitably produces, Bellamy argues.

If Bellamy desires an end to class conflict and sympathizes with the aspirations of the working class, it is logical for him to blame systems rather than individuals for poverty and associated problems. Poverty is the result of unequal distributions of wealth sanctioned by an unfair economic system. Workers are unable to live well because the private control of capital robs workers of their fair share of the value they create, not because they are lazy. Bellamy follows in the footsteps of Marx in arguing that the logic of capital accumulation leads to large inequalities and, ultimately, the impoverishment of workers given that the surpluses capitalists expropriate and use for their own purposes are purely the product of labor. But he also emphasizes the ideological side of this situation: that these inequalities are seen as natural, unalterable, and justified, when in fact they are artificial, changeable, and immoral. As he notes with regard to the intractability of labor conflict, most people assumed that there was no way to meet the worker's demands without greatly increasing the wealth of society, an outcome itself viewed as either impossible or predicated on the existence of large inequalities. Following More, Bellamy rejects this position, insisting instead that the equalization of shares of wealth is the moral and practical counterpart to the duty to labor. The nationalization of capital and the equalization of incomes, along with the mobilization of more of the population in useful labor, the use of noneconomic incentives, central planning, and the elimination of capitalism's boom and bust cycles and periodic wars will result in a significant increase in wealth that will allow everyone to live well. Where Bellamy perhaps departs from More and rejects Marx is in his argument that a change in thinking will result in the rich being satisfied with losing their control of capital. For Marx, interests trump and animate intellectual positions; likewise for More, the initial presence of unequal incomes and individual wealth in excess of sufficiency is likely to spur a greed that would lead its holders to resist parting with unequal wealth.

Bellamy also fundamentally holds that excessive individualism is to blame for the failure of the industrialized nineteenth century to deliver the promise of the good life for everyone. Here he returns to More's position. In the atmosphere that industrial capitalism creates, individualism turns into greed, selfishness, a lack of civic awareness, and general social dysfunction. Unequal shares of wealth, education, and opportunity result in crime, poverty, and conflict, as laborers scramble to gain the necessary resources to live, professionals fight to keep their middle class status, and capitalists engage in full-scale economic combat to keep and increase the economic resources they control. Bellamy also has Dr Leete voice the sentiment that nineteenth-century society was focused too much on the individual in a moral and cultural sense. He argues that too much wealth was devoted to individual enjoyment rather than to civic purposes. The result was the shabbiness of cities that depressed the "public spirit" as well as eliminated the cooperative sense that spurs accomplishments in the arts and sciences and creates an enjoyable life unencumbered by anxiety, conflict, and terror.

This is not to say that Bellamy wants to eliminate individualism. He resists drawing the future citizen as merely one of an undifferentiated mass. Instead, he argues that a future characterized by the collective control of the economy will provide both individual choice and a revitalized public life. These attributes are not contradictory in his mind because he does not accept that social control of the means of production also necessarily entails social control of lifeplans, the elimination of negative freedoms in the realm of expression and other areas, or standardized patterns of consumption. The future allows each person to have the cake of a socialized economy while eating it in an individualized fashion.

Solutions, themes, and the good life

Solutions

While Bellamy notes the role material interests play in the problems of late nineteenth-century America, he does not propose to eliminate them by the forcible nationalization of industries, civil war, or through other solutions that assume that powerful people will resist change. Again, he is not a Marxist revolutionary who believes that violent revolution is the only means to attain a socialist future. Rather, he places his hope in the inevitability of intellectual change that will recognize the moral correctness of equal distributions of wealth and the utility of nationalizing already concentrated forms of capital and centrally directing an already well-organized labor force. While he implies that the continued success of this future society depends on the maintenance of identical material interests (everyone has the same share of society's wealth), he does not see such realizations as stemming from the creation of those interests. Rather, the realization must precede those interests. Correctly understanding the human condition in the context of history, in the form of paying attention to a common sense appreciation of the direction of economic evolution, is a crucial part of the opening to a better society.

Intellectual change will come in several forms. Part of it will be moral and ethical. People will come to understand that unequal sharing of wealth is not defensible if the welfare of others is to be taken into account. In other words, while living an individual lifestyle, people will embrace a sufficiently collective identity such that they will reject material inequality. Another part will come in the form of a different understanding of the world in terms of the prospects for progress and improvement. Bellamy assigns part of the blame for contemporary problems on conservative views that persistently claim that wealth cannot be increased or redistributed. What is taken for granted as natural in terms of economics will be transformed to include the proposition that the world and the human condition are plastic enough to be changed positively. People will understand that the economic pie can be increased and that equal shares need not result in its shrinkage. Bellamy also criticizes cyclical understandings of human progress, which hold that progress is neither indefinite nor sustainable and that humans reach a peak of civilization only to regress to a much lower level. This understanding will change to a linear conception of progress. To accept that a better society is possible and sustainable is a necessary prelude to actually attaining such a society. For Bellamy, some of the most important barriers to the good life are those that exist in our heads.

Materially, Bellamy's future society has a centrally controlled economy. Rather than markets setting prices for commodities produced by private concerns, all production and distribution is controlled by the government, including the price to be paid for goods in terms of a debit, the amount of raw materials fed into the system, and the planning of which products to produce and the amount of every product to be manufactured. There is no private capital and no private property except for personal goods. There are no markets in which money is exchanged. The only private productions are intellectual and cultural. The most important aspect of this central control of the economy is the assumption that the centralized allocation of labor and capital is more efficient than the decentralized distribution of both through markets. Bellamy argues that the centralization of information in the hands of a few decisionmakers allows for the quicker and more relevant movement of labor and capital from place to place and one sector of the economy to another because it eliminates the waste caused by competition and human errors caused by a lack of information. This proposition in turn assumes that relevant information can be easily aggregated, can be acted upon promptly, and yields easily discernible policy directions, production decisions, and resource allocations once it is in the hands of competent central decisionmakers.

The future also organizes labor differently. First, all males labor at materially productive tasks from the time they are 21 until 45, or else make other provisions for their contributions to society if they are engaged in cultural, artistic, or religious activities. Women also are part of the workforce until they have children. There are no situations like that which West and his family enjoyed in the past, gliding through life supported by interest and dividend payments. Labor is a necessary contribution to society. So, as with More's discussion in *Utopia*, the assumption is that the GDP will expand because of additional labor inputs. Labor is also managed centrally. There is no individualized market for labor; rather, young people are organized into labor armies that tackle both routine tasks and extraordinary endeavors. Again, such centralized control is said to be more efficient and productive than reliance upon markets, resulting in additional factors that will have a positive effect on the GDP.

However, the control of labor is not performed completely through a command structure in this scheme. While most workers are part of labor armies, and assignment to particular armies is governed by performance on intelligence and aptitude tests, within those armies the assignment of individual tasks is exercised by allowing workers to choose to engage in particular kinds of activities. In this scheme (which B. F. Skinner later adopts for his own utopia), administrators balance off the arduousness or unpleasantness of work with the number of hours engaged in the work. Workers may choose heavy or unpleasant work that carry short hours, or light or pleasant tasks that carry longer hours. Here, Bellamy draws upon the assumption that people value both choice and leisure and that the people within each unit of the labor army possess sufficiently differentiated preferences that all necessary tasks will be performed through choice; thus, there will be no need for material incentives in the form of either differential wages or the individualized requirement to work in order to survive, nor other forms of necessity or coercion that would force people to take up work they would not otherwise choose.

Bellamy proposes the feasibility and desirability of several other novel economic features. One is the equal distribution of the annual national product among all citizens. Such equality, he argues, is both just and functional. An equal share is just because the only defensible mode of distribution is one that recognizes the common humanity of all citizens. In adopting a wider, collective understanding of the self when it comes to the distribution of income (as did More), the assumption is that everyone counts the same. It is also just because the same standard—that everyone works to the best of his ability—is demanded of all. While the output of each may differ, that is not pertinent in Bellamy's moral economics. Ability and output are randomly distributed among humans and are out of their control. What is in their control is effort, and equal effort is required and is spurred by the application of nonmaterial incentives.

Second, along with choice in the matter of particular duties to perform, Bellamy substitutes social and psychological rewards for hard work. As we shall see, Bellamy believes that people are naturally competitive, but also sees that a situation in which there are no incentives to work hard would result in dysfunctional behavior. People would put their competitive energies into other areas, possibly with harmful results. But Bellamy rejects differential material incentives as the basis for motivating people to work hard in productive activities. As we saw above, he argues that everyone is morally entitled to an equal share of GDP so long as she works to the best of her abilities. Consequently, he turns to other types of motivations to tap into people's competitive nature. Doing so is not problematic in his understanding, for he holds that certain of such alternatives, namely marks of social esteem and disapproval, are both morally superior to and equally as effective as differential material incentives. Reward those who work hard and well and produce more than the average with promotion within the labor armies, marks of social distinction such as medals, certificates and titles (worker of the month, citizen of the year, etc.), and eligibility for managerial positions, or conversely publicly shame those who slack, and people will be motivated to work hard and produce to the best of their abilities.

Another feature of this system is the reduction of commerce to the standardized interaction of consumers and suppliers. Citizens really do not buy goods; rather, they draw on their share of the GDP by obtaining goods from government supply houses. But this is done in a way that mimics the buying and selling of goods, in that while there is no choice among vendors, there is choice among the products the state makes available. The acquisition of goods in the confines of one's share of GDP takes place through the assignment of value to each choice by the use of mechanical value holders (crude debit cards) and distribution points. Value is still measured in terms of money, but this is merely an accounting device because it is not manifested in physical coin, nor are such value measures transferable among private persons. Instead, the real measure of value is labor, as determined by the number of hours spent in producing a product. Thus, each person's spendable income is really equal (and limited) to what is produced by a set number of labor hours arrived at by dividing the total GDP of the nation measured in labor hours equally among all citizens, minus an amount necessary for reinvestment and communal needs. Because different goods are produced by different amounts of labor, the use of debit cards allows for both choice and equality (and the government may lower the "price" of leftover goods in order to get rid of them). People can choose however many goods they wish in whichever form they desire among those available up to the limit of the value included on their yearly debit card.

Bellamy assumes that everyone will be satisfied with an equal but limited share of national wealth as represented by the value of their debit card. This assumption is possible because while he conceptualizes the good life importantly in terms of consumption, he does not see people in this environment as either materially greedy or desirous of unequal consumption in all areas. That is, he importantly links the adequacy of an equal, limited share to a kind of natural pluralism of material desires. Just as he assumes that people will have different ways of balancing the difficulty of work with leisure in the realm of labor, so he argues that everyone has his or her own way of enjoying material goods. To enjoy goods in a particular fashion is to concentrate on one area of consumption or enjoyment. One becomes, so to speak, a narrow connoisseur of goods, the enjoyment of which leaves one little or no appetite for straying deeply into other areas of consumption and enjoyment. This narrowness of appetite allows one to be satisfied with the amount of goods obtainable through a limited, equal share of GDP because one need not spread that share over many areas of intense consumption. This satisfaction is also attributed in part to the dampening of excessive desires that comes with the assurance of material provision, in that everyone is guaranteed an income, education, and health care. In parallel with More, Bellamy argues that anxiety leads to greed; absent the insecurities that preyed upon the minds of citizens in the past, citizens of the future will be satisfied with their share.

A related part of the solution to the problems of the conflict-filled nineteenth century is that in providing everyone an equal but limited share of GDP that can be used as the citizen chooses, Bellamy provides the foundation for the equalization, though not standardization, of lifestyles. But the equalization of income is only a part of the story. In addition to receiving the same amount of credit to spend, everyone shops at the same stores and pays the same price for the same goods. Cultural activities are readily accessible to all. Good food in the form of communal kitchens is universally available. Soundly constructed houses of various sizes and grandeur are available for rent by the state at reasonable rates. Everyone enjoys the benefits of higher education. All men work until the age of 45, when all are eligible to retire and enjoy unstinted leisure. Women as well as men are able to enjoy this life, in part because the realm of "women's work" is also encompassed within the activities of labor armies. Mothers need not spend all their time on cleaning, cooking, and child-minding. Bellamy suggests that this overall, essentially democratic equality is not the result of a leveling down of standards of living, but for most people a significant leveling up. While no one is grandly wealthy in the style of the Rockefellers, everyone enjoys the lifestyle of a comfortably prosperous citizen of the nineteenth century and is content with such a lifestyle. Operationally, this means that everyone enjoys an equal income share, is spurred by social incentives to put forth their best productive efforts during their career, and enjoys the same early retirement age.

Bellamy's new government organization, as with his economic organization, is an outgrowth of what he views as economic and social evolution. With the concentration of capital and control of labor in the hands of society itself, the power over these areas of life devolves to governmental institutions that are understood as the extensions of the people at large. Therefore, government is merely an extension of the organization of the economy, as Bellamy conflates political concerns with economic management. He argues that the main job of the president is to manage and discipline the labor armies, along with enforcing the laws in general (which are minimal and rarely at issue) and helping in economic planning. As such, the president, along with other subordinate managers and the leaders of the labor armies, mostly discharge the tasks formerly performed by the large capitalists. So, while the extent of government powers appears to be expanded into the economic realm, Bellamy argues that it has contracted overall. Government exists for the most part *only* to direct the economy. For the rest, politics follows libertarian principles. There is little provision for checks (there is a Congress that meets to evaluate the reports of departing heads of industrial combines and that of the president, but it appears to sit for only a short period of time and to legislate only rarely) and not much competition for office. The criminal justice process is mostly operated by appointed judges and the maintenance of mental health care facilities. The law has been reduced to "the plainest and simplist legal maxims" because there is no private property (the affairs of which constitute "ninety-nine hundreths" of the laws of the past) and the legal profession itself has withered away.

Of final interest are Bellamy's proposals for the selection of government officials on a syndicalist basis by reference to expertise. Officers are selected through the intermediary of the labor armies based on their demonstrated competence, with the women's army selecting officials who deal with "women's" issues. Importantly, only those who have retired are allowed to vote, not those actively serving in the labor armies. The reasoning here appears to be that activity in a labor army provides people with particularistic interests that must be excluded from the electoral mechanism. Thus, this is an elitist, semi-democratic technocracy with only a limited number of people eligible to vote.

Themes

Bellamy argues that the way to utopia is not difficult or arcane. The problems suffered by people in the nineteenth century are easily understood and when the time is ripe easily resolved. This understanding flows from Bellamy's analysis of social and economic evolution that is akin to understandings put forward by the softer socialists whom Marx criticizes for having an insufficiently clear understanding of social causation. For Marx, social progress comes about through the evolution of economic forms and the clash of people who have different relationships to the means of production. Ultimately, progress comes from the economic base, dragging the intellectual, cultural, and political superstructure with it along a dialectical course. For Bellamy, progress comes about because the movement of society and the economy points in a particular, inescapable direction that people are able to discern by using their native intelligence and then facilitate through their conscious actions. "All that society had to do was to recognize and cooperate with that evolution, when its tendency had become unmistakable," Dr Leete observes. Thus, along with Marx, Bellamy sees people's understanding of the world as ultimately determined by large-scale material factors. People come to understand how to organize themselves by conforming to the movement of economic processes, and economic processes themselves are the motors of change. Until everyone does accept the correct way of organizing society, utopia will not be reached. But unlike Marx, Bellamy sees that process creating a clear and coherent picture that everyone readily accepts and acts upon. So the good news is that everyone is able to recognize the direction of history despite their habitation in a world in which people have different relationships to the means of production because the answers to problems become blindingly apparent. There is no false consciousness among workers, nor any stubborn attempt by the upper classes to cling to their control of capital. The way out of capitalism does not run through the prolongation of class conflict, but through mutual agreement to change. But change does not occur until that agreement happens.

As with the transition, so with the construction of the new society. People do not need to invent it; it is already there in most respects. The creation of labor armies, the control of the economy by a few persons and other basic features of society are ineluctably implemented because they are merely extensions of the organization of the economy that historical processes were already creating under capitalism. As Dr Leete observes, in the late-nineteenth-century capital was already concentrated in the hands of the few, spurring labor in turn to organize itself into huge masses for the purpose of fighting for its interests. The parts of the economy controlled by each capitalist enterprise were already planned. The only difference after the transition is that direction is in collective rather than private hands in the form of elected technocrats. So while the construction of the new order requires an intellectual transition, it does not necessitate the acceptance of exotic or counterintuitive ideologies or radically different economic structures or principles. It merely entails the use and extension of existing management skills, techniques, and structures that capitalist managers and workers had already pioneered.

This future is organized cooperatively. The common good is not conceptualized as a side effect of competition among individuals seeking profits through innovating and squeezing productivity out of economic processes. There is no invisible hand at work here, but rather a conscious set of decisions made by centralized managers. For Bellamy, efficiency and productivity are attained not by the messy and wasteful methods of creative destruction and competition that mark capitalism, but through the self-aware and focused direction of the economy by a set of publicly accountable managers, as is the case in More's utopia. The future state is a managerial, syndicalist enterprise.

Bellamy argues that a cooperative, centralized organization of the economy has moral as well as practical advantages. In a competitive capitalist system, no one is guaranteed the provision of the necessities of life. This point is the focus of an important exchange between Leete and West regarding the maintenance of those who are unable to work due to illness or disability. West on his arrival in the future persists in seeing such people as objects of charity; being unable to support themselves, they must be supported by the compassion of others. Being socialized into a competitive system, he does not grant that they have a right to support from the community. Leete rejects this position, holding that not only is the concept of self-support in general inapplicable in a complex economy based on the division of labor, but also argues that the concept of charity mistakenly ignores the basic moral understanding that all are "brothers." The maintenance of everyone by the community must be taken for granted as an absolute and basic right.

Cooperation and justice also require more than that the economy be organized along collective lines. Education is provided civically. Communal dining rooms are available for all to use. Dr Leete also emphasizes the time, effort, and resources placed in community facilities in general, including civic facilities for the sports and arts, while holding that people's private arrangements are relatively simple. Most people spend the bulk of their time in the community rather than in their private dwellings.

Yet, while Bellamy is at pains to argue that the foundation of this society is collective, life itself is not collectivized. The centralization of economic power and the rejection of a thoroughgoing individualism do not mean the end of individual freedoms or self-expression. People do not live atop one another in communal housing and go about wearing the same clothes and spouting the same slogans. As Dr Leete puts it, "our system is elastic enough to give free play to every instinct of human nature which does not aim at dominating others or living on the fruit of others' labor." While they are organized for work, citizens are not mobilized for political and social affairs. Absent are the mass marches, mandatory meetings, leader worship, and collective discipline that mark *We* and *Nineteen Eighty-Four*. While everyone receives the same income, it is not distributed in the form of standardized goods, as in Utopia. Policy debates continue. People argue over important questions of religion and existence in general. Choice in these matters exists here in ways not available in Utopia, Airstrip One, or the One State.

With regard to this last point, Bellamy has Dr Leete claim not only that there is cultural and policy pluralism in this future America; he holds that there is more freedom of expression in his society than in the nineteenth-century version, in that a broader variety of privately produced periodicals will exist from which to gain information and understandings of the world. In making this argument, Bellamy refuses to concede that a centrally controlled economy will inevitably be accompanied by strict control of public information. Rather, he comes up with a scheme that allows individuals and groups to publish independently as well as to support themselves by engaging in artistic and religious endeavors through the operation of a modified market system in which citizens support artists, writers, and publishers by pledging amounts from their annual credit to support such cultural workers. Of most interest here is the argument regarding the independence of the press and publication, the role of the populace as a whole in supporting publication efforts, and the contention that in the future publication will be more diverse because everyone will have the same chance to pool their resources and publish instead of only those who control large accumulations of capital. In this regard, Bellamy argues that his future society will be both more liberal and more democratic than any that exists under capitalism despite the fact that everyone is in agreement on the broad organization of the political and economic realms.

The good life

The good life for Bellamy is mainly a life of choice and consumption, even though, ironically, it is made possible by the collectivization of important realms of existence. In Bellamy's view, this life is marked by the absence of poverty, anxiety, conflict, and uniformity. That is, one lives a life of generally pleasant work (or if not, very short hours), material sufficiency, companionship with highly educated and civilized fellow citizens, choice in the selection of material things, the enjoyment of social and public goods, exposure to diverse opinions and aesthetic experiences and, ultimately, early retirement and leisure. Or, to put it differently, the good life in Bellamy's future closely resembles the life of choice and consumption that is the popular ideal of contemporary Westerners, but in the context of a collectivized economy, equal incomes, nonmaterial incentives, and labor armies.

As such, Bellamy's vision is often just as liberating and confining as the contemporary American ideal. Despite his emphasis on the plurality of motivational factors and human desires to differentiate themselves, Bellamy underlines the point that people primarily find fulfillment in enjoying material goods and leisure rather than in other ways. People will always want to express themselves through the adornments of their bodies, the decoration of their houses, or the food they consume. One difference, perhaps, is his argument that they also take pleasure in the splendor of public facilities. But in all, Bellamy holds that the citizens of this utopia exist naturally because in large part they choose their lifeplans by deciding how to utilize their share of society's wealth. People fulfill themselves through material choices (how shall I make use of the credits I control) and through display (I find fulfillment in fine clothing, or a nice house, or in eating sophisticated meals) and choosing and enjoying cultural materials. The choice of how to consume goods is fulfilling, and people do so both privately and publicly. Yet, note that this represents only one set of possible lifeplans; other types of lifeplans that would involve material inequalities or "anti-social" competitiveness would be ruled out. Also out of bounds (not only practically, but legally) would be choices to refuse to join a labor army or otherwise engage in productive activity to intentionally live a marginal life. While Bellamy looks forward to a type of pluralistic future, he does not allow for choice among a wide variety of ways of being, or even for all ways of expressing oneself through the expenditure of resources.

Because he does see people fulfilling themselves through choice, Bellamy does not assume that humans complete themselves or find meaning in life through labor. Choice in labor is important and Bellamy makes a certain amount of room for it, but for Bellamy humans are not the essentially creative beings that Marx and Morris draw, and thus organizing production through a system of labor armies that allows for choice in which one balances the arduousness of work with amounts of leisure does no injury to his understanding of human fulfillment. He has Dr Leete dispute the proposition that people find central meaning in their lives through labor, just as he disputes the contention that people are only motivated by differential material rewards. Instead Bellamy, in company with More argues that people find the bulk of their fulfillment as humans when constructing their lives during free time rather than when they are creating economic value. Labor and consumption are ultimately subordinated to leisure. Given a situation in which GDP shares are sufficient for a moderately high standard of living, people will not demand nor accept longer working hours or longer working careers in order to increase the wealth they share because that increase in wealth will not appear as valuable as the leisure that is forfeited. Work is a necessary activity that must be equally distributed, motivated by the correct methods, be made subject to choice and generally rendered as little irritating as possible. Note also that when Bellamy's utopia emphasizes the need for copious free time, it paints a very different picture from Zamyatin's and Orwell's depictions of a kind of collective life in which the community absorbs all time.

Varied consumption is also an important part of the good life. Emphasis is placed on the colorful clothing and plethora of cultural activities available. Public buildings are constructed with an eye for aesthetic consumption as well. This, in other words, is not the life of plainness, sufficiency, and moral and intellectual development found in *Utopia*. It is in many ways a prescient description of contemporary Western life of material and cultural consumption, minus the extreme individualism, income disparities, and, presumably, crudeness.

This final observation brings us to the final important aspect of the good life: the civilized, educated, and generally relaxed atmosphere that Bellamy's utopia is said to create. This theme is emphasized throughout the book, but underlined in the concluding dream sequences. There, West journeys back in time to his fiancé's family and discovers how unsophisticated and rude they really are. In contrast, Leete's family, as well as everyone else with whom West makes contact in the future, are described as refined, cultured, kind, and tactful. Because living the good life does not mean denying the opportunity for others to do so, there is none of the pervasive fear and defensiveness of the old upper classes that accompanies the realization that others envy you and are plotting to confiscate your wealth. Moreover, the educational and cultural attainments that were available only to the rich are provided to everyone in Bellamy's future society. This feature, Dr Leete argues, raises the level of civilization throughout society so that one can enjoy high culture, good manners, refined and educated conversations, and civil behavior wherever one goes. To live in a highly civilized society is in itself an important part of the good life.

Human nature and applications

Human nature

We have seen that while Bellamy embraces many of the economic themes put forward by Marxists and other radical socialists, he is not a complete economic determinist. Instead, he resembles More in his moralistic and psychological approach to anthropology. Indeed, one might argue that Bellamy adopts much of More's understanding of humans and society and updates the latter's prescriptions for the nineteenth century by embracing the importance of choice and consumerism.

As with More, Bellamy assumes that humans, while hardwired, will act on their hardwiring differently given changing environments. In his view, people are hardwired to be competitive, to desire variety and choice, and to want leisure. As we have seen, some of these hardwired characteristics can lead to such problems as disorder, greed, and vastly unequal and unjust distributions of wealth in the estimation of both Bellamy and More. But unlike More, Bellamy does not see most differential behaviors as stemming from the deactivation of hardwired responses, though he does see some important differences as stemming from such deactivation. Instead, he also importantly assumes that environments can be adjusted to provide the optimal grounds for human flourishing. This means that to change environments is not to change what humans are in the sense of making them different kinds of beings either fundamentally or temporally, or by merely subtracting bad traits, but rather to make them better humans by allowing their "essential" good qualities to come to the fore. The story of the rosebush that Bellamy relates underlines this understanding. Plant a rosebush in better soil and its flowers will improve; change contexts and people will react accordingly to become better humans, not because their nature has changed (put them back in a poor environment and they will revert), nor because they are trained differently (it is the soil not the trimming that provokes the change), but because better environments call forth different potentialities. Thus one does not attempt to undo the wiring that makes humans competitive; one merely changes the prizes of competition. Similarly, one does not attempt to change humans to eschew choice or not value leisure. Rather, one creates a society in which those basic human desires can be fulfilled while also supporting a just distribution of income and labor requirements.

An important part of the way Bellamy asserts that we can create such a society through changes in environment is the reformation of economic affairs. The change from a competitive to a cooperative system, marked by central control of the means of production, is meant to underscore humans' natural sociability. As noted above, the related change to nonmaterial motivations also points to a key part of human hardwiring for Bellamy, one that is absent in More's understanding. In Utopia, people work hard because they are trained to do so, they are committed to the community and they are under constant surveillance. This strategy is necessary because More does not see people as naturally ambitious. Bellamy differs. He holds that humans are naturally ambitious and want to differentiate themselves and climb a hierarchical ladder. They want to be recognized, to have power, to win awards, and if these innate desires go unsatisfied, they will see no reason to be productive workers and will likely put their energies into unsocial behaviors. Society must provide those incentives and satisfy that competitive, ambitious aspect of the human character, but do so in a form that is socially beneficial rather than harmful.

Here, Bellamy is in partial agreement with classical liberals who argue that the key to economic growth is individual incentives that allow people to gain individualized psychological rewards for hard work. The difference is that Bellamy rejects differentiated economic rewards. It is not the case, he argues, that humans are only motivated by and satisfy their ambition through economic rewards and goals. Nor is it the case that such rewards are benign in their social impact. He holds instead that ambition can and must be satisfied in a plurality of ways. Nonmaterial incentives, for the most part positive, work just as well as differential material rewards while avoiding the inequalities and attending poverty, envy, and conflict that accompany the latter, as well as privileging the leisure he also sees as natural. He points to the potency of honor, duty, gratitude, and power, as well as the desire to escape public censure, contempt, and discipline as tapping into the better side of human nature. People can gratify their need for getting ahead by seeking social and political marks of esteem and will keep their drives within morally acceptable bounds by avoiding behavior that is accompanied by a loss of face and prestige if given the opportunity to do so. The theoretical result is that everyone will work to the limits of their abilities with none of the undesirable side effects of a competitive economic system.

Bellamy also implies that part of a human's innate ambition is a natural aspiration to a better life. This understanding works itself out in two major themes. In the first, it informs Bellamy's sympathy for the working class. Bellamy does not treat workers as ruffians or uncivilized beasts. Their demands are completely understandable to him because those demands are quintessentially human. Everyone naturally wants to improve his standard of living to a comfortable level. No one wants to work ceaselessly at physically demanding tasks or to live in poverty. The strategy for dealing with these desires is to change society rather than to deactivate hardwiring. The way forward is to allow everyone to live an affluent life through fundamental economic changes. Second, this position allows Bellamy to argue broadly for an important and controversial feature of his future society—that people will accept being drafted into labor armies because they understand that work allows them collectively to obtain the good things which they innately desire. It is an inescapable task. They do not see their service as one of compulsion, but rather as a readily accepted duty to themselves and to the community in the same way that people previously had viewed military service as a duty of self-defense if they wished to live in an independent community. Again, nonmaterial incentives come into play, in this case duty and honor. Likewise, the material incentives are broad rather than individualized: if the community is to prosper and the standard of living citizens enjoy is to be maintained, then everyone must engage in work.

Bellamy also deploys this argument in a different direction, and by doing so again differentiates himself from More, by positing that people will not be satisfied with a life with no material choices. Contrary to More's understanding, Bellamy believes that humans are naturally and strongly pluralistic in their desires, though not necessarily their lifeplans. It is not just that desires *can* be satisfied in different ways; humans are wired such that they *must* be allowed to express themselves through their use and display of material and nonmaterial goods. As Edith Leete notes, "personal taste" is the source of this side of human pluralism. By embracing this assumption, Bellamy is able to construct his communalized society as a fundamentally different place from the drab and uniform societies described in *We*, *Nineteen Eighty-Four*, and *Utopia*. Even though they must work in labor armies and receive the same income, people are able to cover their lives with a necessary variety and texture.

With regard to social discipline in general, Bellamy as with More does assign some responsibility for problematic behavior to human hardwiring that can be deactivated by material conditions. Bellamy assumes that people envy and hate those whom they perceive as unfairly enjoying goods and luxuries they cannot attain. These emotions are corrosive, reinforcing other harmful by-products of competitive wiring (such as violence, a lack of pity, and destructiveness). It is mainly privation and scarcity that lead people to attempt to accumulate wealth and goods and to do so in ways that are ethically unsound. As for disorder itself, Dr Leete argues that the greater portion of crime of the past was committed by those in need because of "the inequality of possession" among the population and thus "want tempted the poor." This includes not only stealing and other physical manifestations of crime, but also softer forms of deviant behavior such as lying. No one finds it either profitable or necessary to engage in such activities in Bellamy's future society. However, it also appears that Bellamy holds that humans can succumb to temptation when the opportunity arises to profit from their position. The wiring that results in greedy behavior can be reactivated if people are placed in situations in which it is possible to accumulate goods. The equal division of the nation's wealth, the elimination of completely portable carriers of value (e.g., money), and the difficulties of storing goods are all important to the elimination of disorder and to creating trust in officials. As with More, Bellamy holds that government officials in the future can be trusted to administer the nation's wealth importantly because there is no way in which they could profit by taking advantage of their position.

With regard to disorder, Bellamy asserts that it arises in general due to circumstances. Given that these circumstances will largely disappear in his future, Bellamy argues that any social disorders that do occur will be caused by individual illnesses. Criminals would be "ill" in the sense that they become unbalanced, either forgetting their moral obligations to others or reverting back to more primitive ways that do not fit modern circumstances. In violating essential social norms, they are acting irrationally. As the products of such organic disturbances, crime would be treated in the same way as the flu or cancer: through hospitalization.

There is some programming that takes place in Bellamy's future. The emphasis on education and its role in acclimatizing people to work in labor armies and to recognize each person's native abilities points to the fact that environmental manipulation of hardwiring is not completely sufficient to the maintenance of the community and to the complete fulfillment of its citizens. People need some assistance in expressing their natural proclivities in the sense that those proclivities must be discovered. But Bellamy shies away from any extensive programming that would mold citizens in any particular fashion. He appears to believe that the bulk of problems that afflict contemporary society have to do with the mismatch between social and political environments and human hardwiring. Extensive social construction of individuals is not necessary. Creating environments that fit hardwiring allows humans to act most naturally; natural behavior, in turn, is generally peaceful and cooperative. The programming that occurs is portrayed as only reinforcing and bringing to the surface these natural characteristics.

Applications

What would Bellamy say of our present situation? He would probably be struck by the many parallels with Gilded-Age America. Despite a higher and more widely distributed standard of living, twenty-first-century America has not eliminated economic depressions, large economic inequalities, long hours of unpleasant work, poverty, the control of vast economic resources by a few private parties, uneven economic development, economic insecurity on the part of the young, large prison populations, war, and violence. He would insist that we acknowledge our failure to eliminate these problems and recognize that this failure stems from sticking with a liberal capitalist state. The stage is set, he would argue, for the transition he had earlier forecast. Would we and should we agree? Are the problems we now experience comparable to those with which Bellamy grappled, or are we differently situated now that we inhabit a globalized world and stand on a more advanced technological platform?

An immediate question to raise is that of outcomes and therefore of Bellamy's overall understanding of progress. If the future Bellamy drew was evolutionary, an outgrowth of existing trends and inevitable, why do we not live completely in the society he envisioned? It would appear that we should, given the continued development of large international corporations and the culture of consumerist expression in which we live. What would be necessary for the peaceful revolution he envisaged to occur? If the change to utopia is more mental than it is physical, as Bellamy argues, what does it mean that the revolution hasn't occurred? Are humans fundamentally different than Bellamy assumes? Does the process of mental change just take longer than he predicted? Has the evolution of economic and social institutions taken a different turn than he envisioned? Or is he just wrong in arguing that ideational factors are primary?

If the transition is to take place on Bellamy's terms, it would be because we recognize that Bellamy's policy arguments are irrefutable. In sum, those arguments are as follows: if we were to nationalize the means of production, centrally control labor, eliminate money, competitive markets and private property aside from personal effects, reduce government to the control of the economy, institute labor armies and noneconomic incentives to work hard, not only would we not change radically the way matters are now organized; we would also receive universal economic security, greater productivity, and a universally high standard of living, more free time, a range of choices with regard to consumption (though more limited than is currently the situation), very low levels of disorder, a lower retirement age, and freedom of expression. Bellamy would argue that such a bargain is enormously advantageous to modern humans. In his mind, we only give up the right to engage in private enterprise, the chance of becoming extraordinarily rich and the right to live without working before the age of 45 to attain such goods. The fact that only a very small number of people would be able to take advantage of such opportunities, along with the high price to be paid for them (economically, socially, and politically) means that common sense dictates that we accept the bargain.

A good place to start in our assessment of this proposition is Bellamy's argument that the solutions to the problems of inequality and class conflict are evolutionary and natural because those problems are really the result of human stubbornness in not grasping the tendencies of economic history. In his understanding, class conflict, market economics, and material insecurity are not necessary for the creation of a prosperous and free society. Economic competition is not something hardwired into humans, nor is it the best way of stirring people to be productive. While people will want to differentiate themselves, they do not necessarily desire to do so by means of economic inequality, but can do so by pursuing social rewards, different intellectual interests, and various consumption patterns within the boundaries of equal incomes. The fact that contemporary society is rent by large ideological differences, experiences protests such as the Occupy Movement and incarcerates a comparatively large percentage of its population should tell us that something is wrong with current institutions and structures. They are warning signs to be heeded rather than inevitable side effects of an otherwise good and natural ways of being. The situation we find ourselves is at best a poor environment for human flourishing, if not a poisonously artificial milieu. We should follow the dictates of our common sense and escape these conditions as soon as possible rather than attempting to salvage them.

What would this mean in policy terms? If we take Bellamy seriously, it would mean policies that seek to break up monopolies of capital and labor are mistaken and attempts to strengthen or prop up markets are counterproductive. We should welcome a consolidation of the means of production in a few hands and the comprehensive organization of labor as preparatory to an eventual collective takeover in the face of a market meltdown. Such developments are manifestations of a better future, and attempting to halt and reverse them is perverse. We should take the rise of the Apples and Microsofts, with their control of large economic resources, productivity, creativity, and organized work forces as indicative of such a future. And even if the results of allowing such organizations to flourish are crises, so much the better, Bellamy would argue. Witnessing and experiencing the contradictions inherent in working to preserve outdated ways of organizing social, political, and economic life will only hasten the common sense realization that we must discard such organizations and the ways of thinking that support them and move on to a nationalization of both capital and labor and the central direction of the economy.

Following such advice would entail, at the least, a certain amount of courage and faith in the future. How do we know that a new and better way of organizing life would arise out of such crises? Bellamy assumes that economic history is linear and follows the contours of his understanding of human nature. In his mind, what is good for humans, the evolution of social and economic institutions, and common sense all point in the same direction. But is this the case? Even Marx, who puts forward a philosophically similar understanding of the tendencies of history, saw important roadblocks to the convergence of economic structures with what is good for humans in the form of the defense of particularistic class interests. Class struggle and possibly bloody revolution stands between the capitalist order and his socialist utopia. Why should we accept Bellamy's more optimistic prognosis? What would lead us to believe that capitalists and labor leaders would willingly give up the power accruing from the consolidation of capital and labor if government allowed such consolidation to occur? We would have to believe that their common sense would tell them that a better society is more valuable than the vast powers they could exercise in an unreformed landscape. The same is true of the attitudes of many ordinary citizens in the United States. They appear even less likely to welcome nationalization than would capitalists, as they equate economic nationalization with a loss of freedom and totalitarian fascist and communist regimes, as well as the termination of their dreams of obtaining and keeping vast wealth. Indeed, the current tendencies are a growing distrust of the existing liberal regulatory state and libertarian calls for scaling it back to a minimal model that does not touch the economy. Would contemporary citizens ever be convinced by Bellamy's argument that his state really is a minimal version? Or is he right that, given enough experience with capitalist crises, people will eventually come to see the logic of economic collectivization?

Of more immediate interest is the fact that the Western world and the United States in particular are once again approaching the levels of economic inequality that marked the late nineteenth century. If such inequality is a problem, what of Bellamy's solution? What would happen if we were to provide everyone an equal share of GDP by means of a debit card, or through taxation and redistribution? Would productivity increase or decrease? Would everyone be satisfied? Would most people be satisfied? Do we have available the technology and managerial skills that would make Bellamy's vision possible? These are all empirical questions that Bellamy assumes he has answered but which are still contentious more than 100 years after his proposal was first formulated.

We can think of some of these topics separately. One important part of Bellamy's utopian ideal is the substitution of nonmaterial for material incentives. The idea is to solve the problem of productivity (how do we get people to work hard) without creating materially unequal conditions among citizens. More's solution was social solidarity and constant surveillance, which has the advantage (in More's mind) of maintaining general equality among citizens. Bellamy is willing to use some types of inequality (public recognition in the form of higher status, or more power) as a spur so long as material inequality is ruled out because he sees humans as competitive and desirous of differentiating themselves. Would it be worthwhile to try such an experiment? Would people really work harder for increases in social status and other forms of social recognition? Would they be as willing to innovate? Would the lash of public opinion be better for the worker and for society than the goad of economic necessity? Bellamy relies heavily on the military metaphor of people volunteering for armies, but this has not always been the case, and often when it has succeeded, it did so during times of extreme crisis. Can such a voluntaristic spirit be maintained indefinitely? Is not this the same tactic of popular mobilization that has been tried and found wanting in the Soviet Union, the People's Republic of China (PRC), and Cuba and which Orwell will later criticize? Or are those extreme cases that also were accompanied by other problematic factors?

As with More, Bellamy argues that a reorganization of social, economic, and political life will result in greater orderliness and fewer laws. Would laws in fact diminish dramatically with the abolish most forms of private property? Would the disputes that appear to animate laws likewise diminish? Are conflicts really about property, or are other factors as important? Dr Leete mentions conflicts that may arise in the labor armies, but suggests that strong expectations of civil behavior, particularly on the part of older officers in their dealing with younger men, will eliminate almost all such incidents. This looks a bit like additional forms of training, which Bellamy elsewhere does not address. Would such training in the absence of larger, systematic attempts at programming citizens be successful?

Assume that the consolidation of capital and labor did result in their nationalization and the creation of the type of system Bellamy advocates. Would it operate as he describes? Bellamy argues that much of what we consider to be the stuff of politics would disappear in such circumstances. Given that everyone will have the same material interests, there will be no need for political parties and while opinions will continue to vary, there will be no gaping differences in policy preferences. Pork barrel politics, bribery (legal or otherwise), and the need to "campaign" will be eliminated. Would this be the case? Can material interests be so uniform that different policy preferences will not arise and political parties and "factions" will remain dormant? Or would people even in such circumstances continue to think about the world in such different ways that intense policy differences would still bedevil us?

The other side of this question is also important. Given that everyone is to acknowledge the importance and necessity of organizing economics and politics in the fashion Bellamy outlines, what room would be left for pluralism in those realms? Would there be any need for elections, or for political journals and other purveyors of political commentary? Even if there were the need, would the community tolerate them given that the basis for the change appears to have been consensus? Perhaps it is from this direction rather than from that of collectivization that the true threats to negative freedoms might come.

As is apparent, one might generate many questions regarding the feasibility of this account, given one's conception of human nature and understanding of the world in general. For example, those who embrace a Lockean, liberal understanding of humans would question why people would be willing to be subjected to the discipline of a labor army, given the understanding of the good life that is promoted. If choice is so important, why not the type of choice that is possible under a market system for allocating labor? Likewise anyone who seriously accepts the proposition that humans are ambitious might question the complacency with which Bellamy thinks about a post-transition governmental structure. Would it really be the case that people in power in the labor armies and in the central government would not seek to consolidate and extend their powers? Is not too much power given to particular people with insufficient checks on that power?

With regard to living arrangements, Bellamy attempts to square the circle of strict equality, communal life, and centralized decisionmaking with choice. Note that More did not attempt this feat, being content to have everyone dress the same and rotate housing to ensure equality and nonattachment to property. Is Bellamy successful in his attempt to create an alternative? Or does the strongly democratic element he injects into the distribution of income necessarily lead him to the same conclusions More drew—that if the aim is to build community and social justice on the basis of economic equality, the community cannot allow for differentiation?

A different set of questions might be asked of the attempt to combine choice with the concept of an equal share in terms of its practical application. Would Bellamy's scheme of a debit card work? It appears interestingly close to some contemporary conservatives' emphasis on providing public services by means of vouchers rather than in-kind goods or services, though Bellamy's debit card is used in the context of government supply points rather than in a market economy. The latter appears to be a key difference, not only in terms of undermining the conservative case for vouchers (the argument that market competition would provide the goods and services that are supplied more efficiently than would direct government provision) but also in terms of actual variety. Would the central control of manufacturing really result in a sufficient variety of goods that would make choice meaningful? Bellamy has Edith hold that while there is variety among goods, there is not too much variety because too many choices would be detrimental to the act of choosing. Is this a backdoor way of saying that the choice of goods would be greatly limited? If so, are we back to the uniformity that More, Zamyatin, and Orwell identify? Or is it the case that choice and variety can be limited and still be meaningful? To put the question from Bellamy's point of view, what do we give up now by insisting on so much choice and variety, and consequently tolerating so much waste and inefficiency? Might limited variety still constitute the basis for sufficient choice while making resources available to raise the standard of living for everyone?

It is also interesting to note the larger question of labor here. It is still the case that some people do menial labor, such as cooking, waiting tables, cleaning clothes, and tending to industrial machinery. This is not a Land of Cockaigne story. Nor is it a case of complete labor democracy, for while some only engage in manual labor for a short time while very young, others, being deficient in other skills, must do so for the entire length of their service. In other words, equality is not pushed to the point that everyone always shares in manual labor. Instead, there is the ethic that all labor is good and to engage in one type of labor is as good as engaging in another, as well as the dicta that engaging in unpleasant work results in reduced hours and that everyone receives the same income no matter what labor they perform. So Bellamy proposes democratization in this area in the sense of stipulating that everyone must work (for a significant portion of one's life) rather than living on inheritances and dividends, that all work is equally valued such that those who do perform menial tasks are not relegated to a lower social or economic class, that engaging in heavy and unpleasant work is the result of a free choice that is compensated by more free time, and that all received the same income. Much of this appears to be an advance on our current ways of viewing and valuing work. Sanitation workers, elementary school teachers, and those who care for the ill and aged really are more useful than pop singers, athletes, and reality show actors, but their value now is rarely correctly assigned either socially or economically. Bellamy's society would appear to value them appropriately while still allowing for differentiation. Perhaps we might consider the utility and wisdom of emulating it in this regard.

Finally, Bellamy assumes that creativity and change in economic matters will take place more rationally under central direction than under a market system. Bellamy condemns the destructiveness of capitalist competition, as firms not only strive to sell merchandise, but also to drive competitors out of business, resulting in the waste of time, effort, and capital itself. Defenders of capitalism would reject this criticism, arguing that such creative destruction is a dynamic necessity and thus a strength not a weakness of the system. A centrally controlled economy in this latter analysis would be too slow to discard old technology, to invent new products and services, and would continue to invest limited resources in existing industries and product lines out of habit and a lack of alternatives. It would fundamentally lack creativity as was the case, it appears, with the Soviet system. From where would the Bill Gates and Steve Jobs of this future arise? Would they only be managers, or would the lure of social honors and prestige lead them to work as hard and as creatively as they did under a late-twentieth-century capitalist regime? Even if such figures would flourish, what of other inventors and entrepreneurs who may not have such an oversized impact on life, yet also make possible a dynamic and creative economy? Would they be smothered by their enlistment in labor armies, either during their time as ordinary workers or during a stint as manager? Or would they be freed from the constraints that a capitalist economy now imposes on them in terms of differential access to education and capital? Bellamy would probably argue the latter. He might also add the assertion that nonmaterial rewards may act to spur more innovation because the satisfaction that people derive from benefiting society may not have the limits inherent in piling up individual stores of wealth, as well as the observation that in his society, innovations truly would benefit all of society and would contribute to a larger sense of justice.

Notes

1   A discussion of West's mental state that explores these and other topics is contained in Jonathan Auerbach, "'The Nation Organized': Utopian Impotence in Edward Bellamy's Looking Backward," *American Literary History*, Vol. 6, no. 1 (Spring 1994).

2   Gib Prettyman, "Gilded-Age Utopias of Incorporation," *Utopia Studies*, Vol. 12, no. 1 (2001).

3   Peter Beilharz, "Looking Back: Marx and Bellamy," *The European Legacy*, Vol. 9, no. 5 (2004).

4   Auerbach, "The Nation Organized."

5   Matthew R. Davis, "Remaking the Nation through Brotherhood in the Utopian Fiction of William Dean Howells and Edward Bellamy," *Contemporary Justice Review*, Vol. 8, no. 2 (June 2005).

6   Justin Nordstrom, "*Looking Backward's* Utopian Sequels: 'Fictional Dialogues' in Gilded-Age America," *Utopian Studies*, Vol. 18, no. 2 (2007).

5

News from Nowhere

Introduction

Morris describes *News from Nowhere* (1890) as "chapters from a utopian romance." This gives us several clues as to his purpose and meaning. First it appears that he means this work to be unfinished. This is not to say that as a story it is unfinished, but that he does not want the end of the story to be the end of the story, for several reasons. First, as with Bellamy, Morris has a perhaps naïve faith that description will help lead to realization, even if that is not exactly the way that the good society described in the book comes about. Morris sees writing as a form of political action; this story is his attempt to act, and so he wishes that action does not end with the story's conclusion.[1] Second, as we shall see, he appears tentative regarding both the possibilities for attaining the good life he describes and the likelihood that the conditions he outlines supporting that good life can be maintained. He is skeptical of revolutions, revolutionaries, and the overall restlessness of human nature, and thus his account is unfinished in the sense that he is fearful for the beginnings and the possible demise of this good life.

Morris also embraces the notion that his story is romantic and utopian. He places it in the future even though the environment described in the story resembles late medieval or early modern Europe. Thus, Morris's story asserts that environmental changes will help transform human behavior. Where Morris differs from More, Bellamy and others in his approach to environmental changes is in his less-is-more stance. Morris does not advocate innovation, more rationality, or organizational improvements. He wants to simplify. He wants a cleaner environment both physically and socially. This comes about through less technology, a less sophisticated economy, a simplified form of government, and fewer people. The good life requires that we remove important innovations that make life unappealing. But, of course, going backward is difficult, perhaps more difficult than making a leap forward.

This prescription has interesting parallels with *We*. In both stories, innovation, technology, and civilization, at least beyond a certain (often ill-defined) limit, are seen as increasingly harmful rather than helpful. Morris concurs with Zamyatin in accusing us of outthinking ourselves, of being too clever to be intelligent. The good life, he suggests, is one of simplicity and elegance, and he indicates that an essential part of such a life is simply being. So, this time in contrast with *We*, Morris does not pose an either/or situation in which we can have either civilization or freedom and simplicity. The good life contains both and is attainable if we can somehow strip ourselves of the superfluous without reverting to barbarism or a primitive standard of living, or give in too much to the restlessness of spirit that is accommodated in his good life through the concept of free and easy wandering. Wandering through life is good. Wandering away from the particular environment that makes the good life possible and allows us to live simply, freely, and well is not.

The story and interpretations

The story

News from Nowhere has important parallels with *Looking Backward* in terms of plot, in part because Morris writes his story as a response to Bellamy. In both, utopia is set in the future. In both, a person from the past is somehow transported to the future by sleeping. In both, the story unfolds as the main character explores the differences between the present and the future. It is the endings of the stories that contain the difference. Where Bellamy teases us by creating a set of false awakenings that move the protagonist back and forth between utopia and ordinary society and ultimately creates a happy ending, Morris brings us back with a crash. *News from Nowhere* is merely a dream of the protagonist, who must accept his bitter fate at living in a decidedly non-utopian present. It is the contrast between the awakened state and the dream that is the heart of the book. Its message emphasizes both—that one must awaken to the fact that ordinary society is a nasty place in which to live and that one must dream of something radically better, even if the way to this better life is unclear. This lesson differs from the message of *Looking Backward*, which holds that utopia is not a dream and that the road there is not difficult to find.

In *News from Nowhere*, the contrasts between ordinary society and utopia are revealed in the form of journeys within the dream. These journeys serve to expose the protagonist to the different way of life enjoyed by its inhabitants, provide excuses for his guide to explain matters, underline the freedom in which inhabitants of utopia live, and importantly demonstrate the radically altered physical environment of the place. This gives the story a somewhat random shape because the action takes place in the context of these forays. But this is intentional because journeys are important to the book in more ways than organizing the plot. They are meant to sharply contrast life in ordinary society with that in utopia both in terms of the quality of the experience and with their purpose. Utopia can only be experienced and understood through journeys. In ordinary society, journeys are utilitarian—one engages in them for a specified purpose, to reach a destination. In utopia, journeys are ways of life. To borrow a phrase from the Daoist *Zhuangzhi*, the good life for Morris is about free and easy wandering.

Life in this future is also about creativity. Bellamy has the future go back to the past to reconstruct, for the most part, a crafts economy that puts a premium on productive, creative labor. People work because creative activities fulfill them. They delight in making beautiful, hand-crafted objects. They have discarded most industrial processes, but because people do not spend all their time consuming, the amount of goods required and the general amount of work needed to be performed is much less than in modern society. People in this future have also restored natural beauty as the usual human environment. Humans have abandoned modern urbanism in favor of scattered settlements, villages, and cooperatives. There is no money or money equivalents, and government is stripped to a minimum, with an emphasis on direct, consensual democracy.

We know Morris privileges physical nature from the beginning of the book because the protagonist gains relief from the stifling experiences of modern existence in the outdoors. Such contact with Nature, when the latter has not been polluted or otherwise distorted, renews the self. It removes psychological burdens and clears the mind. One is no longer weighted down, having escaped what is artificial. Yet old man Hammond also speaks of humans mastering Nature through architecture. Nature is not entirely the answer to human problems, and one does not want to strip humans of all civilization. It is here that the themes of

Nature and creativity cross. Because humans are creative beings, taking material from Nature to fashion into objects of beauty and utility, their good life is not that of a purely agricultural or hunter/gatherer existence. While being human does not mean completely conquering Nature, it also does not mean submitting to it. Open spaces and woods are abundant in the future and the mega-cities are gone, but human spaces are also clearly delineated. Nor does the need for simplicity yield crudeness of life. There is no cult of the primitive in this future. The question then is not that of abolishing civilization, but of living at the right stage.

The right stage of civilization for Morris is that of late medieval Europe. He idealizes this as a time of craftsmanship, community, beauty, beneficial contact with Nature, harmony, and productivity, but without either the roughness of previous ways of life or the industrial coarseness of modernity. He does not attempt to resurrect the ancient cultures of Rome or Greece, or argue for a return to the wilderness. That is to go back too far and to adopt a way of life too alien to modern Europeans. The clearest symbol of his preference lies in the architecture he describes. The building style is clearly medieval in both the materials used (mostly stone) and the emphasis on craftsmanship. Here, the contrast of bridges he describes serves to introduce this theme. While awake the protagonist finds ugly the modern nineteenth-century steel bridge that he sees when crossing the Thames, while in his dream the stone bridge that replaces that artifact is described as beautiful. It is not so much the contrast of stone with steel, but that of craftsmanship versus rote work, solidity versus shoddiness and grace versus gracelessness that makes the dream bridge better and thus symbolic of this vastly superior culture and its aesthetic norms. It is Morris's contention that a civilization that produces such works of craftsmanship and beauty best accords with human nature.

The beauty of clothing and of people is also important to the story. Here Morris risks falling into the mindset satirized in *Erewhon*. Utopias always seem to contain beautiful people. That outward beauty signifies inward satisfaction is a cliché. But Morris also means this literally, as to some extent do other utopian writers. Outward beauty is said to be a product of the impact of changed environments on humans. To live a life in which food, clothing, and shelter are not worries, work is a game, and no one need labor at things they do not enjoy reduces stress. Morris argues in effect that it is modern society that is the cause of our aging. To be decrepit, wrinkled, twisted, and otherwise worn out is not a natural phenomenon. Once we recognize this and change our environment, our inner selves will be at ease, our outer selves will reflect this and we will appear as we naturally should—as beings whose beauty is intense and does not fade as quickly with age.

The story unfolds as the narrator journeys to what is left of London to speak to an old man about the past, then accompanies his guide to help gather hay. He becomes attracted to a young girl they encounter—a symbolic representation of the good life. The story ends as the dream fades and the narrator awakens again in the nineteenth century.

Interpretations

Most interpretations see this story as fitting in with Morris's larger political or aesthetic agenda. Some see it as mostly aesthetic, with Morris working out the implications of his involvement in the craftsman movement, as exemplified by the emphasis on craftsmanship, creative labor, and beauty in the story. Thus Vaninskaya draws a connection between Orwell and Morris, holding that both privileged Nature, aesthetics, and libertarianism.[2] Delveaux also notes the connection between Morris's ecological orientation and his opposition to a machine-like government, such as the one Morris saw in Bellamy's work.[3] Watkinson meanwhile marks the importance of the depiction of work as unalienated play performed in the context of egalitarian society.[4]

Others place the emphasis not so much on the nature of the good life as on the descriptions of how people attained this better society and thus dwell on the extended descriptions Morris provides of revolutionary activities, the deceitful nature of bourgeois governments, and the alternately ineffective and ultra-violent character of revolutionaries. These commentators hold that the story is largely important because it marks a turning point in Morris's relationship with the radical political organizations (particularly anarchists) he had previously patronized, acting as either a response to more radical reformers who long for revolution (and thus the lengthy discussion of the perils of violent revolution) or as a break with anarchism, with the emphasis on actual government organizations, decentralized and consensus-based though these are, that are central to the utopian experience itself. In these arguments, attention is not focused so much on the attractive aspects of the vision Morris lays out, but on his political motivations and the limitations of that vision, including observations that his ideal community would not be as tolerant as it first appears.[5]

The interpretation here differs in the holistic treatment of the story and on the characteristics of the utopia Morris provides us. We are interested in the assumptions Morris makes, how all the pieces of the utopia Morris presents fit together, whether political, social, or economic, and the nature of the good life he describes. Different as well from some interpretations is the emphasis here on journeys and in particular, the emphasis placed here on free and easy wandering and the subsequent understanding of the relationships among creative work, leisure, and journeys.[6]

Contexts and problems

The contexts of this utopia are much the same as those in which Bellamy worked. As with Bellamy, Morris levels a devastating criticism of nineteenth-century Western society, but unlike the former he also finds little to praise in modernity. The first topics he raises are the disjuncture between classes and between the government and ordinary citizens, and the consequences of these rifts for society. Life is portrayed as a continual struggle between capitalists, who control money and political power, and workers, who supply labor. The former are only interested in accumulating capital, recognizing obligations neither to other humans nor the environment. The former are subjected to conditions that are little better than slavery. In contrast, Morris implies, during the Middle Ages lords and serfs shared a vision of the world and lived in much the same surroundings, but the technological and administrative advances of early modern times have torn that solidarity asunder.

This disjuncture is manifested in various ways. One is through social and economic inequality. The last part of the book is mainly devoted to documenting the blessings brought by equality to the future and, therefore, the baleful consequences of inequality in the past. Inequalities come in various types. Morris takes them all on. He condemns inequalities of consumption, workload, enjoyment, leisure, status, and power in the modern world. Governments exist to protect the interests of the wealthy rather than to further the common good. Those in most need of help—the poor, the old, the unemployed—are victimized rather than assisted. Only the rich are able to enjoy leisure or find fulfillment in creative activities. Disorder is artificially stimulated through the manufacturing of an inhuman environment that benefits the rich and powerful and forces others to break laws in their struggle for dignity. Economic and political inequalities create poverty, disease, resentment, violence, and greed. Inequalities also have psychological effects because they create an environment in which everyone is dispirited and unhappy. Attempts to change this situation through collective action are ruthlessly suppressed.

Importantly for Morris, modernity's economic system and its foundation in inequality turns most work into a chore not a pleasure because work has been robbed of both creativity and utility. It is mostly rote factory work in which people must engage merely to survive. Such an environment drains labor of its expressive function. Work in a capitalist system is also not on the whole useful, resulting in badly made and mostly useless goods. Morris condemns modern industrial society for manufacturing goods merely for the sake of perpetuating and manipulating a money-based market system. Products are produced to be sold, not used, and if people do not desire them, those desires are artificially awakened within them with the aim of gaming the system, with capitalists harvesting labor so as to control immense amounts of wealth. Participating in that system is not fulfilling, and labor comes to be regarded as a burden rather than a pleasure because the most important part of human nature, the creative urge, remains unexpressed.

A final problem is ugliness. Capitalist society offends Morris's aesthetic sensibilities. Manmade structures are ugly because ill-designed. The physical environment is ugly because polluted and built over. People are ugly because they are stressed and unhappy. This problem also manifests itself in the scarcity of sound and beautiful material goods. Ironically, while Morris excoriates industrial society with producing too many things, he views it as a society suffering from scarcity of quality goods. To live life well, people must have at hand useful, sturdy, and beautifully designed things, objects that capitalism is unable to produce. Ultimately, Morris argues that modern capitalism breeds a lesser kind of life in that the very measures of beauty are debased. This is a somewhat different attitude than the one Bellamy adopts. Bellamy argues that capitalism is productive, it does produce useful things, and that its general organization principles can be adapted to the new socialist reality. The rich in his account both understand beauty and will acquiesce to changes because they cannot enjoy their lives when in the midst of inequality. They recognize at the least that it is better to live an elegant life where everyone enjoys the same lifestyle, but more generally are able to grasp the moral implications of the new system. Morris argues that capitalism is more insidious in its effects on aesthetic appreciation and its infusion into morality. This argument, of course, in part stems from

Morris's more complete denunciation of modern industrial life, but it also indicates a general understanding of the class system as inhuman and vicious in ways that Bellamy does not accept. Bellamy's capitalists might be warped by the economic system and generally callous in their treatment of the working class, but they are sufficiently rational and in touch with their sensibilities to grasp the direction of economic evolution and to appreciate the moral correctness of a more socialized life. Morris's capitalists are in contrast completely dehumanized by capitalism and are more like those Jack London describes in the *Iron Heel*— ruthless, violent, without scruples, and completely incapable of grasping a truly human morality. Their presence is another reason why utopia and the good life require a clean break with the modern, industrial world.

Solutions, themes, and the good life

Solutions and themes

Unlike Bellamy, Morris sees little hope that either capitalists or the middle class will experience a utopian epiphany and embrace a new world of equality and craftsmanship. Morris also rejects the conventional socialist route out of this box, which is to have the lower classes take over industrial society. Such a move would merely perpetuate the alienation people experience in their working lives, particularly that between themselves and the physical environment because it would not yield the type of fundamental changes to the economy and society that Morris thinks necessary. It would retain the fundamentally problematic industrial, urbanized society with its system of labor alienated from human nature and living patterns alienated from physical nature. More generally, the problem is not just who is in charge, but also what they are in charge of. Capitalism is not the primary problem in Morris's view. Industrialization and its attendant features are the more fundamental obstacles to the good life—capitalism is a product of the larger economic and civilizational process that Morris blames for humanity's difficulties. The structural solution Morris advocates, therefore, involves going backward in terms of civilization, landscapes, and economic development. Eventually, the landscape must be changed back to an earlier condition, and this transformation involves the clearing of houses and deliberate de-urbanization and de-industrialization. In this sense, the move back to a more natural state requires artificial action to counteract the artificiality of modern society. Humans created the mess of modern life; they must consciously change what they have wrought in order to regain contact with their natural selves, and this includes more than discarding capitalism. However, because capitalism gives some people a material stake in the *status quo* and causes others to misunderstand the nature of the human condition, many will resist the change and many will suffer in the course of the change, making the transition dangerous and costly.

Morris's proposal to revert to an earlier stage of civilization therefore entails a whole cluster of concepts and remedies as well as costs and risks. It involves the adoption of a largely crafts-based economy, which does several good things. One, it creates things that are durable and useful. As the product of human hands and ingenuity, made one at a time by people who are invested in their labor, items produced by a handicrafts economy are qualitatively better and are responsive to real needs. Second, a handicrafts economy produces things of beauty. Things made by hand, or at least with a minimum of mechanization, Morris holds, are inherently more beautiful than those mass produced by machinery, thus satisfying the human need for aesthetic creation. But it is not only physical products that are more beautiful as a result of such an economy. De-industrialization in this understanding re-beautifies the physical world. The environment is clean because it is no longer polluted with industrial products. The Thames is clear and contains salmon. The riverbanks are no longer choked with pollution-spewing factories. The ground is reforested. The air is clear. The same is true of the people. They are no longer required to work long hours, so they are rested. They no longer have to labor all their days indoors, so they are healthy. They are no longer slaves to machinery, so they are strong and are happy with their work because free to express their creative urges. Because they are happy, largely worry-free, exposed to the clean air and fully exercised, they are young looking and beautiful.

Another outcome of a crafts economy is the variety of different kinds of work available. People are able to work with different kinds of materials, work with their hands and with their minds, employ both brute strength and dexterity, and exercise their creativity. Morris argues that this variety provides another bundle of good things. It allows all sides of the person to be exercised, not just the intellectual or the physical alone. It allows people to expand their horizons and understand many things—for example, one character is interested in weaving, printing, mathematics, and history. It helps develop different parts of the personality, such that one neither becomes too intellectual and asocial, or too physical and thus boorish. Variety of work socializes the introvert and polishes the extrovert. Such variety also mitigates the creation of social ranks and hierarchies based on work or family status. Well-dressed men are also scholars and garbage collectors in the story. Writers of novels row boats. All perform useful work, and work that is not always considered pleasant. Everyone naturally and eagerly engages in activities traditionally associated with the lower classes as well as those connected with the upper classes.

But getting to that place is difficult due to the resistance of capitalists and the power of states. Therefore, politics is also in need of transformation because of the capacity of states to accumulate power and provide some in the community with the ability to create and defend an unjust and inhuman system. Morris vigorously displays his disapproval of conventional governments, though he is less clear in his description of what he actually wants. We do know many things that the future does not have. There are no states; rather, the world is filled with diverse and interesting cultures that employ only local self-governing structures. Each exists in harmony with others because there is no competitive national system to set them at odds, nor the attempt artificially to join disparate cultures together into a national unit. Prisons are also gone, not only because of the understanding that antisocial behavior in the environment of the future is accidental or the product of errors of judgment, but also because their very existence would create unhappiness among the people from the knowledge that others are suffering within them. This statement, along with others, implies that Morris assumes a great degree of social solidarity and psychological empathy among people in this environment. People will, if not distracted and persecuted by a dysfunctional environment, derive happiness from the happiness of others and suffer with the suffering of others. In turn, those who do commit violent acts out of error, emotion, or accident are naturally remorseful. But this only emerges when society does not engage in disciplining the wrongdoer. Rehabilitation is spontaneous and individual because it stems from the naturally generous disposition of humans.

Natural sociability, with its overtones of an automatic regard for the common good and happiness, a lack of self-centeredness or exclusive devotion to individual material interest, and a desire for compromise, turns governance from the task of exercising authority to one of facilitating cooperation. Morris insists that while differences of understanding will exist in his utopia, they will not be as deep or systematic as the old system of political parties suggested. If people possess such deep differences of understanding, created either by individual desires or by external interests, they would not be able to do the "business" of everyday life, he insists. Such business is ultimately rooted in an unadorned confrontation with events and conditions that enable people to settle differences based on empirical observation and pragmatic reasoning—Morris's example is that of a collective decision on when to gather a harvest. Through this metaphor and other arguments, Morris insists that the fact of living together in a common physical environment, along with the innate human sociability identified earlier, is enough to make differences of understanding or competing desires for public goods either trivial or of very short duration. Public business is ultimately of a technical and pragmatic nature and can be resolved easily by using basic technical means. The same would be true of people in the nineteenth century were it not for the power of the state and the games of ordinary politics, which in the course of creating conditions in which only the few may enjoy the good life masks genuine sociability and the simplicity of public affairs with the appearance of complexity, innate competitiveness, and inevitable difference.

Morris reinforces this position with arguments regarding the reach and nature of communal decisionmaking. He argues that this future society is libertarian—in matters of individual taste and lifestyle people are left alone to do what they wish. Unlike Utopia, the community here does not pass judgment on the topics of sex, attire, or entertainment. Only those matters pertaining to the common good are decided collectively. Here, the method is that of majority rule in the context of direct democracy. Decisions are made in commune or ward meetings in which all neighbors are allowed attendance, voice, and vote. Minorities are respected; if votes are close, decisions are postponed for further discussion. Indeed, decisions usually will not go forward unless the minority agrees, even in opposition, that they can.

Moreover, as there is no property, Morris holds that there are no laws and no courts in his society. Here, in common with Bellamy, Morris suggests that ordinary political organization is the result of the concept of property. Bring exclusive rights to objects or people into society and laws are required to sort out those rights, and along with laws come courts, lawyers, policemen, and other officials, as well as prisons. Get rid of property as a mistaken innovation and once again human's natural sociability takes over. People will not be forced to try to take from others, as no one will attempt to monopolize wealth. Thus, Morris treats the creation of the law as a mistake; it presumes a scarcity of things and in operation ironically creates that scarcity. This artificial scarcity, along with the artificial concept of ownership, destroys natural sociability. Remove property and one can remove laws; remove laws and almost all the violence and disorder experienced by nineteenth-century society disappear. Thus, rather than the answer to a problem that arises naturally in human existence as liberals such as Locke would have it, Morris depicts the law and property as the creators of the problems they are assumed to solve. Discard them and there are few instances of disorder, no criminal classes, nor habitual criminals of any kind.

With regard to economics, Morris theoretically solves the problem of production by relying upon three principles: (1) people, being creative beings, like to work and will create items of value; there is no need for social or economic incentives of either a positive or negative nature; (2) people like a variety of kinds of work, and are in themselves diverse, so everything that needs to be done or produced will be,[7] and (3) people prize beauty and elegance more than quantity; therefore, large amounts of goods need not be produced.

These three propositions converge into the justification for a crafts-based economy. Such an economy satisfies the natural human urge to create by working directly with materials. While such an economy is labor-intensive, this presents no problem. People want to work and the quantity of products is not as important as their quality. Moreover, because the economy is not capitalistic (and with only a few necessary items mass produced by machinery), the drive to produce more things in order to accumulate capital in private hands is absent. Only what is needed is produced. This allows for the leisure to pursue a variety of creative activities. Finally, because everyone wants to labor and will labor, there is no social or economic penalty attached to physical or difficult labor. Everyone is willing and eager to perform laborious tasks, and because this is the case, there are no social or other class stigmas attached to any type of productive labor.

Equally important is the absence of money as a holder of value or as a rationing system. No specie is circulated. It is not needed because of the nature of the material desires each person possesses. People want high-quality goods and services, but are content with a sufficiency of each. Not needing large quantities of things due to limited desires and the absence of a system that awards prestige to consumption, one simply goes to the market (supplied by the spontaneous labor of everyone) and gets what is needed. Likewise, if a service is needed, one either calls on a relevant specialist (who will be happy for the exercise), or one gets together with friends to do the deed in a convivial atmosphere. Morris follows More here and rejects Bellamy's argument that some type of rationing device is necessary. Greed has disappeared. Everyone being supplied with what they need and none taking more than they need, there is no need for currency or debit cards.

Being entities who find fulfillment in creative labor, people work to fulfill themselves and as a service to others. They see a need and work sufficiently hard and sufficiently long to address it. Physical labor is no longer viewed as a burden. Rather, it is a sport akin to rowing or playing rugby. So there is no need to use economic incentives to force or to entice people to work. Neither is it necessary to draft people into labor armies and motivate them with social incentives (as with Bellamy) or to subject everyone to the beady eyes of neighbors and officials (as with More). Nor is it necessary to entice people to engage in laborious or unpleasant work by dangling the prospect of more leisure, as Bellamy also suggests. While leisure is important for rest and variety, it is not the venue through which people construct themselves. Rather, they create themselves through labor. People spontaneously, because naturally and innately, wish to labor over tasks that are useful to society as a whole, no matter their nature. Given a sufficient number and variety of people, everyone will have a sufficiency of high-quality goods and services that allow each to enjoy the good life, and can have them for the asking, without money and without the need to ration them, and everyone will have a sufficient supply of leisure as well.

The good life

The good life in Morris's society of the future is one of beauty, enjoyable physical labor, good health, material security, contact with Nature, and free wanderings. At bottom, therefore, it is free, creative, and expressive. This characteristic cuts across the concepts of production and consumption that we usually find in these stories. It appears that Morris wishes life to be stripped of much of the influence of technology that Bellamy would keep and which then and now mediates between humans and the natural environment. But people are not thrown out into Nature. They still live in solid buildings and wear elaborate clothing. And as with the society of *Looking Backward*, the good life here includes consumption. People are happy when they possess and use beautiful things. The key to this utopia is therefore finding the right amount of direct interaction with work and Nature that yields creativity, beauty, and the things necessary for consumption. Too much interaction, in the form of constant labor, routinized labor, or labor that is destructively associated with low social status, and humans are overwhelmed; too little and they equally suffer from scarcity of either goods or creative expression. Morris argues that nineteenth-century industrial society has separated humans too much from the creative and aesthetic connection between humans and physical Nature, with the result that their lives are unhappy, their bodies worn out and prematurely aged and their social relations frayed, even if large quantities of (ugly and often useless) goods are produced.

To live in Morris's future is to live a freely creative life. Unlike More's utopia, people travel freely. They learn spontaneously, taking up subjects as they please and continue the learning process throughout their lives. They associate together in cooperatives, drop in on each other, live without laws, and order themselves in the absence of courts and prisons. They deliberate in direct democracies, pursue consensus, and avoid confrontations and conflict. They exchange services. They seek out work and throw themselves into it. They engage in a variety of endeavors and pastimes. They enjoy the beauty of the countryside, the goods and buildings they create, and the untrammeled countenances of their fellows. They live free of greed and experience little conflict, jealousy, or violence. They do not accumulate goods or money. They marry (and sometimes separate), have children, and live to ripe old age.

Living in this utopia requires that one be highly social, appreciative of labor and intensely energetic and curious. One must also be able to conceive of a good life in the absence of much technology or rigid structures. One must be satisfied and fulfilled by a life that potentially swings between intellectual stimulation and physical labor. One must have a well-rounded psyche. Are people naturally that way? Is our current penchant for specialization really a later accretion to human nature? Morris thinks so. A natural and happy human is one who is not confined to a life of the mind or of the body. Living the good life means having the opportunity and unleashing the ambition continuously to sample the fruits of a wide variety of experiences and behaviors.

Thus, the good life here does not consist only of consumption or the gathering of riches. It is also not only about abundant leisure. Rather, it is more about creating and enjoying a simple life that is filled with beauty, spontaneity, and change. One does not need gadgets to save labor—labor in itself can be a game. One does not need many things—it is better to have a few, beautifully made things than to have many, poorly manufactured and ugly articles. One does not need the police or the state to remain orderly or to enjoy a safe life. More generally, the good life means enjoying the balance that comes from free and easy wandering through physical and creative spaces.

Human nature

While Morris discusses the creation of norms and the development of culture in his dream future, he is not speaking of socially constructing humans. Hardwiring is most important to the human character, and he seeks to return to what he thinks are natural, authentic humans. In particular, he holds that no matter the advantages of various types of civilization, humans can only be happy and fulfilled in one type of social and physical environment. This environment must allow people to express their creative urges, to engage in many different activities, to wander freely and to experience beauty. Thus it is not a matter, as with Zamyatin, of people being torn between their desires for security or freedom. Human nature is coherent, and all parts of human nature point to a single way of organizing people that allows them true fulfillment. To put it in terms of hardwiring versus software, programming, and social construction, Morris not only believes that humans are strongly hardwired and thus environments are very important in terms of which responses they stimulate. He goes further to argue that only one type of environment is truly compatible with human hardwiring. All others are dysfunctional and end up warping humans by diverting them from the fulfillment of their potential. More generally, he appears to believe that there is no need to socially construct humans because their problems can be solved and their potential fulfilled by changing their physical, social and economic environments. Thus in a moral sense, hardwiring must be strongly determinative of the type and level of civilization chosen. Failing to choose the right civilization results in humans who are deformed, in that they display inhuman types of behavior such as greed, hostility, burning ambition, cruelty, and callousness.

This understanding of human nature informs the most important aspect of Morris's discussion of environments and behavior. For Morris, industrial society is "artificial" (meaning not in accordance with human hardwiring) in a highly destructive fashion. Natural humans, he holds, are not greedy. Nor do they naturally need external motivations to work, nor are they combative or generally disorderly. Humans naturally are productive, sociable, aesthetically sensitive beings. Economic systems and modes of production that depend upon competition twist people. This judgment produces a description of the relationship between environment and behavior that is subtly different from More's. More argues that most people are greedy in ordinary society because they are put in situations of scarcity. That situation is natural; therefore, society must produce an artificial atmosphere that deactivates this hardwired response by providing economic security. Morris, in contrast, argues that it is only in the highly artificial atmosphere of modern industrialized society, with its competitive economic system, that people come to be greedy. Greed, in other words, is an acquired characteristic. Eliminate the unnatural environment that created that characteristic and the characteristic will disappear, for good. To reveal the best in humans, one does not manipulate the environment by creating an artificial situation; one strips it, going back as far as is necessary to a simpler way of life that reveals humans' natural grace and sociability.

The flip side of these assumptions is the position that, absent uncongenial environments such as those created by modern, industrial capitalism, people will spontaneously cooperate. They do not need incentives to abandon egoistic behavior, nor do they need to be socially constructed to fit into a pluralistic direct democracy. They enjoy being with one another. There are few natural frictions among them—they do not see material interests as exclusive, they view themselves as naturally part of a larger organism, and they would rather recede in the face of potential conflict than to pursue their own ideas. That is not to say that humans are naturally perfect in Morris's understanding. There are problems in utopia. But these, Morris suggests, are the products of emotions or "perversity and self-will." People become angry or jealous and lash out. They experience problems in their relationships with the opposite sex. In extraordinary circumstances, such problems lead to violence. While Morris has old man Hammond agree to a comparison between antisocial behavior and disease, this is not the same as the concept Bellamy embraces. Morris does not literally mean that violence and crime are diseases or are the products of disease, but rather agrees to the metaphor because it denies authorship of violent acts. Such behaviors are accidents or errors of judgment. As such, they are not intentional; therefore, punishment is not warranted on grounds of either deterrence or retribution. Accidents are unforeseeable calamities, uncontrolled by those who experience them. They cannot be deterred. Nor ought they be the cause for retribution. Punishment for either of these reasons would be arbitrary and, therefore, unsociable. No police, trials, or prisons are necessary in this natural environment. Nor is medical treatment for the disorderly necessary. Rather, society depends on the natural sociability of the perpetrator to emerge in the form of remorse and atonement.

Another important part of human nature in Morris's understanding is the ability to learn spontaneously, without structure. Morris argues that in the future education will take place outside institutions. Humans are curious and can and will learn on their own, with no need for formal schooling and the "boy factories" of contemporary England. This human characteristic is connected with another most important proposition in his understanding of human nature: that humans are creative beings who find the most meaning and happiness in creative activity as labor rather than in possessions, leisure, or consumption. Where other utopias will rely upon mechanisms (surveillance, nonmaterial incentives) to ensure that hard physical labor is performed and distributed in an equitable fashion, Morris sees people being eager to embrace any opportunity for work that arises when labor takes place in an atmosphere that is free of economic competition, industrialization, and a money economy. Such activities as constructing houses and paving streets, instead of being shunned as too strenuous, uninteresting and the mark of lower social orders, are considered "genuinely amusing" and sought after by both young and old because work allows for creative expression and exercise for the physical body.

Thus, Morris argues that people fulfill themselves through creative labor, both skilled and unskilled. While Marxian at its source and productive of Marx's contention that people in a fully communist society will be able to enjoy a variety of creative pursuits, this position ultimately takes Morris to a different place than Marx. Where Marx argues that this trait drives humanity forward through the various stages of economic development until it finds its satisfaction in a socialized and industrialized society, Morris holds that industrialization is anathema to it. The creation of value when regimented stifles humans. To be forced to work for a while in a factory, then live the life of an artist or critic is unacceptable to him. One sacrifices too much of life and too much of satisfaction unnecessarily. All life is creative work.[8] It must be done spontaneously, outdoors if possible, and with the minimum of interference from technology and organization. To be creative ultimately means working directly on material with one's hands and mind rather than creating and working with capital. To sacrifice creativity for quantitatively measured productively in order to generate more time for leisure is not acceptable, for such an attitude assumes that "Nature" is entirely outside of us, to be wholly mastered and completely separated from us in order that we might seek fulfillment elsewhere. The correct understanding posits a closer interrelationship between humans and Nature that is facilitated by labor. Humans can only live the good life if they can enjoy this relationship in all its parts, which entails the continued engagement with creative, physical and mental, labor.

This picture allows Morris further to suggest several things. It allows him to argue that a crafts-based economy is sufficient, as it will produce enough things to satisfy the nongreedy needs of natural people. It allows him to argue that people will not need money as rationing device, as they will not take or consume more than they need. It allows him to argue that both material incentives and even the nonmaterial incentives to work that Bellamy identifies are unnecessary. It also allows him to argue that people will be satisfied with a nontechnological society. They will not want to surround themselves with labor-saving devices. They can dispense with trains, machinery, gas lights, and other features of modern nineteenth-century life and not only be happy, but infinitely happier. By extension, he would also argue that people would be completely fulfilled without the electronic means of amusement (radios, televisions, computers, and cell phones) that are ubiquitous in our modern, technologically savvy society.

Finally, an important reason why Morris's utopia is characterized by free and easy wandering is because people there are naturally curious and restless. They are not content to do one thing all the time, or to stay in one place for long periods. They must be up and about, trying out various kinds of work and moving from one type of activity to another. They are intellectually and physically energetic. Most of the characters (some women appear to be more domestically oriented) move about from one place to another and work in a variety of environments and in a variety of modes. People are not confined to one profession. People combine the activities of manual laborer with writer, garbage collector with mathematician, boatman with historian. They are eager to try new jobs, to engage in seasonal work, to branch out into new intellectual endeavors. Thus, Morris argues that in this environment free from the chains of capitalism, industrialization, and urban civilization, people are allowed to display their natural flexibility and explore their innately complex intellectual, emotional, and physical make-ups.

The problem from Morris's point of view is the effect of this restlessness on the future of such a utopia. When characters like Ellen (the personification of utopian life) express anxiety about the future and an interest in history as a way of thinking about human mistakes, they display disquiet with the capacity of humans to inhabit this place for long. Being restless, humans may wish to try something different, transferring their wanderings from their individual lives to society as a whole. Just as humans left the original Middle Ages during their journey through types of civilization, so Morris appears to fear that humans would do the same here, expressing their restlessness with a push to transcend the civilizational boundaries of this good and necessary environment. The only environment that can make humans happy may, ironically, be insufficiently structured to prevent them from discarding it.

Applications

Morris sees contemporary modern humans as artificial perversions of the true type. Their competitiveness, individualism, violence, and disorderliness, pervasive jealousies, greed for physical possessions, aversion to work, ill health, and ugliness are the products of their modern, industrial environment and not at all indicative of the basic material. To that point, Morris argues that the state, laws, social strictures, armies, factories, cities, schools, prisons, and civilization, which we tout as the answers to the problems of human nature and as the highest accomplishments of our flawed species are actually the causes of our problems and should be a source of shame and disgust. Morris would condemn us for preserving a failed civilization and perpetuating (and pushing forward with) a dysfunctional and inhuman economic model. Insofar as the twenty-first century is an extension or magnification of the nineteenth century, this historical outcome is a catastrophe rather than a triumph, and we have only ourselves to blame.

Taken literally, Morris's recommendations go far beyond policy proposals, extending to advocacy of wholesale revolutionary change that even in his story was the outcome of a long and bloody war that depopulated and otherwise devastated society. Few have had the desire to pay that price for utopia; even while accepting Morris's condemnation of modern industrial (and postindustrial) society, one could argue that if such destruction is the cost of being truly human, it is better to exist at a less than fully human level.

But we can look at those recommendations as suggestive of somewhat more modest proposals. Morris encourages us to think differently about how we see human fulfillment and flourishing. We assume that more technology is better, in large part because it saves labor. We assume that a higher standard of living is constituted mostly by access to more goods or better goods as defined by higher technological standards. Morris thinks in other terms, emphasizing how we live our lives more than what we possess, and when he does address possessions elevates aesthetic appreciation over technological wizardry. In his mind, there should be no separation between work and play because work should be enjoyable, even if accompanied by physical exertion or unpleasant smells.

It is only when the creative and useful aspects of work are masked that labor becomes unpleasant; such unpleasantness disappears when people control what they create, in the sense that they freely give away the products of their labor. How is it that we could attain such a mindset? Would it be possible without radical structural changes to the economy? Morris would reject the proposition, but might the change he seeks be much like that which Bellamy identifies, being just as much in our minds as in our environment? Such understandings might already be occurring in the realm of publication, as writers take advantage of technology to create and then give away the products of their creativity. Might the same apply elsewhere, and be possible, ironically, due to the presence of the technology that Morris generally dislikes?

On a larger scale, Morris points to different priorities. We should encourage less industrialization and more crafts-based production. We should promote de-urbanization. We should move toward a more libertarian and consensus-oriented political structure. We should tap into our natural desire to learn rather than housing ourselves and children in education factories. There are many questions regarding such recommendations. Would a crafts-based economy create enough material goods for people to live as Morris describes them? Would changing the environment as described, to emphasize creative labor and equal living conditions, really banish most violence and antisocial behavior? Can we live in small, self-sufficient economic units and have the quality and standard of life that Morris describes? Will people spontaneously work to provide for the needs of themselves and the community? Can we get along without armies, policemen, courts, and laws? Can we live cooperatively in a direct democracy? Are people really naturally social and creative, willing and eager to work and loathe to harm one another? Is the good life composed of free and creative labor? Will people in such an environment really retain their youth and beauty and find happiness?

Moving beyond such skepticism, we can examine some of the possible solutions to our ongoing problems that Morris proposes. One is to embrace the libertarian approach to lifestyles that he describes. While American society has moved progressively in that direction over the past 100 years, one might argue that more needs to be done. Perhaps the way out of the problems with the war on drugs is to declare it over. Allowing people to make their own choices regarding such substances may bring use above ground and rid society of both the criminal element that flocks to black markets and remove the burden on both society and individuals bear when users are criminalized.

Likewise, is it possible that a greater emphasis on seeking consensus and attempting to reduce politics to technical questions might remove some of the dysfunctionalities of modern government by reducing levels of partisanship? A more exacting norm for passing legislation and engaging in public policy initiatives may reduce political temperatures. Such a move would also reduce government activities as a whole. A reduction in activities coupled with a process of consensus-building might refurbish the image of public institutions and restore some of the trust in them that has been lost over the past 50 years by all elements of the body politic.

Could we go further in the direction that Morris indicates in terms of education and do so on a broad scale? Remember that Morris approaches education on the assumption that children and people are natural learners. Adopting Morris's understanding would entail ridding ourselves of conventional schools, focusing on apprenticeships, as well as allowing people (both young and old) to follow natural aptitudes. It would also mean promoting manual labor as good for everyone and completely compatible with intellectual pursuits in other parts of one's life. Perhaps a more relaxed, practical, and well-rounded approach to education would spur younger students to learn more and more deeply than they do currently in a classroom setting and entice people who have an aptitude for mechanical and manual labor to obtain training in those areas without discouraging them from thinking that such training rules out the simultaneous or later pursuit of more abstract intellectual pursuits, or to see participation in such activities as marking a disadvantaged and disdained lower social class.

Morris would also have us place a greater emphasis on the quality of products rather than quantity. Would this increase our enjoyment of life and provide the stage for more fulfilling labor? It could. To embrace such a shift would, however, probably also require a change in the broader culture. Are people capable of doing so, or has culture and experiences with recessions, unemployment, and uncertainty inevitably molded modern humans such that they equate security and the good life with a large quantity of goods, and with consumption itself as the marker of the good life?

Aside from thinking through these practical solutions to the problems we face, we should grapple with a larger set of questions: does Morris really set the stage for a good life? Morris's idealization of creative labor and the economy of the Middle Ages may strike the observer as artificial. At the very least, Morris must inject into this life many elements of a later industrial age, as he himself admits when it comes to some types of machinery and practices of mass production.

The Middle Ages were also not necessarily a time of health and vigor. Would we want to give up modern medicines that have helped tame many of the diseases that cut short the lives of earlier humans? To think of the Middle Ages as a time of equality is also fundamentally wrong. Morris may well accept this point and argue that his vision is not the recreation of the Middle Ages in toto, but rather the resurrection of certain understandings of beauty, culture, and labor that would be found there. Yet, can these be recreated outside the historical, social, and political context in which they arose? Is an equalitarian, communist Middle Ages possible, or are the good things about the Middle Ages inevitably connected with what was undesirable? The danger is that what Morris describes is really a tarted up, Disneyfied version of the past, at odds with both the experience of that past and of its underlying conditions.

Other questions are also pertinent. Morris argues that a high culture and high degree of intellectual attainment will be in the grasp of everyone in such an economy. Yet this is again dependent on the assumption that the demands for physical labor will be satisfied even in the absence of large-scale industrialization and the routine use of modern technology. If these assumptions are wrong, then there will be no time for most people to indulge a movement back and forth between producing goods, providing services, and engaging in the study of mathematics, aesthetics, poetry, and history. Earlier experiences with such a crafts-based economy showed that such luxuries were available only to the very few. No one else had the leisure or energy for such pursuits.

There is also the question of beauty. One could discard this as frivolous, but that would be a mistake. Morris is here making a serious argument in a rather superficial way. His contention is that our physical and mental problems are largely artificial and the product of our modern way of life. Disease, disabilities, and aging will largely disappear if we were to live psychologically and physically healthier lives. No one, of course, would dispute this last contention. The real question has to do with Morris's understanding of what constitutes and what contributes to such a life. Will working with our hands help? Will being able to engage in a variety of activities help? Is the removal of urbanization and industrialization necessary? Would the removal of economic anxieties and competition help? There is also the larger question—overall, does modern, industrial technology and science offer us a net loss or gain of health? Morris points to a health deficit in modern times. Is he right? Would going backward really allow us to live healthier and happier lives? Or have the technological and medical breakthroughs of the last century rendered Morris's position ridiculous?

As noted in the introduction, the story is open-ended in terms of its description of change. As emphasized here, Morris does not see "progress" as a moving forward to ways of life that are unknown. The future, if it is to be good, must in important ways resemble a past that has already been discarded. To live the good life means to go backward to an existence that removes problematic additions to human behavior. Yet despite the realization of this on the part of many characters in the story, some of them also admit to an uncertainty with regard to the maintenance of this ideal way of life. Morris, it appears, is uneasy about the future of the future. Would people, having attained this happy life, be content with it? Or would they once again be tempted by technology and the promise of material abundance?

Notes

1 For another understanding of Bellamy's view of this book as a political act, see M. Holzman, "Anarchism and Utopia: William Morris's *News from Nowhere*," *ELH*, Vol. 51, no. 3 (Autumn 1984). For a general discussion of attempts to characterize the story in terms of genre, see Roger C. Lewis, "*News from Nowhere*: Arcadia or Utopia?" *The Journal of the William Morris Society*, Vol. VII, no. 2 (1987).

2 Anna Vaninskaya, "Janus-Faced Fictions: Socialism as Utopia and Dystopia in William Morris and George Orwell," *Utopian Studies*, Vol. 14, no. 2 (2003).

3 Martin Delveaux, "O Me! O Me! How I Love the Earth: William Morris's News from Nowhere and the Birth of Sustainable Society," *Contemporary Justice Review*, Vol. 8, no. 2 (June 2005).

4 R. Watkinson, "The Obstinate Refusers: Work in *News from Nowhere*" in S. Coleman and P. O'Sullivan, eds, *William Morris & News from Nowhere: A Vision for our Time* (Bideford, Devon: Green Books, 1990).

5 See Michael Holzman, "Anarchism and Utopia: William Morris's *News from Nowhere*," *ELH*, Vol. 51, no. 3 (Autumn 1984). On the limits of toleration, see Marcus Waithe, "The Laws of Hospitality: Liberty, Generosity, and the Limits of Dissent in William Morris's *The Tables Turned* and *News from Nowhere*," *The Yearbook of English Studies*, Vol. 36, no. 2 (2006).

6 For a discussion of Morris's understanding of the relationship between work and leisure, see Ruth Kinna, "William Morris: Art, Work, and Leisure," *Journal of the History of Ideas*, Vol. 61, no. 3 (July 2000).

7   For more on this point and its origins in Morris's reading in various socialist literatures, see Kinna, "William Morris," 504–505.

8   Kinna, "William Morris," underlines the proposition that the later Morris of *News from Nowhere* had come to accept the importance of leisure as the complete cessation of work and the importance of having some mechanization available that will allow for the discharge of certain types of large-scale manufacturing. This position is certainly present in *News from Nowhere*, but I argue that the main thrust of the story is the natural creativity of humans and that it is through work, rather than leisure, that people ultimately express and develop their humanness.

6

We

Introduction

The dystopian novels discussed in the following chapters, Evgenii Zamyatin's (1884–1937) *We* and George Orwell's (1903–1950) *Nineteen Eight-Four*, describe how the quest for the good life is turned upside down by the growing power of a state controlled by a small group of people. Links between the two are rife. We know that Orwell had read *We* before embarking on his own dystopian writing venture. Both stories at least in part take the Soviet Union as their model, though Orwell's tale is not as much about the Soviets as is sometimes thought. Both are troubled by the impact of modernity on human freedom and see in the natural world a contrast with a dehumanizing future. Both are concerned with privacy and the intrusion of the state into the most intimate details of one's life. Both, therefore, raise some of the same fundamental questions. Where is the state headed? What are the problems associated with powerful institutions, mobilization of the population, and the growth of coercive organs? Will the problems and crises of the present and future empower the state such that it will escape the control of ordinary citizens? Does the quest for material and physical security give the larger community the leverage it needs to dominate human lives, leaving little or no room for freedom and individuality? How can we prevent the state (or those who control it) from becoming too powerful?

A further set of questions concerns the place of rationality and logic. Is rationality good? How useful is it? To what extent do we use it and to what degree does it use us? Zamyatin is suspicious of the totalizing potential of rationality, particularly in its connection with the innate desire for security and subsequent codification in culture and the state. Rationality run amok is the seed of his dystopian vision, with technocratic minions of the state morphing into guardians of orthodoxy. Orwell, in contrast, sees rationality as one of the keys to remaining fully human and autonomous. In order to control its inhabitants and impose orthodoxy, he argues, the dystopian community must destroy the capacity to reason and substitute for it a radically subjective and flexible understanding of the world.

The story and interpretations

Story

We (ca. 1921) is written in the form of a diary kept by a scientist in a future that is dominated by mathematical logic and the state. People do not have names, only designators comprised of letters and numbers and are known as ciphers. They live under a regime, the One State, which came into being as the result of a "Two Hundred Years War" and claims to have created utopia. The narrator, D-503, lives in a city enclosed by a wall that keeps an uncivilized, uncontrolled, and nontechnological Nature outside; inside, it is filled with transparent buildings and a dominating state apparatus. D-503's job is to supervise the construction of the *Integral*, a spaceship that will bring the benefits of the One State to the rest of the universe. In reality, the One State plans to embark on the same project in extraterrestrial spheres that it has accomplished on earth—to impose its way of life willy-nilly on others. As D-503 records in his diary, the One State promises that if alien races "won't understand that we bring them mathematically infallible happiness, it will be our duty to force them to be happy." This theme is the key to the government's relationship with its own citizens. The One State forces them to be happy by the power of mathematical logic. As a result, citizens live, work, procreate, and die for the state and its rational, technical understanding of the good life.

The One State is ruled by the Benefactor, the predecessor of Orwell's Big Brother and the heir of Jack London's Oligarchy and possibly Plato's philosopher king, Machiavelli's prince and More's King Utopus. Through him, all citizens join with the state. He is at once leader and high priest. D-503 accepts this political order and way of life for the most part, though the tone of his journal reflects from the beginning some latent uneasiness, identified later as the development of his soul and imagination. This uneasiness facilitates his participation in an adventure that takes up the bulk of the story. It begins when he is jolted out of his passivity by a strange woman, I-330, a musician who is employed in re-creating and ridiculing old and therefore "primitive" pieces of music. I-330 exposes D-503 both to a world of irrational emotions and to an underground resistance that plans to use the *Integral* to blast open the city's wall and open its inhabitants to the wonders and messiness of Nature. While this initial scheme fails and I-330 is executed, the resistance does succeed in blowing up part of the wall, unleashing a period of total freedom that the state struggles to contain. Despite this setback, the One State forges on with its final solution to the problem of attaining human happiness and security—an operation on each citizen in which her imagination is removed. The book closes with D-503, *sans* imagination, once again enjoying the ascetic beauty of mathematical precision.

We is a story of dystopia from the inside. The narrator does not have to undertake a journey to find it, but as with *Looking Backward* and *News from Nowhere* makes excursions within and outside the city to flesh out the experience. D-503's movements in the story are between the two poles of existence Zamyatin stakes out—the safe, clean, secure, yet sterile, regimented, and unimaginative life of the city and the dirty, dangerous, but exhilarating and sensuous world of the countryside.

Interpretations

A variety of differences influence interpreters' understandings of the ultimate message of this story and the immediate targets of its satire. Chang Hui-chuan's "Zamyatin's *We*: A Reassessment" contains an interesting and informative discussion of the literature on the story. For Chang, the story is not typical of a dystopia in that it is neither completely pessimistic nor a satire. Rather, it is an open-ended and "heretical" story which through its very text attempts to break through the ossification of dogma represented by modern understandings of science and civilization.[1] Amey likewise does not see *We* as a prototypical dystopian story. Emphasizing the importance of surveillance and transparency for the immersion of the individual into the collective in the One State, Amey nonetheless argues that the all-seeing, Panopticon-like surveillance apparatus the state uses serves to set the stage for the creation of an individuated identity, and thus there is a glimmer of hope for humans in such a setting even if that hope in the story is extinguished by the state's desperate act of removing citizens' imaginations.[2]

In Aginsk's view, the message of the story is immediate and aimed at contemporary figures and conditions. The story is about the mechanization of people in the contemporary Soviet Union, the loss of rights and individuality experienced there, and the political and economic views of the members of the Proletkult group, whom Zamyatin believed were championing that process.[3] Natasha Randall also sees *We*'s targets as immediate, in the form condemning the contemporary fascination with the industrializing and assembly-line methods of Henry Ford and Frederick Taylor that was rife in the Soviet Union in the early 1920s.[4]

For Slusser, Zamyatin's targets were larger and less immediately topical, though he argues that Zamyatin couches the delivery of satirical messages in the new and popular medium of science fiction. In this interpretation, it is not just the Soviet Revolution or the Soviet Union that is the ultimate source of the problems Zamyatin identifies, but rather a "totalitarian world founded on an extreme application of the quantifying logic of Western rationalism." In this understanding, Zamyatin is located within the ongoing cultural debate within Russia that pitted Westernizers against Slavophiles, with Zamyatin generally taking his place with the latter.[5] Stefani, in contrast, sees the story as participating in a contemporary Russian literary trend of engaging in a dialogue with Plato's *Republic* and in doing so providing a critique of Plato's understandings of critical political and social values. Here the thrust of the book is taken to be philosophical, with underlying political implications pointing to the problems of state control, conformity with state values and the loss of individual autonomy that are associated with a discredited, Platonic way of thinking about the world.[6]

The interpretation used here tends to side with the broader, philosophical reading of the book. I take Zamyatin as seeing in modernity, and not only the new Soviet regime, a threat to the fundamental character of humans. More broadly, I take him as critiquing the artificial nature of civilization itself, and the role of governments and rationality as the possible purveyors of an ultimately problematic way of life that, nonetheless, has its roots in a divided and incoherent human nature.

Contexts and problems

Zamyatin is writing not only in the aftermath of the Russian Revolution, but also in the trail of decades of socialist thought. Many who adhered to a socialist way of thinking shared the modernist assumption that progress equals the complete triumph of humans over Nature through the application of rationality. Socialism in its Marxist form and in the Soviet Union embraced the industrial revolution and science. Factories, machinery, and technology embodied the way forward because it was assumed that if the forces of production were correctly understood and communally controlled, they would deliver the goods and the leisure necessary for everyone to live the good life. A socialist society would entail life in the city, industrialization, technical innovation, and the final escape from the idiocies of a rural existence. Socialism would complete the historical human project of building a human civilization that would allow humans to live an unalienated life.

Zamyatin appears to pick up on the themes of scientific socialism and technical industrialization that were promoted as the core of the socialist experiment in civilization in the newly established Soviet Union. He saw the state, armed with a messianic understanding of science, displacing all prior ways of human living with a rationalized, streamlined, process-oriented lifestyle in which all activity must pass the muster of the state's understanding of logic and productivity. As it turns out, the phase that Zamyatin satirizes had a short life in the Soviet Union, as not only did Lenin turn away from avant-garde understandings in art before his illness, but Stalin's rise as Lenin's successor led to a decisive switch from futuristic policies and grandly progressive conceptions of civilization in general to the embrace of traditional understandings of morality and nationalism.

Nevertheless, some aspects of what Zamyatin feared did come to pass. The Soviet state expanded its range of activities to include control of many otherwise private aspects of individual life, with service to the state raised to the highest level of importance. Faith in science and technology, in the form of the "super-industrializing" model of modernization Stalin eventually championed, also came to dominate Soviet economic thinking for decades, with the result that individuals were reduced to the status of state workers and mobilized to carry out state activities. And while the regime discarded the modernist and avant-garde trappings of the concept by the end of the 1920s, the Soviet government continually promoted thereafter the "new socialist man" in its educational policies, cultural offerings, and propaganda campaigns. More to the point, a modernist worldview dominated the minds of some of the most important figures in the Party and government in the early 1920s. These visionaries rejected the romantic yearnings of the peasant parties for land and local communities and the anarchist attempts to turn back the clock to a mythical, preindustrial time of stateless governing through universal participation, consensus, and village autonomy. In their circles, to be revolutionary was to embrace the cutting edge of all endeavors. Revolutionary art was modern; revolutionary morality was new-fangled. Revolutionary life had to be innovative, which meant technologically advanced, sophisticated, and built around institutions of the modern state.

Zamyatin, while a Bolshevik, a member of a circle of prominent Bolshevik artists, and admirer of some aspects of modern technology, writes against such thinking. He appears to have sympathies for the old, the natural, and the rural as capable of touching and developing the core of humanness even if they do not provide the comfort and security that modern cities furnish. He is afraid of a future that banishes a natural life in favor of a completely mechanized, artificial existence (though he also does not see a natural life as unproblematic). He rejected a future in which workers would become Taylorized productive units, work would be mechanized, and city life would be totally isolated from the country. If the New Soviet Man would as closely as possible resemble a machine, Zamyatin was not in favor of that construction. In critiquing this future, Zamyatin hoped to dissuade his fellow intellectuals from fetishizing the scientific, the rational, and the mechanical.

Given both its message and its format, *We* was not a democratic work. It was not meant for the workers and peasants, or even ordinarily educated, white-collar Soviet citizens. It is too experimental and fragmented to have had wide appeal, much less be universally accessible. Even today it is not an easy read. At the time, it would be extremely difficult going because it contains a literary sensibility that would only come into its own in mid-twentieth-century science fiction. But even in his limited effort at reaching intellectuals, Zamyatin was unsuccessful. *We* was panned by his fellow writers, and he was eventually forced into exile and died in Paris at an early age.[7]

With its attempt to demonstrate the problems of the society the new Soviet regime initially idealized, *We* introduces us to scientific dystopia. Where Bellamy paints science and technology as crucial means by which to attain the good life for everyone, Zamyatin resembles Morris in viewing science and its accompanying language of mathematical reason as problematic with regard to a truly human existence. But it is not primarily because science and technology pollute the earth that causes Zamyatin to question science, nor does the danger Zamyatin identify come, as it does in later science fiction, in the form of animate technology running amok, but as the invasion of the human habitat by technical ways of thinking and living. This is not the fear that our tools escape our control, but that we will descend to the level of our tools while believing that we are advancing to a better way of life. Machines do not become human; humans become machines.[8]

Themes in dystopia and dystopian life

Themes

Zamyatin paints an intimate portrait of dystopia's state-controlled life through D-503's journal. Of particular importance to this life is the Table of Hours—the communal schedule of the community that orders the time of every person in the community. With the exception of the two personal hours, everyone does the same thing at the same time. As such, the Table is the coordinator of the communal body, the nervous system that ensures harmony through uniformity. Zamyatin makes a point of tracing the Table to train schedules. This equation of humans with trains has significance on several levels. On the first, it represents a change in understanding progress and movement. The chapter that discusses the Table starts with a disquisition on travel, with D-503 musing on the historical demise of the conception of travel as progress. To travel freely means to scatter the components of the corporate body. Progress is no longer seen in those terms. Coordination rather than scattering is the goal, and it is in this sense that train schedules rather than travel itself has come to signify progress. The second level of significance is related, in that train schedules are a way of coordinating mechanical devices. They are not necessary because trains possess autonomy and may wander off on their own. Rather, they are required because trains are tools in the hands of others and must be kept in motion and coordinated by an outside agent. The Table of Hours reduces humans to the level of trains, in large part because it assumes that they do not possess autonomy. They are machines to be run to a schedule for the convenience and purposes of the state. Here, while exaggerating for effect, Zamyatin points to the regulation of time by authorities as an important threat to freedom and full humanity. To coordinate time, to order the day through scheduling, is to remove the contingency that allows us to explore our lives. In this sense, the Table of Hours is the ultimate refinement of thousands of years of attempts by officials, bosses, teachers, and civilization itself to control time and master humans. It is the heir of the calendar, timepiece, clock, the obviously mischievous factory whistle and stopwatch in the hand of the efficiency expert, and perhaps the anticipation of the Personal Digital Assistant.

A second important theme of the One State experience is the merging of culture and politics represented by the entities known as the Benefactor and the Guardians. The Benefactor is the leader of the One State, reelected in the ritual of the One Vote. He performs all the general duties of leadership—the provision of state security, the supervision of manufacturing, the maintenance of order. But the Benefactor is more. He is the chief of the Guardians, those who ensure that citizens do not stray from the One State orthodoxy. He is a high priest who does not always punish, but usually leads transgressors back to the fold through repentance. Even when experiencing the capital punishment that turns the criminal back into his basic physical elements, prisoners do not struggle but accept the rightness of the act, taking it as a kind of atonement that will bring them a secular salvation. The religious-like rituals and images manufactured around the Benefactor soak up all the emotion that cannot yet be pushed aside by mathematical reasoning while serving to join together all the ciphers into an orthodox whole.

The Guardians, in turn, are the heirs to a jumble of different types of social stewards, including Plato's rulers and the Tsarist and Bolshevik secret police familiar to Zamyatin. They are Platonic Guardians in the sense that they are concerned not just with order grossly understood, but also with the very conception of the state. When people denounce others to the Guardians, they accuse those transgressors of treason. They betray people who are different, who are not, in Plato's sense, in tune with the One State ideology. People inform on others willingly and joyfully, for they do not see this as a betrayal of their fellows but as the provision of salvation, the putting of the misguided back on the road to health and righteousness. Zamyatin undoubtedly has in mind examples of revolutionary zeal and justice, as well as accounts of religious enthusiasm from the past. There is in the concept of the Guardians an element of the confessor figure and Dostoevsky's inquisitor. To confess one's sins or to help others to make good their transgressions is to unburden the soul and psyche of uncertainty and doubt. Koestler will pick this theme in his dissection of the Soviet purge trials and Orwell will recycle it in his portrayal of Airstrip One. Of course in the language of the One State, the soul is not involved here; rather, it is rational orthodoxy, or as D-503 puts it, it is a matter of making rational again an equation that has fallen into incoherence.

The most important theme, however, is that of civilization and its discontents. *We* is heavy with illustrations of Zamyatin's ultimate suggestion that civilization has been a colossal historical mistake. An important part of this larger story is the subsidiary argument, equally well illustrated, that civilization entails movement away from Nature as facilitated by the state. The thematic separation of humans from physical nature represents an important part of the state's social construction of citizens into a preferred mold. The state separates humans from the messiness of Nature and calls it a good thing. Generally denied contact with elemental forces, humans are susceptible to the state's totalizing imposition of mathematical logic as the stuff of artificial construction. Straight lines must be normative; mathematical consistency can alone be the measure of correctness if the randomness of interactions between the body and untamed natural environments are eliminated. Early in the story, D-503 goes into raptures over the disciplined "unfree" dance of motors and machinery. To be unfree and follow mathematical discipline is the height of human attainment in this conception, and to attain it one must be immersed in an artificial environment that the state creates and controls.

In making this argument, Zamyatin more generally connects the problem of attaining happiness with artificial constructions wrought by civilization, science, and the conquest of Nature. Those constructions are the consequence of the choice to reach for happiness. In Zamyatin's world, the One State represents the apex of human civilization, defined as the means for overcoming humans' natural condition by an artificial and hence more perfect (because more orderly and happier) existence. To be civilized means improving our situation, substituting for the filth, pain, hunger, and danger of our beginnings the security, comfort, and logical sophistication of a modern, man-made artificial environment that is made possible by the core civilizational tools of rationality and science. It also means moving away from our atavistic emotions, needs, and desires toward the clean, clear, ordered realm of scientific reasoning.

In drawing rationality and science as the core of civilization, Zamyatin departs from the usual social science conception that equates civilization with a broader understanding of culture as including art, literature, religion, and philosophy, as well as instrumental and scientific understandings. Zamyatin instead sees the moving force of civilization as human's continued intellectual mastery of their physical situation, and the motor of that understanding is rationality in the form of scientific reasoning. If humanity's ambition is happiness through physical security, it is rationality, science, and the scientific language of mathematics that provide that good, and everything else that distracts from those ways of understanding the self and the world must be eliminated or taken over. The physical presence of the city comprising the One State incorporates the triumph of man over Nature, just as the "city" has done throughout history. This city is separated from manifestations of physical Nature by a wall and citizens need not wrestle with the earth to find sustenance—they do not hunt, fish, or farm, but are fed, like machines, with petroleum-based food. Likewise, citizens are separated from atavistic human nature by the imposition of scientific rationality—they are not to grow angry, indulge in jealousy, or love one another, but exist, like machines, in an environment characterized by mathematical precision.

A final theme is the choice between happiness and freedom that Zamyatin argues is part of the human conundrum. Zamyatin has D-503's friend, R-13, compose a poem wherein he argues that the Eden story illustrates a basic choice between being happy and being free. Humans at first chose freedom, but thereafter yearned for happiness until they finally understood that happiness entails unfreedom. This position, of course, represents One State orthodoxy, but it also reflects the tragic dualism that Zamyatin sees in humans. It is entirely plausible in his understanding that people would be tempted to sacrifice freedom in order to escape the disorder, hunger, and violence that prevents them from being happy. He also implies that people might accept that freedom need not be an intrinsic part of happiness. If happiness and the good life are conceived in mostly material terms, then this makes sense. Recall that More did not incorporate much individual freedom in Utopia. Zamyatin extends this understanding to have the One State emphasize the peace and security that comes from a wholly civilized psyche at the cost of freedom. Zamyatin appears to fear that the same choice of happiness and security has already been made by humans in general through our embrace of civilization and the state, though the example of I-330 and others suggests that the choice is difficult and dissidents will choose nature and freedom instead. Ultimately, however, Zamyatin argues that we cannot have both. Being free means not only enjoying life but enduring contingency. Being happy entails the elimination of disorder and the possibilities of pain, suffering, and disappointment that inevitably accompany freedom. To live without an imagination, soul, or emotions is the price of being happy because only in that condition will the possibility of unpleasantness, brought about by the choice of the wrong thing and the consequent experience of ugliness, be banished. That one cannot experience happiness in a naturally human way in such circumstances is only one of the many ironies of aggressively pursuing happiness.

Alongside this dichotomy, Zamyatin constructs a corresponding opposition between reason and freedom. To be reasonable and rational is to be constrained within the iron bounds of logic. Reason demands conformity. To be free entails enduring randomness and disorder. The two, therefore, cannot coexist, nor is a coherent compromise between the two possible, thus D-503's rejection of jokes. In one reading, Zamyatin takes this opposition only to exist in terms of the ideology of the One State. That opposition certainly characterizes the beliefs of those who are most deeply trapped by that ideology, and it is those in the resistance who argue that some compromise between the reason and freedom may be possible. But I think that such an interpretation is mistaken, as it also appears that Zamyatin himself thinks that the roots of this opposition are embedded in the nature of the concepts themselves and wishes to paint the dissidents as at best mistaken romantics and at worst (as with I-330) just as manipulative and uncaring as the One State. While he clearly is satirizing the rational man and grossly exaggerating the effect of rational thinking on humans, it also appears that he believes the environment he describes is not just the creation of the One State; it is the product of rationality itself in the service of the quest for progress, happiness, and security. It is this combination that creates the power of the One State and the aesthetic of its mathematical precision.

It would not do, however, to overstate Zamyatin's opposition to rationality. He is not in favor of "unreason" and he does not romanticize the natural. Nor does he wholly condemn the rational in preference for alternatives. Rationality appears to be an important part of the human character. It is good, just as are emotions and Nature. The problem is that it is imperialistic. Insofar as we pursue rationality as a way of attaining what we want, namely happiness and safety, we give up freedom. This is the tragedy of the human condition: that in the course of building a community we must continually choose between rationality and freedom, between happiness and freedom, between civilization and expression, between security and a fully realized human life.

The dystopian life

Unlike *Looking Backward* and *News from Nowhere*, I argue that the targets of *We* are larger than industrialization and capitalism. Zamyatin takes aim at all aspects of modern civilized life, which rationality and technology symbolize as well as embody. In this understanding, Zamyatin is importantly concerned with the rise of the modern all-encompassing state as the agent of civilization.

Nothing is outside the purview of the One State in this story, making it more powerful than even More's government—this is partly the point. The state provides food, housing, and medical care. Everyone's movements are open to the state's scrutiny at almost all times. The state schedules sex, sleep, and recreation. The state attempts to rid people of such uncongenial emotions as jealousy. The state controls what people read and write. Citizens eat at the same time, sleep at the same time, and rise to a common alarm clock. The state even generates music electronically to keep it within the bounds of mathematical rationality.[9]

The state in this dystopia does not control mindlessly. What the state controls is what it thinks important to the maintenance of order and civilization. This is not new. What is striking is that the state considers so many things important. While the state does allow for a small slice of personal time, that personal time is marginal in the day is itself a powerful statement. How the state controls is also of interest because it does not proceed by manipulating and stratifying the population. Its methods are not so indirect and lacking in ambition. The state instead directly controls people by means of the Guardians (another allusion to Plato) and the imposition of mathematical reasoning. This control is mainly moral in character, though physical manifestations of power and the dread they cause are also in evidence. Obedience to rules and the state is engrained into the population. D-503 reacts to the presence of Guardians in the same way that truly devout people react to religious authorities—he is pleased by their presence because their loving surveillance will help him adhere to the state's rules and regulations. They are, in his words, akin to angels. The state has succeeded in training its citizens to love their chains as they previously loved their service to the gods.

Government in the One State is ostensibly formed and held accountable through elections. These, though, do not represent the exercise of choice; instead, through the mechanism of the One Vote, they manufacture and demonstrate solidarity. To vote in the same way for the same person who is already in power is to manifest one's connection with fellow citizens under the tutelage of the state. Dissent in the form of a "no vote" is dangerous. It threatens the oneness of the state and citizens, creating disharmony, disorder, and mental confusion. Zamyatin may be satirizing several targets here. First, this could be a criticism of what he perceives as a lack of true choice in the elections of capitalist states. One must keep Zamyatin's revolutionary background in mind and not reach for the conclusion that his intention is only to criticize the Soviet state. Yet, the Soviet system does seem to be an important target of Zamyatin's criticisms. It was in the

Soviet Union that the conception of a single leader in the context of "democratic centralism" was most prominent (the Italian fascists were only beginning to gain their reputation) and dissent was becoming increasingly dangerous. It was in the Soviet Union that the concept of solidarity was pushed the hardest and where the ritual of voting took on the religious overtones that Zamyatin invests in the One Vote.

The One State also controls sexuality and procreation. It controls who may actually reproduce, excluding from the process everyone who does not meet particular norms. D-503's regular partner, O-330, is forbidden permission to have children despite her desire to do so because she is slightly too short to meet the "maternal norm." Her decision to have a child in defiance of the state would have earned her a death sentence had she not escaped to the outside. The state likewise regulates the time and place of sexual encounters, and in the name of eliminating jealousy mandates that everyone has the right to engage sexually with anyone else. All this is strongly reminiscent of early Soviet policy and, presciently, of Communist Chinese regulations.

Zamyatin's obsession with this subject both underscores and goes beyond his arguments about the extent of the state's reach. He has D-503 join sexuality with hunger as basic urges the state seeks to control in the name of bringing happiness and fulfillment to humanity, though in actuality satisfaction of physical and psychological needs are the state's way of controlling citizens. The state took care of hunger by inventing oil-based foodstuffs, thus making possible unlimited supplies (and extending the metaphor of humans as machines). Its efforts to take care of sexuality have similar overtones. It cannot and does not want to eliminate the sexual drive. It wants to rationalize and satisfy it. Nor does it want deny the sexuality of its citizens and attempt to harness the resulting nervous energy, as Orwell has it in his dystopia. Rather, it seeks to reduce sex to a function. Satisfaction comes through sanctioning regular sexual activity and by promulgating the rule that everyone has the right to sexual intercourse with anyone else. Reduction of sex to a function comes by making it the object of the state's care and instruction. The state portrays sex as a necessary activity engaged in for purposes of health and procreation. It diminishes sex to a hygienic and necessary procedure that has nothing to do with exclusive or emotional attachments between partners or between parents and offspring. The state robs sexuality of its potentially destabilizing effects by co-opting it.

Simultaneous with the effects of the control of sex as a potential source of subversion is the larger debasement of humans. In the hands of the rationalist state, sexuality becomes another instrument for their mechanization. Here, Zamyatin takes aim at the ongoing political interest in eugenics. Some of this was crudely classist and racist, holding that "inferior" races and ethnic groups should be sterilized. Zamyatin satirizes this concept in D-503's account of the One State's ideological dismissal of the ordinary and natural reproduction of families. But Zamyatin also condemns eugenics for a larger reason. There were others (including Soviet officials), ostensibly more generous, who advocated eugenics as a way of cleaning the race of "mental defectives," the disabled, the weak, and the unhealthy. These advocates of racial hygiene are also Zamyatin's targets, as D-503s rendering of the "humane" side of the One State's ideology demonstrates. To scientize the human race in the name of eliminating alleged suffering is, for Zamyatin, to chop off important parts of what it is that makes us human. Part of our humanity, he would concede, is our ability to reason, to understand the world, and to make our lives and environment better. But other parts have to do with experiencing the world in all its texture and being whoever it is that we happen to be. Churning out humans according to a mold or norm reduces their variety and not coincidentally also reduces the possibility of exploring what it means to be human in ways that fall outside the state's comfort zone. The power to standardize humans both physically and socially is a product, Zamyatin wants to argue, of the state's participation in the larger process of scientific advancement and civilization. To regularize and restrict artificially what it means to be human physically is the culmination of civilization's goal of subjecting humans in general by constructing them.

To push the point, *We* importantly chronicles the problem represented by the transformation of humans into pliable minions of the state through a process of social construction that humans themselves have accepted in their quest for the good life. This is the upshot of many of the other problems outlined in the story—the loss of freedom, the control of sexuality, the scheduling of time, the end of privacy, and the eclipse of individualism. In the course of devising ways of ensuring security and happiness, members of the One State must give themselves up to outside control. Put in a larger, historical context, Zamyatin is arguing that to pursue science and civilization as integral to the good life is to end up with humans that are the creatures of the state, without wills or even thoughts of their own. Zamyatin has D-503 remark that life in the One State is not yet perfected because things still happen. In this statement, D reflects the prevailing orthodoxy of the state. Life in which nothing occurs, that is, in which everything is foreseen and all events and conditions have been planned and are under control, is the ideal. On one level, this security is understood conventionally. It means the absence of physical dangers that come from violence, disease, starvation, and war. Zamyatin portrays the One State as providing those material things that More, Bellamy, Morris, and most conventional political philosophers argue the best state furnishes everyone. But Zamyatin extends this understanding to a deeper level. To attain perfectly this security, he argues, the state must provide itself with its own brand of safety—the confidence that comes when officials know that citizens will not disturb the operations of the state. To create material security, the state must also create perfect conformity, perfect harmony, and perfect predictability among its denizens. It socially constructs humans to obtain these goals in the name of the good life by instilling in citizens an exaggerated respect for rules and uniformity expressed as intolerance for randomness. D-503 is an example of such construction when he considers an unplanned event in his own life a problem rather than an opportunity. It upsets his equilibrium, making him feel insecure. He conceives of it as the implanting of an irrational number in his brain and as such a threat to a civilized and scientific good life.

With no names, only indicators and conceptualized as ciphers, the citizens of the One State have difficulty thinking of themselves as unique, individuated beings. They exist only as parts of the state, as units of a cell. D-503 cannot conceive of the adventure he lives as anything other than a collective experience. This is not the record of D-503, but of We. The reduction of individuals to parts of a mass being is crucial here to the reduction of humans to beings to be dominated. The central method Zamyatin identifies in that domination process, as well as the symbol of the method as a whole, is the imposition of mathematical logic as the compulsory way of conceiving of the world. In criticizing this situation, Zamyatin is highlighting the importance of alternatives to rationality and civilization in the form of senses, sensibilities, emotions, and imagination to the self-construction of unique beings. To remove uniqueness and autonomy from that process of constructing the self, the state or any other powerful entity must remove the various alternative paths one can take to conceptualize the self and its experience in the world. Mathematical reason is particularly well-suited to this task in its abstractness, its insistence on precision, and its association with the advance of civilization. As the ultimate expression of scientific materialism, rationality is the tool Zamyatin feared the Soviet state would use to reduce humans to good socialist units.

Zamyatin rubs in this point throughout the book by illustrating the substitution of mathematics for ordinary discourse. As the diary of D-503, the book is a reflection of a citizen's thought processes. In recording of his thoughts, experiences, and conversations with others, D-503's reveals how in the daily course of life the use of ordinary words, grammar, and narrative structures is often pushed aside or invaded by the use of mathematical symbols. O-90 is not chubby—she is a circle, to be described in terms of the roundness and arcs. I-330 in her apparent difference with O must be an X—not circular but angular, and her capacity to discomfort D must be the same as the mental distress caused by "a displaced irrational number" or an undefined variable. As with Orwell after him, Zamyatin uses this play of different symbolic systems to illuminate the importance of language to the individual's processing of experience, development of values, and autonomy. Because the language D-503 uses is the mathematical language of the state, he is almost always led back to the conclusions the state wishes him to draw. It is not so much brute force that makes the One State so powerful; it is this ability to destroy alternatives to conceptualizing the self that empowers it.

The removal of names in tandem with social construction through mathematical reason is one practical technology the state uses to destroy individualism. The inescapably public lives of its citizens are another. Collective life and the loss of privacy go together in this understanding. Glass walls, uniforms, permits to have sex, communal recreation to tune of the "March of the One State," the synchronized mastication of food in communal kitchens all (satirically) contribute to the understanding that citizens live their lives as part of a larger and more important being. Individual activities are exceptional. If the community is to be all powerful and citizens only parts of it, then there should be nothing kept separate from the collective. The exceptions are holdovers from the past. More accepts this point while Morris and Bellamy refuse to concede it. Zamyatin condemns it. All this, of course, is exaggeration, yet as with all dystopian fare, it has its origins in practices in place (or being seriously discussed) in the Soviet Union at the time. Its communal kitchens, collective farms, voluntary Saturdays, and a whole host of other institutions and activities drove home the point that a Soviet citizen had her existence as a member of the community and that expectations of privacy and private time should be minimal.

One could argue, and this also seems to be part of Zamyatin's purpose, that the constant attention to the doings of citizens betrays unease on the part of the One State. It cannot be comfortable that people are really in tune with its ideology. Why require listening devices on the street to record conversations? Why require glass walls? Is it that the state must be suspicious given the separate physical bodies humans occupy? Is it because it suspects there is a hardwired human desire to act autonomously within that body? Or is it jealous of any energy its members bestow on things other than the state itself? Here and elsewhere, Zamyatin argues that while the logic of the state moves in one direction, it appears that something in humans instinctively resists that course.

Human nature and applications

Human nature

As we can see from the discussion above, Zamyatin, unlike Bellamy, Morris, and More, sees important contradictions in human nature. We have been put together with a collection of incompatible pieces, in that we desire many different things, the pursuit of any one of which leads to conflicts with others. Zamyatin in part embraces this contradiction because it reflects the raw materials of humans. But he is also concerned that the flow of history has pushed us down a particularly difficult path, one that leads us, in his mind, to turn on ourselves. While Zamyatin argues that there are a bundle of characteristics that make people fully human (the capacity to reason, to experience emotions, to take responsibility for actions, to act freely), he also holds that society can suppress certain key characteristics such that, while outwardly human, people no longer qualify as wholly human. Thus, he has people in the One State sacrifice their freedoms, sublimate many emotions (including jealousy), and delegate moral responsibility outside themselves even while he seems to say that these are inherent characteristics of humans.

Zamyatin appears to argue that many human characteristics are hardwired and therefore must be ripped out if the state is completely to control them, but also that many are programmed and must be reprogrammed if the state is to have its way. It is clear that he, at least satirically, depicts imagination as hardwired, for the One State initiates operations to remove physically the parts of the brain that contain that capacity. We will also see later that he believes the desire for happiness, security, and freedom are hardwired. But his extensive arguments about ideology, the role of the Guardians, the rituals in the Cube Plaza, and the success of the Table of Hours suggests that much of human behavior can be controlled by different kinds of programming, and even if humans are hardwired, their responses can be twisted, turned around, or shut off by social processes.

Where Zamyatin differs from all those who argue that hardwired behavior can be changed through environment or that human software can be reprogrammed is in his opposition to the entire project. He is not concerned with the wrong programming or the correction of environments; he thinks that changes to human nature are intrinsically harmful. To be human must mean to be fully human, with all the problems and faults and contradictions that come from being a member of that species. If some parts of our human nature sometimes express themselves in the commission of crimes, the creation of insecurity, and the infliction of pain, then we must deal with these as they manifest themselves, not by seeking to avoid them by identifying and excising undesirable parts of our nature. People come with hardwiring and are programmed by their surroundings; he seems to argue that it is best to leave these as we find them. To attempt intentionally to construct humans directly or indirectly leads to dehumanization.

As noted above, Zamyatin also appears to argue that humans are contradictorily hardwired. One hardwired characteristic is their desire for happiness and security. In the beginning, security came through the gradual conquest of external, physical Nature. With the peak of human civilization, this quest extends to the conquest of internal human Nature through the elimination of all elements in the human character that create risks, pose dangers, or create uncertainty. Thus, he depicts the flow of civilization as the attempt to find material and physical security that is motivated by a fundamental human desire. People want to be fed and to feel safe. The development of laws, religion, rituals, and ceremonies are part of this process, as is the development of economic systems, technology, and industrialization.

But Zamyatin also portrays people as inevitably craving freedom and an accompanying individualism. I-303 is the most egregious example of this, but other characters betray the same tendencies. O wants the freedom to have a baby. R wishes to write his own poetry. Even S (an undercover Guardian) appears to have some agenda that is supportive of freedom and the realm outside the wall, while the One State's scheme to remove imaginations is met with general panic and resistance among the state's citizens.

The problem is that these are incompatible impulses. Humans' hardwiring is inconsistent and incoherent. To act on one part of our hardwiring means to neglect the other part which, in turn, continues to nag at us. To chase single-mindedly after happiness and security means abandoning an essential part of what makes us human—the freedom to explore our emotions, sensuality, and sense of individual self. To pursue freedom in turn means putting in doubt many things we crave in a good life: security, comfort, health, consumption, solidarity and intellectual achievement, and the happiness that accompanies these. We are left in the extreme with either a civilized but sterile existence, or a free, but primitive life. Zamyatin appears to opt for freedom as preferable, asserting that a free and primitive human is more authentic than a completely civilized and secure entity, perhaps because a free individual can still pursue security and respect rationality while a secure, thoroughly rationalized human must abandon liberty and individuality.

Finally, Zamyatin assumes that humans are fundamentally characterized by their capacity and need to understand the world and the information that comes their way. D-503's journal is a description of how he processes his life. What interests Zamyatin most is how information is processed and who controls the processing. He wants to argue that humans process in a variety of ways—through reason, through emotion, through the senses, through memory, and through imagination. The One State seeks to strip its citizens of the capacity to engage in any but the approved method. For an outside agent to insist that processing equals and can only equal mathematical reasoning is to control what constitutes citizens and thereby to construct them.

Applications

It is in the One State's alleged transformation of citizens into nonhumans that we find the elements that have come to define modern dystopias. An all-powerful state, the loss of privacy and individualism, the control of time, the overwhelming figure of the leader have become clichés, but Zamyatin was plowing new ground in the early twentieth century. It is particularly surprising to find him at the helm of this plow given his radical background, for his dystopia is in many ways a liberal's and humanist's nightmare. To be turned into a machine is the dread of those who reject the concept of intense social solidarity. Zamyatin does not want to be absorbed into a larger entity and serve as cog in a bigger machine. He does not want his freedom to be curtailed down to a few minutes of personal time and be at the service of the state the rest of the day.

In the course of describing this dystopia, Zamyatin criticizes the promises of modern ideologies and modern civilization itself. Civilization left to its own devices cannot provide us the good life. It cannot put together the disparate pieces that make up human nature or give us happiness and freedom. It cannot create a technologically sophisticated life based on science and rationality that also makes room for emotions and autonomy. Accepting Zamyatin's views means abandoning faith in civilization and modernity. It is to think radically about how we organize our lives. It would mean going back to some point in our social evolution before we developed sophisticated institutions and cultures and rethink the terms of our coexistence together as humans. Maybe this would result in a rejection of society itself and entail living as isolated beings. Perhaps it would mean rejection of the state as something that promises more than it can deliver. Perhaps it would entail a rethinking of civilization as something that attempts to develop all aspects of atavistic humanity rather than, in Zamyatin's understanding, subordinating one part of human nature to another.

In painting civilization as dehumanizing, Zamyatin creates questions that are currently topical. What do we give up in pursuing a comfortable life? What is the price to be paid to attain an environment in which we do not have to deal with the dirtiness of Nature? At what cost do we purchase industrialization, air conditioning, cars, the internet, and high-rise condos? What do we pay for genetic therapy? What is the charge for civilization itself? Zamyatin suggests that the price is too high because it is our very humanity, and we do not even know that we are paying it. That is not to say that Zamyatin is in favor of inflicting pain and suffering on humans in order to increase the intensity and worth of their experiences, or as Neville would suggest to provide the necessary challenges that enable humans to fulfill their potential. Nor is he saying that the goal of reducing pain and suffering is wrong or harmful in itself. Instead, he argues that progress conceived as happiness and security requires us to give up freedom (for freedom entails risks and discomfort), autonomy (for autonomy implies the possibility of making the wrong decision), and possibly emotion (for emotion leads us into ways of perceiving that are at odds with rational certainty).

Initially it appears that in making this point, Zamyatin provides us with a rather banal argument that has already been digested. Such observations are at the heart of every contract theory explanation for the rise of the state—people experience so many inconveniences without a state that they sacrifice some of their freedoms in exchange for the security that a state's coercive capacities can bring. It can also be put in terms of scientific progress. Humans lose their illusions regarding themselves and the universe as they become more scientifically aware. One cannot be totally free and autonomous and be secure, and one cannot have knowledge and retain romantic fantasies. The conventional lesson drawn is that we recognize and accept the disparate natures of security and freedom but have found various ways in which we are able to enjoy both. The same is true of the conflict between civilized existence and romantic freedom, and enlightened understanding and playfulness.

But Zamyatin pushes this position further than does either contract theory or a theory of scientific disillusionment. His story asserts that humans can only be secure and comfortable if they allow themselves to be reduced to machines, losing their individuality and neglecting their nonrational capacities by becoming part of an all-encompassing state. Security and freedom cannot coexist, and thus the artificial existence that is civilization is dehumanizing.

Zamyatin pursues this argument in two ways. First, his position is that those who control the state at any particular time can use the innate desire for physical and material security as a way of controlling people. People want guaranteed social order as well as housing, food, medical care, etc., and in providing those goods, the state can gain the means by which to remove people's autonomy. If it is the state that provides these basic goods, then (1) citizens need not exercise their own will, ingenuity, and energy to obtain them, thus removing opportunities for people to claim and exercise their own powers (a point that is reminiscent of Neville's), and (2) the state also is provided reasons, made good by its monopoly of power, to remove from citizens their control over those powers. Events in which citizens exercise their powers autonomously are only episodes in which those individuals interfere with the working of the state and deprive the collective of its ability to provide physical and material security. Do we accept this argument? Has the state become such a focus of various types of security that individual efforts are seen as unhelpful or harmful? Is it a problem that some people view the state as an engine for attaining security and therefore are suspicious of most of its activities? Or to look at it from another viewpoint, are officials actually providing security (by means of state pensions, welfare payments, health care) as a way of gaining power? Even if we were not to accept that argument, would we accept the proposition that the provision of security provides both an unanswerable justification of and irresistible opportunity for a dangerous expansion of state power? If we accept either argument, what should we do? Again, note that even the provision of police and military protection responds to our desire for physical security and entails trade-offs of autonomy and the empowerment of officials. As Locke would put it, we no longer decide as individuals the meaning of right and wrong because we participate in a political organization that requires obedience to known and written laws. Though modern conservatives would agree with Zamyatin's larger point, they would also argue that there is a primary distinction to be made between the provision of physical security and the provision of material security. The first is minimal enough to preserve individual autonomy; the other is a threat to freedoms. Is that the case, or are both equally threatening and conservatives (and perhaps everyone except anarchists) insufficiently aware of the empowerment of the state that flows from intense concerns over crime and terrorism?

On another level, Zamyatin appears to argue that the pursuit of happiness and security has a larger logic of its own that operates on the grand scale, pushing humans to create increasingly elaborate and sophisticated states and civilizations that, in providing us with more social structures, political institutions, technology and culture, inevitably squeeze our autonomy and identity. Even if he is satirizing and exaggerating in fleshing out the consequences of such a process, at bottom there is a serious argument. Zamyatin does not see the state resting with only partial control over citizens and civilization as merely informing people's lives. If the desire for happiness and security creates the state and enveloping civilization, he argues, why would this dynamic end with a minimal or even a conventionally powerful state? Why would it not continue to push us into the arms of the ultimate state and a civilization that resembles that which informs the One State? If progress entails the loss of our illusions, will not science and civilization eventually sweep away all competing ways of conceptualizing life, leaving us with one understanding alone, such as mathematical logic? If the two—the state and civilization—combine, will they not reduce us to their construct rather than allow us to remain their producers? Zamyatin fears that this is the case. Is this a relevant fear? Has the sweep of progress through the ages with humans emerging from a scattered and primitive existence to a life that we recognize as civilized and advanced really been an exercise in a loss of pluralism and autonomy and a gradual dehumanization? Once we gathered ourselves into groups with institutions, did we place ourselves on an unstoppable conveyer belt that will inevitably lead us to a mechanical existence? Is ultimately our only choice that between an inhuman life as a living machine and truly human life in a primitive, uncomfortable and insecure state of nature? Or does Zamyatin tumble into a romantic way of thinking (reminiscent of Rousseau) that fetishizes a natural existence that has never and never will be satisfactory?

While he importantly differs from Neville and Orwell, Zamyatin has in common with them a strict and ascetic moralism that we should take into account. This stance on his part appears ironic, in the sense that he appears to advocate large realms of individual freedom. Yet, it is this desire to see humans free to make choices and inhabit environments uncontrolled by others that lies at the root of his moral stance. Even if human autonomy brings pain, confusion, and even death, it is better in his eyes to suffer these while taking responsibility for one's actions than to enjoy the regimented and pain-free existence that science and civilization seek ultimately to bring. The development of the state and civilization, he argues, as the embodiment of the project of eliminating pain and discomfort, is ultimately the attempt to avoid paying the price of being human. He sees their pursuit as irresponsible and cowardly as well as profoundly ironic, for in attempting to evade our existential bill, we end up losing ourselves. Where there is no pain and no discomfort, there are no humans because no room for individual responsibility.

This is a disconcerting argument to confront. It appears to turn upside down everything we take for granted as good. Who is not in favor of civilization, and who but the most hardcore anarchists and eccentrics would say that the state and science, for all their faults, are in their essence harmful? If we take Zamyatin seriously, we see that he anticipates some of the postmodernists by not only questioning whether we are mistaken about the overreach of officials and the state and must reform our political lives to shrink the state, but whether we are also mistaken about the things associated with civilization and political life that we value, and must face the prospect that the future holds nothing of intrinsic worth if we continue to participate in civilization's march of progress. Caught in the flow of history that is driven by our hardwired instincts, we may continually be caught in a basic battle of happiness and security with freedom, and because the instinct for the former empowers institutions that can construct us, our ability to control our lives will progressively shrink. Do we see this now? Do the instruments of civilization and culture drive us to take up one understanding of life and the world rather than many? As More might put it, are we being molded to equate a good life with material possessions, to see the conquest of physical Nature as always good, to believe that the products of technology are superior to those things physical Nature provides us? Are we in fact being molded and programmed, and should we object to the entire project of molding and programming that Zamyatin attributes to civilization and the state even if we disagree with him regarding how that project is being carried out?

In thinking about these questions, we must confront and evaluate the story that Zamyatin provides us. Gauging its plausibility is difficult given both his satirical exaggerations and the intentionally fantastic platform of science fiction he employs. Yet we can still pose relevant questions. Does the elevation of scientific thinking and pragmatic rationality limit our understandings? Is there deep-seated friction between logic and imagination? Can we envision a state that is so committed to rationality that it would attempt to impose such a fierce conformity on us that we would begin to think of ourselves as machines? Is our time being increasingly controlled by the state, corporations, and technology?

While to some degree these concerns are importantly raised and explored by postmodernists as well as the heirs of modern liberalism (particularly libertarians), one can also find counterarguments to them. It is not the case that our experiences with those who are most dedicated to the application of rationality and science to the world show that they are devoid of other human characteristics. Newton had a wide variety of intellectual and aesthetic interests. Einstein was far from Mr Spock. And to a great degree it is the demands of individuals, often working through markets, that has created time-management devices, pushed forward science and technology, and created norms and rules that increasingly govern our behavior. Might all this be part of a way of constructing ourselves that is both legitimate and coherent?

One could further argue that even if Zamyatin is right, an effective way of combating the hostility to pluralism he detects in rationality is to emphasize that rationality itself must be dependent upon emotion and imagination for its utility. Would not a completely rational understanding of humans and their motivations be forced to be pluralistic, entailing an acknowledgment of the ineradicable and necessary place of emotions, the imagination and different ways of conceiving of the world to any rational strategy for understanding the human condition? Without imagination and some tolerance for pluralism, science would at the least have a narrowly configured research agenda. Pushing the boundaries of our understanding of the world entails thinking beyond the limits of our present understanding, that is, to fantasize about what lies beyond the horizon. One could argue that a society based strictly upon science, technology, and rationality could not, for internal reasons, get rid of imagination. Conversely, one could make the argument that those states or organizations that have come closest to reducing their members to ciphers and machines (such as North Korea, the People's Temple, even the Soviet Union itself) have not been founded upon science and rationality, but upon romantic fantasies. Indeed, one might argue that many of the political problems we now face, including fiscal problems, stem from the injection of emotion and fantastic stories into politics along with a rejection of rationality rather than an overabundance of rational analysis.

Yet, it does pay to think closely about the dangers of the quest for happiness and security and their association with science and rationality that Zamyatin warns us against. It is those goods that aspiring all-powerful leaders usually promise to deliver. Are we innately prone to follow such leaders despite the other sacrifices they extort from us? Is the specter of the Benefactor always before us, beckoning us to live a life of ordered prosperity, or have we learned in the process of our becoming civilized to recognize and avoid such characters? There are also dangers in buying into systems of thought that promise us those ultimate benefits. It is good to remind ourselves that if we accept a system with a particular set of assumptions, ways of conceiving the world, rules of argument and particular definitions and assumptions, we trap ourselves. Systems of thought, be they mathematical logic, political ideologies, or religious dogmas, are self-perpetuating, totalizing, and quintessentially sticky. Once we accept them, there is no outside place to stand to evaluate the ways they lead us to process information or arrive at conclusions. They are, to put it in modern parlance, echo boxes. Everyone parrots the same line, thinks the same thoughts, makes the same criticisms of rival systems, and delivers the same judgments. As with D-503, their adherents cannot but conform. Yet, similar to the lure of leaders, such systems summon us to embrace them. Must each generation learn anew the consequences of accepting the intellectual comforts such leaders can bring? Is it possible that the only choices we have are those among various greedy leaders and totalizing ideologies?

Other questions are equally important to thinking through Zamyatin's story. Can the quest for happiness, security, and order be so overpowering that humans are willing to sacrifice significant physical and intellectual freedoms in its pursuit? Would people be willing to conceive of the good life in ways that exclude freedom? Is the One State plausible in this sense? Here, Zamyatin appears to be on firmer ground. In some ways, we can view the One State as a technologically advanced and greatly less accountable form of the government More proposed in *Utopia*. Insofar as the latter appeals to us (and it does have its appeal), we are vulnerable to the slippery slope that Zamyatin identifies. Paternalism can be just around the corner. The trick is to recognize it and not confuse it with effective government.

At bottom, Zamyatin encourages to ask the fundamental and increasingly important question: is civilization and technological progress goods we wish to retain and continue developing? We take a "yes" for granted, but he, at the least, would like us to rehearse and think about the reasons why. If we enjoy the ease and sophistication of civilization, is that a sufficient reason given the effort civilization requires? If civilization of the kind we have developed is not available to all because of its expense, and if even the provision of it to those who now enjoy it threatens eventually to bankrupt the planet of its natural resources, can we morally sustain it?

We should also confront the other fundamental question Zamyatin poses because it likely yields a somewhat different answer. Given the dilemma he presents to us, would we choose to live in the One State or outside it? Zamyatin implies that we have already, both as a species and as individuals, made the choice. People in the West and increasingly elsewhere in the world live mostly in urban areas, cosseted by air conditioning and assisted by machines, informed by modern technology and medicine, living lives that are confined and molded by the strictures of civilization. Very few of us are willing to pay the price of living primitively, and we automatically conform to the norms the state and civilization impose on us. Yet, almost everyone whom I have asked this question instantly and forcefully argues that they would live outside the One State. They insist that they prefer freedom over security and comfort. Why is that? Is it that we do not recognize what Zamyatin sees, that we have already given up significant parts of ourselves in the quest for those goods? Or has Zamyatin missed something fundamental that allows us to dissolve the tragic choice he presents us, allowing us to choose happiness, security, and freedom?

Notes

1   H. Chang, "Zamyatin's *We*: A Reassessment," *Philosophy, Literature and History* (May 2003).

2   Michael D. Amey, "Living under the Bell Jar: Surveillance and Resistance in Yevgeny Zamyatin's *We*," *Critical Survey*, Vol. 17, no. 1 (2005).

3   Faith Aginsk, "Zamyatin's Novel *We*, in the Context of Works and Ideas of the Proletkult," *Canadian-American Slavic Studies*, Vol. 45, nos 3–4 (2011). Hutching makes a similar argument while providing an informative background on Zamyatin's aesthetic views and his complicated relationship with the artistic avant-garde. In Hutching's understanding, Zamyatin was uncompromising in his dedication to the avant-garde in art, but objected to the tendency of cutting-edge Soviet artists to glorify machinery and the instruments of production and to lapse into solipsism rather than remaining grounded in social reality. See William Hutchings, "Structure and Design in a Soviet Dystopia: H. G. Wells, Constructivism, and Yevgeny Zamyatin's *We*," *Journal of Modern Literature*, Vol. 9, no. 1 (1981).

4 N. Randall, "Introduction," *We* (New York: The Modern Library Classics, 2006).

5 George Slusser, "Descartes Meets Edgar Rice Burroughs: Beating the Rationalist Equations in Zamiatin's *We*," *Canadian-American Slavic Studies*, Vol. 45, nos 3–4 (2011).

6 Sara Stefani, "The Unified State and the Unified Mind: Social and Moral Utopia in Zamiatin's *We* and Plato's *Republic*," *Canadian-American Slavic Studies*, Vol. 45, nos 3–4 (2011).

7 For the story's publication history, see Yukio Nakano, "On the History of the Novel *We*, 1937–1952: Zamiatin's *We* and the Chekhov Publishing House," *Canadian-American Slavic Studies* Vol. 45, nos 3–4 (2011).

8 A comparison with *Erewhon* is of interest here. Butler makes the belief in the animation of technology a point of fun and satire. To fear technology is to indulge in irrational apprehensions that lead us to turn our lives upside down for no good reason. For Zamyatin, the fear of becoming a piece of machinery is both a manifestation of our hardwired desire for freedom and a defensibly human concern for threats to our essential character. It is not fear that we should fear, but technology and rationality itself.

9 This is perhaps an allusion to both Plato and the emerging, state-controlled socialist aestheticism in the Soviet Union.

7

Nineteen Eighty-Four

Introduction

George Orwell's dystopian work is partly the product of his own reading in the genre. He had carefully read London's *The Iron Heel*, Huxley's *Brave New World*, and Koestler's *Darkness at Noon*, as well as *We* before embarking on his own effort. Orwell is sympathetic to important parts of Zamyatin's message and shares many of the same concerns, namely the control of the processing of information, the loss of privacy, and separation from Nature. But *Nineteen Eighty-Four* (1949) is not a twin to *We*. Not only are Orwell's experiences and politics different, but his purposes in writing his dystopia are also at variance with Zamyatin's. *We* is a vision of people becoming machines through the forces of civilization and rationality; *Nineteen Eighty-Four* is a morality tale about the consequences of fanaticism and the loss of rationality.

While this observation points to important differences in the way the two evaluate the role of rationality, at bottom is also a difference of scope. Zamyatin's is the more sweeping vision. In attacking progress and civilization, he puts into question large human goals. Is civilization worth it? What price do we pay for inhabiting the City? Orwell, in contrast, is more concerned with power and the loss of the self in a larger cause. His is the more technical work, filled with observations of how people become blinded to the faults of the leaders and systems they follow, and how leaders manipulate intellectual and emotional environments and engage in programming to gain complete control over citizens. He is closer to classical liberals than is Zamyatin. Moreover, while Zamyatin is more pessimistic about the possibility of progress and creates a more deeply dystopian society, Orwell depicts a more realistic scenario. This is not just because Zamyatin's picture is fantastic in its foundation in science fiction, but also because Orwell is able to grapple more directly with the psychology that leads to dystopia. We never really know how the One State arose out the Two Hundred Years War other than the observation that it is the ultimate expression of civilization. But we know why people revere and support Big Brother. Not only are they afraid; not only are they psychologically and emotionally manipulated; they also and primarily *want* to believe in him because they crave certainty. That is why he is Big Brother, not The Benefactor.

The story and interpretations

Story

The protagonist of *Nineteen Eight-Four*, Winston Smith, lives in London in a renamed England known as Airstrip One, itself part of the larger entity of Oceania. He works in the Ministry of Truth readjusting records to accord with the state's ever-changing presentation of reality. His flat is dingy, his marriage over, his health indifferent. Like D-503, Winston keeps a diary in which he records his experiences, illicit in part because it gives him an independent account of time as it passes. It is also illicit because he fills it with his hopes, memories, fantasies, and misgivings regarding the state, the Party, and Big Brother. As private musings, these are forbidden. To live publicly is the credo of Airstrip One. Love of Big Brother is as well, so the hatred he professes for the leader is the source of extreme danger.

Technology is much less well developed here than in the One State. A modified form of a television does beam the state's propaganda into people's homes and provides the state access to their personal space. The same technology is placed in offices and outside areas as well. But for the rest, Airstrip One is a tired, threadbare, flyblown place stuck in the 1930s. It is drab, dirty, colorless, and hungry. It is far from the One State's sleek and shiny technotopia. While the instruments of the state continually argue that things are getting better and better, materially and physically things are getting worse and worse.

The story itself chronicles Winston's slide from a covertly unhappy denizen of Airstrip One to an enemy of the state, then his forcible conversion back to good citizenship. The narrative reveals all the dinginess, pettiness, general boredom, and moments of terror an ordinary person experiences in a totalitarian society.

We learn how experienced citizens control their facial expressions, shop on the black market for scarce items, avoid intimacy with their neighbors, and even come to fear their own children. We also learn of the elites' manipulation of information, their demands for complete loyalty, and their division of society into classes despite their egalitarian rhetoric.

Within the claustrophobic atmosphere of Airstrip One, Winston finds solace in a relationship with a girl whom he initially suspects is a member of the Thought Police. With her, he finds a semblance of an individual life without the Party or the state. They discover the joys of the countryside and find themselves entwined with what they think is a resistance movement. They come into contact with someone whom they believe is a leader of this movement and receive from him the "Book," which systematically describes the origins and foundations of the Party and Big Brother. But Winston's foray into unorthodox activities is not sufficient to explain this entry into the "resistance." While he believes in the existence of the resistance, he does not actively seek to become a resister; left to himself, he merely toys with the idea as a fantasy. In fact, he is lured into joining the group, which itself is a provocation meant to suck in and neutralize all those who have independent thoughts and aspirations.

As such, Winston is not a revolutionary in the ordinary sense of the word, though he is, as with all humans, prey to some forms of fanaticism. Left on his own, he is not a threat violently to overthrow the established order. But the state, nonetheless, considers him dangerous. It cannot abide him because he harbors an inner skepticism and a secret desire to live as an individual. To not be with the state is to be against it. He is not a pro-state fanatic and must be retrained. The story ends with Winston marginalized. He has yielded to the demand to follow orthodoxy and succumbed to the temptation to give his total being to the state and to Big Brother. In professing his love for Big Brother, he completes his final conversion. He becomes what the powers that be want of him, a besotted follower of the orthodox line.

Interpretations

In common with *Utopia*, *Nineteen Eighty-Four* has been the subject of such a vast quantity of scholarship that any attempt to summarize or survey all possible interpretations far exceeds the limits of this study. I therefore confine myself to reflections on a few interesting constructions.

Of recent attempts to think about and apply the concepts Orwell provides, *On Nineteen Eighty-Four: Orwell and Our Future* is perhaps the most comprehensive.[1] An older but still useful contribution is Elshtain's survey of some of the ways we can use Orwell's treatment of politics to think about the problems of power and manipulation, particularly those associated with the patriotic lure of war.[2] In contrast, Gleason, in a piece also written in the mid-1980s, treats *Nineteen Eighty-Four* as part of the literature on totalitarianism and so provides an interesting argument questioning its broader applicability, suggesting that what Orwell described were political phenomena confined to the 1920s, 1930s, and 1940s, and thus his work is at best of limited usefulness in reflecting on current problems.[3]

Most of the literature on this story focuses on particular aspects of the work. Roback provides a good overview of Orwell's economic views, helpfully emphasizing his criticisms of both capitalism and socialism.[4] Gottlieb provides interesting insights into the story by stressing both the exaggerations and religious symbolism it contains. Viewing it as in the tradition of English satirists, she sees it as "a parody of mysticism, highlighting the perverse nature of religious rituals and modes of seeking for religious and mystical truth," an interpretation that accords closely with parts of the interpretation used here.[5]

Somewhat different are Kateb's views. Kateb is one of several critics who see the story as importantly a reflection of Orwell's deeply held personal beliefs and psychological state of mind rather than a literary work or the product of a critical distance from political events. In his interpretation, the story is colored by Orwell's increasing disillusionment and deepening skepticism that also distorted his idealist commitment to democratic socialism, a combination that made him a less than trustworthy analyst of politics.[6] Shklar shares some of Kateb's doubts, though she rejects the attempt to link the work to Orwell's psychology or physical state of being. While she argues that it is an interesting attempt to grapple with key political problems in a theoretical fashion, she ultimately is unconvinced of the story's utility for those who study politics systematically due to what she perceives as its lack of originality and depth.[7]

Contexts and problems

Orwell is writing at the end of a short, though active, life filled with many political twists and turns. His early experiences in Burma and with the underclasses in

London and Paris have given him a healthy distaste for imperialism and unbridled capitalism. His association with socialist movements and participation in the Spanish Civil War likewise has made him suspicious of the Soviet Union and contemptuous of avant-garde radicals. He is committed to socialist reform in Britain, but pursues that goal inconoclastically. His disillusionment with both ordinary and radical politics was reinforced by his most recent experiences. By 1947, his earlier hopes that the Depression and World War II would lead to fundamental changes in British society were dashed. While some of his desired economic reforms, such as the nationalization of natural resources and important transportation systems, were initiated during or after the war, not only were most of the structural changes he championed not forthcoming, but the increasing power of the government did little, in his mind, to overcome the class differences that marred English society. Wartime comradery did not translate into permanent or deep manifestations of equality; they merely strengthened the class system, and those who already had power and social status in prewar society continued to occupy their same positions in the postwar world.

Thus, his dystopian society is not the Soviet Union transported to another place, as so many readers tend to believe. Scholars have convincingly demonstrated how closely Orwell bases many aspects of Airstrip One on wartime England.[8] Big Brother is just as much Churchill as he is Stalin. Minitruth is the Ministry of Information, where Orwell worked for a period during the war. The rationing of food, the bleak housing conditions, and the endless propaganda are part of what Orwell experienced during the war and its aftermath. *Nineteen Eighty-Four* really does follow in the pattern of dystopian stories by projecting forward troubling trends rather than acting as a criticism of a society that already exists elsewhere. That is not to say that Orwell only draws on his wartime and domestic experiences. There is also a good mixture of other materials, ranging from those derived from his adventures in Spain to his observations of Germany and the Soviet Union. But this, again, moves us away from viewing the story as only a criticism of the Soviets and Stalin. Unlike *Animal Farm*, which is transparently a satire of the Russian revolution and its aftermath, *Nineteen Eighty-Four* is about human problems generally and British problems in particular, not just about the troubling experiences of Russia.

The fundamental problem with which Orwell concerns himself here is the fanaticism created by the quest for certainty. This concern shows up early in his writings in the form of a rather nasty anti-Catholicism. Orwell's critique of Catholics is based on his argument that they give away their intellectual freedom in exchange for the infallible truth that the Pope and church provide. Catholic believers, he holds, so greatly desire certainty and so greatly fear the disquietude that comes from even the mildest skepticism that they allow others to control their understanding of the world and their sense of morality. There are many problems with this, he argues. First, this attitude removes from believers any sense of moral autonomy or responsibility. Second, it turns believers into uncritical followers who blithely do the bidding of their masters. Third, it releases leaders from any sense of accountability, providing them license to inflict harm on anyone who may stand in the way of their schemes.

While Orwell never substantially softened his view on Catholics, he did move away from his earlier notions that they were somehow unique in their behavior. He instead began to extend this criticism to other organizations, gradually changing his formulation of the problem. In this later understanding, the desire for certainty is not manifested only in the yearning to join a hierarchical religion, but in the development of a general fanaticism in pursuit of goals, whether it be in the context of religion, socialism, vegetarianism, or patriotism. This position leads him to a general condemnation of a whole variety of orthodoxies. But the association of both fanaticism and orthodoxy with religion persists in this story, as illustrated by the religious connotations of various displays of devotion to Big Brother.

Another central problem Orwell attacks is hierarchy and the persistence of class. Orwell is careful to argue that his dystopia is one in which economic, political, and social inequality is in play. Where Zamyatin's city levels the population in terms of living standards, Airstrip One contains significant differences of lifestyle, material wealth, and power. The entire experience of living there is dominated by brushes with hierarchy and competition. One lives at the expense of others, gathering power and wealth to the self even to the point of killing fellow citizens. Hierarchy and class mark tyranny; large inequalities of wealth and power are both the result of tyrannical action and tools by which tyrannies attain and retain control. This is surely a criticism of both the West and East at the time. Orwell was never reconciled to the basic inequalities and destructive competition that capitalism generates. The words he puts in the mouth of Symes, that the proles are not human, comes from his experience with colonialism in Burma. He was equally dismayed, as *Animal Farm* clearly illustrates, by the continuation of political and economic hierarchies in the Soviet Union. But, again, while this serves as a critique of the Soviets, it would be a mistake to read it as an argument against economic and political egalitarianism and for the concept of an inevitable class structure, as do some readers in America. The existence of classes and hierarchies in Airstrip One does not signify the inevitable failure of socialism in Orwell's understanding; rather, it describes an important part of the dystopian experience. Where there are classes, there is no hope for a good life for all, whether the society is capitalist or socialist in name.

Orwell was also disturbed by the ways the British state was entering into the lives of ordinary persons during World War II. While police powers in England had increased in the 1920s and 1930s, it was the onset of stricter methods during the war that concerned him most because they represented the tie between national emergencies and police snooping. He was also well aware of the elaborate systems of observation practiced in the Soviet Union and Nazi Germany. Orwell exaggerates this trend, as did Zamyatin. However, he does not convert this into a case of technology run amok. Part of Airstrip One's arsenal is indeed technological, in the form of the ever-present telescreens. But Orwell wants to underline the fact that the same danger exists in low-tech forms. The old-fashioned use of spies and informers can be as effective as gadgets in laying open one's life to the gaze of the state, as More also indicated. Indeed, such tools can be even more effective. One can evade technology by hiding or finding places outside the range of surveillance, but with spies and informers about one is never at ease. When the state takes over one's children as it minions, even the family no longer serves as a refuge.

States do not just control by means of physical coercion and surveillance, Orwell argues. They also do so more subtly and fundamentally. One way is to attack rationality. In this story, such attacks come in the form of undermining the objective basis of rationality, seen most clearly in the misuse of the principle of correspondence. Correspondence is the equation of two things. The objective basis of the principle holds that equivalence must be established by a consistent method and in a disinterested manner. To equate two entities, whether quantitative or qualitative in nature, one must establish the similarity of their constituent parts. If no similarity can be established on independent grounds, they cannot be equated. They are different, not similar. By promulgating such slogans as *War is Peace* and *Freedom is Slavery*, the state systematically uses the correspondence principle but violates the objectivity rule by equating very different concepts. It drains of its meaning the logical relationship claimed. Such proclamations, while retaining the shell of logic, in reality randomize the thinking process, allowing the state to claim the mantle of objectivity while it subjectively manipulates the labels it uses.

The state must use this method because the labels available to it still carry connotations and meanings that escape its control. Freedom is viewed favorably; slavery not so. Equating the two helps the state portray activities associated with the second as associated with the first (or vice versa—depending on the circumstances, it may want to emphasize that freedom is a kind of slavery). Ultimately, however, through its creation of Newspeak, the state no longer need indulge in such overt attacks on rationality. Because all labels will, in their connotations and relations with one another, be strictly defined, the necessity of using rational operations will be limited. As Symes puts it, orthodoxy means not having to think, and the shrinking of vocabulary achieved by Newspeak will eventually mean that unorthodox thoughts will not be possible. In other words, at some point Doublethink (the reconciliation of contradictory propositions) will not be necessary; the intellectual resources at the disposal of citizens will be so sparse as to make everyone Goodthinkers (those who automatically adopt the position of the state). Orwell detected such attacks in the ordinary politics of the 1930s in both the capitalist and Communist worlds and in wartime propaganda. He worries that these attacks, having proved efficacious, would continue indefinitely. He fears their dehumanizing effects, believing that eventually they will rob most humans of the ability to think clearly and independently, thus denying them their identity and autonomy.

Associated with these attacks is the manipulation of history and language. We know from the first sentence of the story ("the clocks were striking thirteen") that time is under the control of the state, quite possibly changed to the 24-hour clock used by the military. But it is not just ordinary time, in the form of schedules, which worries Orwell as it does Zamyatin. He is also concerned with "history" as the storehouse of objective reality and important data, and language as one of the means by which we process those data. Orwell was well acquainted with the efforts of powerful entities, whether states or other organizations, to take control of the way people understand the world. He had witnessed the erasure of history in the course of Stalin's purges and in what he took as the rewriting of the narrative of the Spanish Civil War. He saw it again in the British government's manipulation of descriptions of events during World War II. He wished to push this insight further in this story by portraying the control of history and language as one of the keys to maintaining power.

Control in his description follows two somewhat different paths. The control of language is meant to restrict the conceptual means by which judgments can be made. As we saw above, Newspeak is a kind of censorship. To use words in

Newspeak is to only use the concepts of which the state approves. This function is reinforced by the evolution of Newspeak, wherein vocabulary is increasingly restricted. The fewer the words available, the better. History is treated differently. It is not as if "information" is not available; rather, the state is all too eager to provide facts, figures, reports, and observations. It does so in part while shading this information in whichever direction serves its policy best at any particular time (here we get a description of "spin"). It also does so by changing that information. History is no longer a single record of events, but is now a malleable database, at one time saying this, at another the opposite. This manipulation of history does at least two things to citizens. One, much as with the One State's insistence on mathematical logic, the state's control of history means that any analysis of events must eventually come around to the conclusion it favors. There can be no independent judgment when the basis of all judgments can be changed or erased. Second, the malleability of the past puts the individual off balance. There is no place to stand in which to make judgments or assert one's individual capacity to make judgments competently. The evidence one would wish to reference will no longer exist in tangible form. Such flux is confusing, disorienting. There is no way that one can defend an individual existence, for meaning is tied up with the collective's control of the basis for understanding existence itself.

Influenced by geopolitical writers of the time as well as by Jack London's discussion of the subject, Orwell also saw the future as possibly marked by perpetual war. Centers of power arise that dominate particular parts of the world and draw to themselves important human and natural resources. While Orwell saw in this a continuation of the earlier wars of the late nineteenth and early twentieth centuries that were sparked by the ambitions of capitalists, he saw perpetual war in the future as exploiting more fully the potential for domestic advantage. Taking his cues from the mobilization of citizens achieved by all participants in World War II, as well as by London's analysis in *The Iron Heel*, Orwell argues that war is the best means of disciplining and controlling a population. By putting their lives and livelihoods in danger, by threatening the identity established by modern patriotic myths, and by activating atavistic instincts to hate enemies and outsiders, wars serve to galvanize citizens, recruiting their energies and again tying them to the state. Wars help free political elites from accountability and allow them to pursue whichever projects they see fit. A mobilized, emotionally charged, outwardly focused population does not have the time, energy, desire, or means by which to evaluate a government and hold it accountable. In this anticipation of a beefed up "wag the dog" thesis, Orwell sees the pursuit of war as not only the continuation of competition by brutal and bloody methods, but also a tool of power, a weapon to be used by rich and powerful elites, and a means for the cultivation of fanaticism.

Dystopian themes and life

Themes

Orwell is a pioneer of the experience of the modern dystopia. His portrayal of how modern political systems can be manipulated for private gain, the perils and experiences of being mobilized constantly, and the terror of being continually monitored are rightly seen as commentary on how even ordinary politics in the twentieth century have gone wrong. The terror he depicts is more immediate and real than Zamyatin's portrayal of mechanization; even Zamyatin's use of mathematical logic can be admired as an alternative language and found amusing, whereas Orwell's depictions of Ingsoc and Doublethink emphasize their brutality. Among the most important of the themes Orwell associates with the perils of modern politics are fanaticism, impoverishment, and the communal nature of the modern dystopian experience.

The Party and Big Brother both demand fanatical devotion to themselves. Fanaticism means the total devotion of the self to the object of attachment, the complete giving over of intellectual, emotional, and moral energy. Everyone, at the least, attempts to display a total commitment to the regime for safety's sake. The children of Winston's neighbors are trained in fanaticism by the state's youth organizations. Their sweaty father provides them with another example in his complete devotion to state-sponsored sports. Members of the Anti-Sex League dedicate their minds and bodies to the state. Ultimately, some members of the Inner Party such as O'Brien are allegedly so devoted to the Party that they depict themselves as powerful and immortal because the Party is such. In Orwell's rendering, fanatics discard their obligations to everyone else in their total dedication to a single cause. They mow down all obstacles, disregarding all competing moral arguments in their quest. Here, according to O'Brien, the Party's goal is power. But while Orwell is particularly interested in power, fanaticism can be attached to anything, including the pursuit of otherwise noble goals. This conception of fanaticism differs in its effects from the mechanization of humans that Zamyatin describes. Where the latter talks of transformation through the elimination of emotion and the winnowing of understanding to mathematical logic, Orwell points to the manipulation of emotion and the transformation of logic and reason to a subjective and flexible way of thinking dominated by human authorities.

Orwell is particularly interested in the recruitment of emotions in fanaticism. He does not view fanatics as stoic, even if he describes them as sometimes attempting to cultivate a stoic exterior. Rather, he sees fanaticism as importantly incorporating emotion. For one, emotion creates energy. The manipulation of sexual energy is central to his understanding of the state's ability continually to mobilize the population in collective work and individual sacrifice. Rather than having the state disarm citizens by allowing them to satisfy sexual desire through the means of state regulation (in the One State through means of pink tickets), Orwell has the state cultivate that nervous energy by elevating abstinence as a civic virtue. The Anti-Sex League is the culmination of this effort. But fanaticism is also about the intentional display and controlled discharge of emotion. The Two Minute Hate and Hate Week are the means by which the state strengthens its ties with citizens, preparing them for any type of activity or sacrifice through the channeling of emotional displays. Emotional expressions of hatred toward the enemies of the state do several things. They externally bind people into a single entity—people express the same emotion at the same time with regard to the same object. Not to do so is to be conspicuously different, an outcast. Through such displays, the state recruits a sense of righteousness to its side. It also firmly establishes the state's enemies as the enemies of each individual. The state can and does make this connection intellectually, but the manipulation of reason is not sufficient because doubt may always enter. But there is no doubt in emotion; hate brooks no qualifications. Finally, emotional displays against enemies carries one away despite intellectual reservations, as Winston describes in his recollection of a particular Two Minute Hate. Emotional displays reinforce fanaticism by removing inhibitions and all other barriers to one's devotion.

Where leaders use fanaticism as a tool for recruiting the energy and identity of citizens for their own purposes, they also use it to free themselves of scrutiny and criticism. A fanatic devotes herself completely and without question. A fanatic wishes to be controlled, welcoming discipline, surveillance, and efforts to enforce orthodoxy (as we saw, a theme that Zamyatin also explored). A fanatic, as Winston demonstrates at the end, accepts that the world can only be understood subjectively by means of the vision the leader supplies. This position liberates leaders not just in their relations with such people, but also in all their other activities. A fanatical following demands no accountability. Everything the state does will be by definition right, good and correct. However, Orwell does differentiate among the ways people become and remain fanatics. Some are in Orwell's Newspeak parlance Goodthinkers, people who will never be tempted to deviate from orthodoxy because they accept without question everything they are told. To be blunt, they are too stupid to be unorthodox. Others are more intelligent and require mental gymnastics to remain fanatical and orthodox. Winston is not turned into a Goodthinker in his time in the Ministry of Love; rather, he is retrained in Doublethink.

While fanaticism marks life in Airstrip One, the inhabitants of this dystopia experience material conditions closer to Engels's description of the working class than Zamyatin's mechanical humans. Rations are always short and continually cut. Uniforms are shabby. Living spaces are cramped and squalid. Food is bad and there are shortages of such basic necessities as razorblades. The very air stinks. This depiction is intentional because Orwell sees poverty as a tool of control just as powerful as plenty. He had explored this theme previously in his meditations on the poor in capitalist societies. To be poverty-stricken and hungry is to experience a restriction in one's horizons.[9] One no longer thinks independently about politics because the promise of food and better living conditions becomes a spur for obedience or a source of distraction (witness the proles and their fascination with the lottery), as does the threat of even worse conditions, and the quest for the necessities of life absorbs what physical and mental energy one has left over from work for the state. As we saw with regard to sex, a community that aims for total control does not try to satisfy human desires as a way keeping order and preserving power in Orwell's reckoning; drawing a different conclusion from Zamyatin and to a degree Neville, Orwell holds that the state keeps those appetites alive in order to sap energy from potential troublemakers, manipulating their material appetites, distracting their attention, and dividing potential rebels. Here it is the lack of material security not its provision that poses a danger to autonomy.

Related to this impoverishment is the experience of standardization. Clothes are uniform; food is plain and unvarying, and days follow one another in dull succession. Part of this uniformity is the similarity of experiences across people of the same social strata. Winston's fellow workers have much the same life as he. Part of it also has to do with plainness itself. Where More saw plainness and uniformity as creating the possibility for a materially better life because such features eliminate waste, tamp down greed, and lay the groundwork for a truly familial solidarity, Orwell paints them as condemning people to a physically and sensually impoverished existence. It is true that Airstrip One is not the same as Utopia, with the latter's well-kept housing, parks, gardens, wide streets, hospitals, and cozy communal kitchens inviting us to stay. But, for Orwell, the lack of variety would have been stultifying even if there had been more of everything.

Orwell is also concerned with poverty in this and other contexts because he wishes to underline the judgment that fanaticism does not bring the good life. For Orwell, material security is good, but fanatics cannot achieve such a goal. To devote oneself completely to a cause or political movement is not the answer to the problems humans experience. Fanaticism is a destructive rather than a constructive force, for it empowers people who have no intention of making life better. No absolute leader is compelled to, is willing to, nor will feel obligated to care materially for his followers. Fanatics, by giving up their autonomy, abdicating their responsibility to use their critical faculties and empowering absolute leaders, get what they deserve. They are tools to be used, used up, and discarded. So while Orwell departs from More in his assessment of uniformity, here he is in close company with More. He does not argue that the pursuit of material security in itself is problematic. He does not categorically conclude that a government that controls important natural resources, transportation networks, and other elements of the economy is dangerous. He espoused such moves in other writings. Rather, it is the pursuit of such a goal fanatically and the concentration of power in particular institutions and officials that would pose danger in his mind. On the larger scale, he would agree that the overall desire for security can be problematic, but is not directly dangerous; it is dangerous only when that desire becomes associated with the need for certainty and thereby promotes fanaticism.

It is also the case that while Orwell was a critic of twentieth-century capitalist individualism, he also held fundamental liberal tenets among his socialist principles. His depiction of the relentless communal facade of Airstrip One shows his commitment to a liberal appreciation of negative liberty. In that Airstrip One, no citizen is officially anything more than a part of the larger community; individualism and eccentricity are effectively outlawed. As Winston remarks, "In principle a Party member had no spare time, and was not alone except in bed." And indeed even that statement undershoots the mark, as witnessed by the belief by Winston's wife that such sexual relations as are to be had are a "duty to the state." There are a variety of reasons for the Party's emphasis on creating an artificially collective life. Such a life, as Winston notes, is physically, mentally, and emotionally exhausting in ordinary times. One must always be on stage, minding all the officially created and ever-changing customs and rules of social interaction. This is heightened by the atmosphere in Airstrip One, where one could run afoul of authorities by an incorrect facial expression, a lack of proper enthusiasm, or a fleeting indication of doubt. A tired population is one that has no thoughts of resistance. Such a communal life allows elites more easily to control the physical movements of citizens. To be a part of a group in places where groups are supposed to gather eases the tasks of surveillance and manipulation. To be alone, to not be in places where other citizens are gathered, is to complicate such tasks. Thus to be alone in Airstrip One is to invite even more scrutiny.

An artificially communal life also and most importantly reinforces the foundations of fanaticism. As we have seen for Orwell, to be a fanatic means ceasing to be an autonomous individual and instead someone who finds complete understanding and identity in a corporate being. The manufactured collectivization of Airstrip One cultivates that foundation, identifying the state as that larger, better, and infallible entity in which one invests hopes and aspirations. Note, however, that Orwell is not saying that every society that has collective characteristics is marked by fanaticism and a loss of individualism and negative liberties. Nor does he necessarily equate socialism with the type of dehumanizing communalism he depicts here (he, in fact, comes close to accepting the communal anarchy, with its marked individualism, that Morris promotes).[10] However, Orwell does believe that every fanatic understands himself as part of a larger, organic being, and thus every fanatical organization will be collectivized and exhibit the pathological characteristics of Airstrip One.

The dystopian life

The state appears to be the dominant actor in Orwell's understanding of dystopia. Everything appears to be done for its benefit. People are obliged to follow the state's rules. The state controls information, rationality, history, and language. The state, rather than individuals, seems to be the main actor here. But this is not really the case. While it is easy and necessary to speak of "the state" in *Nineteen Eight-Four* as shorthand for understanding the attack on individualism Orwell describes, there really is no such separate entity. While the identity of both Inner and Outer Party members is collective and society itself is collectively organized, neither the state nor the party is really an actor in itself. The state is really controlled by a group of individuals using institutions to further their own ends.

In this portrayal of those in power as well as in his discussion of how Winston and his colleagues live, Orwell departs significantly from Zamyatin, who really does portray the state as the embodiment of the collective and an active agent of science and civilization, and does describe ordinary people as sharing many aspects of a single mentality. In contrast, one may say that Orwell in part uses an understanding similar to that of the "pluralist" school of thought that attacked the description of mid-century dictatorships as monolithic totalitarianism.[11] In his understanding, there is no reality of corporatism behind the rhetoric and display of party-states. There are only individuals both at the top and the bottom who use the institutions of the state for their own purposes. Dictatorships in this understanding keep control by physically separating people from one another through suspicion and fear even while denizens participate in collective activities and those in power use collective institutions and projects as ways of controlling and manipulating them. While citizens are never allowed to be comfortable as individuals in Airstrip One, neither are they at ease when in the presence of their fellow citizens. At the top, factions struggle for power and engage in balancing activities. Among the Outer Party members, people treat one another with suspicion. They have common experiences, face common threats, and work on common projects, but find no emotional or intellectual connection with one another. While they live in collective conditions, there is no solidarity or shared consciousness. To put it in the words of a Machiavelli or a Rousseau, they are not a "people."

The institutions that Orwell references are, in comparison, closer in tone to those conventionally associated with dictatorships and associated organizations, though their actions are exaggerated. One such institution is the Party. It is clear that Orwell models the Party after the German National Socialists, the Soviet Communist Party, and organized religious communities. It has different levels of membership, a system of "democratic centralism" in which power and decisionmaking are concentrated at the top, and is characterized by discipline. It is also subject to periodic purges, ostensibly to cleanse itself, but more probably as a result of power struggles among various factions. Thus, Orwell does not portray the Party as the perfect organ of subjugation, just as he refrains from describing any institution in Airstrip One in those terms. The Party is made up of humans, all of whom have separate interests, desires, and appetites they attempt to satisfy, and others both inside and outside it feel the brunt of those attempts at satisfaction as well as the effects of their mistakes and bumbling.

The ministries in Airstrip One, meanwhile, are dedicated to preserving the power of the Party. In doing this, they may incidentally benefit the general population. For example, the Ministry of Plenty does preside over the creation of food and goods. But it does so not because it is serving the population. If goods and foods are produced, it is because leaders require that citizens be fed, lodged, and clothed. Without these, they would die or rebel, neither of which leaders wish. Similarly, the Ministry of Truth provides books, poems, films, and plays for the population not because of any concern on its part that people be educated and stimulated, but because without the official provision of such materials, people would look elsewhere and that would be a dangerous development. But for the most part, there is very little connection between what goes on in the ministries and the public good. The Ministry of Truth provides little information useful to the population, as Winston argues when speaking of the completely artificial nature of official statistics. The Ministry of Love does not provide order—not only are its own methods disorderly and violent, and not only does it allow other organs of the Party to cultivate violence and disorder in citizens, it does not care to curb the real disorderliness of the proles. All the energy, time, and wealth the ministries consume are, from the point of view of the general public, wasted. Winston's own work, which entails the destruction, rewriting, and reprinting of material that people likely will never read and which are all equally false, is typical of the tremendous squandering of resources.

The Thought Police is the exception to the general description of institutions as ineffective. It is a combination of the Inquisition, the Soviet Secret Police, and the SS. It is powerful, ubiquitous, and wily. Its wiliness sets it apart from the stupidity that many attribute to policemen. The Thought Police are several steps ahead of any potential dissident. It is they who tempt any who have unorthodox potential to reveal themselves. They set up the spy networks and set family members against one another. They have refined torture and reprogramming as well as surveillance. Their role, as their name implies, is not so much to keep physical as mental order. They do not patrol the streets looking for robbers; they invade people's houses and workplaces looking for deviations from orthodoxy. For Orwell, this is the more dangerous and tragic manifestation of power. A nation of laws in which the police heavy-handedly assert physical order is far more tolerable to him than a state with no laws whose police seek to enforce love and devotion to the state. The first affects one only outwardly and can be systematically evaded by guile or close adherence to laws. The latter cannot be eluded and it goes to the very core of being human in terms of the use of intellectual faculties and the expression of emotions.

Orwell pushes his analysis of this kind of internal control to its ultimate end to assess the attempt not only to control information, history, and logic, but also the meaning of sanity itself. His purpose is somewhat different from others who have made this point. London's position in *The Iron Heel* and Zamyatin's in *We* resemble that of postmodernists (particularly Foucault) in that both wish to establish that the definition of sanity is an exercise of power. There is no objective definition of either sanity or insanity. They are malleable concepts that have their existence by institutional acts of creation. One cannot take shelter in them, just as one cannot shield oneself from the state through the invocation of laws. None of these have an objective existence and are used by the state to mold society in a desired image. This is not the position Orwell adopts. While he sees the concept of sanity as a weapon in the state's arsenal, he insists on the reality of an objective world of history, logic, and common sense. To be sane means to remember accurately, to process information in a reasonable and independent fashion, and to adhere to logical consistency. There can be governments that understand and respect this objective understanding of sanity, just as there can be governments that create useful and necessary laws. These meet one of the criteria of good government. But for a government to play with the definition of sanity, to subjectivize it, to decree that someone who uses common sense and rationality to process information is insane, is for Orwell to make a fully human life impossible; thus such a government is both different from a good government and objectively undesirable.

Looming over everyone in Airstrip One as the arbiter of right, wrong, sanity, and the common good is Big Brother. Big Brother is a mythic figure whose public persona has little to do with his own person. That persona has been constructed to provide a human focus for fanatical devotion, providing a face that can be associated with guidance, assurance, knowledge, a plan, surveillance, and ultimately certitude and security. In that sense, Orwell does not wish to draw attention to the phenomenon of Big Brother as a dictator. He may or may not be one—we do not know. As with Stalin, he may be dependent upon a group of people for support and therefore is not the all-powerful decider of the country's policies. He may not exist at all anymore. The important point is that he functions publicly as the touchstone of all important things. He is depicted as the font of orthodoxy. He is said to watch over everyone continuously. He grants awards, awards punishment, and provides all material goods. He is not a priest like Zamyatin's Benefactor. Rather, he is a secular god, and Orwell's complaint is not that he is secular, but that he is a god. No one should be treated as a god or speak for a god in his mind. If they do, the stage is set for fanaticism and the imposition of orthodoxy, for gods or their equivalents are jealous and satisfy perversely the human desire for certainty.

As with everything in the book, these institutions are exaggerations, part of Orwell's satire on fanaticism. One need not have the Thought Police to experience the dehumanizing demands of government. Yet even in his exaggeration, Orwell was often closer to events than he may have realized, as Solzhenitsyn's work has shown. People in the Soviet Gulags were forced to betray everything they treasured for the sake of the Party. Some did so willingly, acting the part of Goodthinkers in the same way Orwell portrays Parsons and Winston's wife. The Soviet penal system during the Great Purges did spend inordinate amounts of time on prisoners in seeking to break their will and substitute for other beliefs an overriding allegiance to the state. There is something profoundly correct in Orwell's understanding of both the psychology of the prisoners and the jailers that goes beyond the effectiveness of torture and sadism themselves. Of course, the physical pain and psychological pressure administered in the Ministry of Love's establishments are not meant as punishment, but for reformation of the person into a willing servant of the state, whether his destination is outside or inside the labor camps. Orwell sees this as the wave of the future. States will not be content to make examples of people, but will ultimately demand love as well as obedience or the acknowledgment of power. In this stance, Orwell stands with Zamyatin against the views of such utopians as Bellamy (and to some extent Morris), who hold that treating crime as a sickness is an advance rather than another tool in the arsenal of those who seek to gain and keep power.

We see that Orwell attempts to paint dystopia as a mixture of experiences. One part is drabness and poverty. Even members of the Outer Party, relatively privileged as they are, have a lower standard of living than the middle class of the early twentieth century and live much less colorful lives. But another part has to do with extreme passions. The naturally fanatical among the population keep themselves in a state of fervent admiration for the state. For the rest, the artificial means of Two Minute Hates and other interventions mobilize their emotions. In addition, there is the fear the Thought Police engender, manifested in the absolute necessity of keeping up with the ever-changing information, judgments, and orthodox views the Party generates. Those who do not display the compulsive behavior of natural fanatics must always keep on their toes so as not to stumble across an unorthodox thought, act, or expression. There is a low, but persistent, and quite real sense of terror that such people experience.

This all takes place in the context of a life in which people experience little privacy. In More's Utopia, the nonstop presence of others is to serve as a source of comfort and security. In Airstrip One, it is a font of discomfort, insecurity, stress, and danger. In Utopia, the collective nature of life allows people to have enough goods and time on their hands so that they can develop themselves intellectually. In Orwell's dystopia, the artificially collective nature of life means that there is never enough time for individual development and, rather than abundance, what is shared is chronic scarcity. In Utopia, a collective life means that ordinary citizens are able to hold government accountable and be autonomous in a large sense. In Airstrip One, the politics of the collective forces everyone to prove herself a good citizen over and over again through compulsive immersion in civic affairs.

While on the whole Orwell's descriptions here are meant to be exaggerations with a serious political point, there is also in Orwell's description of life in Airport One an element of farce. The character of Parsons in particular is clearly a satire on several types of people Orwell found irksome in contemporary England. He is part public school hearty, interested only in sports, and part Old School boy, never able to move past the experiences of his youth. But he is also part fruit juice-drinking, sandal-wearing, bearded, exercise-bent, hiking-obsessed crank. While his character helps illustrate the dangers posed by enthusiasm, he is also Orwell's shot across the bow of both the establishment types and leftist countercultural bohemians of the 1930s who created their own demanding and competing sets of orthodoxies and rules of conformity. To a degree, Airstrip One is Orwell's description of the kind of ridiculous world such twits would create if they were ever, by some twist of fate, be left in complete charge.

Human nature and applications

Human nature

Orwell sees humans as vulnerable to outside control in their character as processors of information. Likewise, Orwell sees in human nature elements that can lead to problems in realizing the whole person. There is also in Orwellian humans an innate desire for security and certainty that leads them to invest their judgment and identity in powerful leaders. In holding these views, Orwell agrees with Zamyatin that humans are equally hardwired and programmed. He believes that the need to process information and the desire for certainty are hardwired in humans, but that other characteristics are provided by culture and training. Also in common with Zamyatin, he does not see hardwiring as immune from outside control and manipulation. The hardwiring he identifies is dependent upon resources outside the individual. Manipulate information and one can control the way individuals process information. Interfere with the way they process information and one can control the outcome of the processing. Provide humans with objects of veneration and one can control them through their need for certainty.

On the surface, Orwell appears to follow much the same understanding as More. Just as the latter sees people as hardwired, but also sees their behavior as changeable through changes in environments, so Orwell argues that the way people act on their hardwiring can be affected by outside agents and environments. The difference between the two, aside from the fact that More sees this as a beneficial thing and Orwell describes its abuse, lies in how this happens. More sees the process in terms of eliciting particular responses from human hardwiring by creating specific social, political, and economic environments. Orwell goes somewhat further. He sees the community enacting fundamental changes in people, in that by manipulating how people process information, it creates people who cease to be autonomous. It appears, however, that he does not think it possible to change human hardwiring (the electronic device used in Winston's interrogation appears to be a comment on the impossibility of attaining a permanent result using technical means, even though corrupt elites would covet such a result) or to deactivate such hardwiring. It cannot be the case that elites can completely prevent people from processing information by structuring the environment in a particular fashion. When people process information in the way the Party desires by acting as Goodthinkers, that result is importantly the result of characteristics already present in the person's particular makeup. One cannot manufacture Goodthinkers; thus, people are not socially constructed in the way Zamyatin describes (in which he describes a process by which elites control an environment such that one part of human nature is expressed at the expense of the rest). Instead, elites both encourage the deluded behavior of natural fanatics and train the rest to act like fanatics, in part through coercion and in part by encouraging the natural desire for certainty. Orwell does not show Airstrip One going as far as the One State in trying to rip out hardwiring. Instead, he illustrates those in power massaging the information available for processing, controlling the language by which people describe events and conditions and engage in processing, and training people to use the accepted understandings of rationality and logic when they do the processing. It is not their hardwiring that is changed, but the way people use that hardwiring.

There is also a close connection here between the use of hardwiring and programming. Hardwiring is often activated and managed through the programming that comes from culture and training. However, while the presence of particular types of collective environments and situations in which the processing is not freely engaged will impact hardwiring, it is not the case that Orwell emphasizes the presence or absence of particular economic or political systems. Rather, it is in the relationship of those systems to the resources and programming human hardwiring requires in order to operate that is important. Thus, Airstrip One is importantly a mixture of capitalism and socialism—no single type of environment is to blame for dystopian conditions, but all potentially can be culpable if elites who create and control them indulge in the kinds of activities Orwell identifies.

Importantly, Orwell paints the desire to believe in something and to rely on some power or institution as a source of certainty as a hardwired attribute. He even describes this in Winston, skeptical as he is, through the certainty he possesses regarding the existence of some resistance movement. He believes in it just as others believe in the Party and Big Brother. Orwell appears to assign this trait to our survival instinct. Everyone innately desires to be cared for, to feel safe, and to have others make decisions for them, just as was the case when one was a child. The familial connotations of the label "Big Brother" are not accidental, nor are the passages in which Winston is described as remembering his mother. The desire for certainty is connected with an emotional desire for protection and safety.

Orwell also, of course, fundamentally sees people as entities that process information. To live in the world humanly means to take in information, analyze it, and then form judgments, thereby completing the process of constructing oneself. Whether or not people do so independently and rationally is another story. To live the good life, one must be able to process in those ways, but people can process under constraints. Winston, for example, is able to enjoy some parts of his job because they involve higher order processing functions. Yet in working for the Ministry of Truth and living in Airstrip One, Winston is not processing information independently. Where Zamyatin attacks the monolithic control rationality exercises over humans, Orwell reverts to the autonomous use of rationality, or common sense as he would put it, as one marker of the good life. To be fully human is to be able to make independent judgments as to the origin, nature, and meaning of events and conditions. Rationality is the means by which such judgments are made because the objectivity of rationality (as opposed to the subjectivity of ideologies or religions) allows one independently to make consistent judgments. But physical environments and emotional spaces are also important to autonomous processing. Orwell agrees with Zamyatin that humans, as processors of information, do not only process with their minds, but also with their bodies, senses, and emotions. While they are importantly rational beings in Orwell's understanding, humans not only must consume intellectual goods untainted by manipulation, but also must freely experience the world with their bodies.

Therefore, while Orwell usually identifies "Nature" with the physical world, he can also refer to what is "natural" in humans. Orwell seems to identify emotions as more natural and often purer than the results of intellectual efforts. It is true, of course, that he portrays emotions as being manipulated from the outside, but if one can stay true to one's own emotions, as he portrays Winston's mother, then one will be a better, because more moral and more independent, person. That is why Orwell has Winston ultimately idealize the proles—they remained in contact with their "primitive emotions," just as he has Winston and Julia hope they will retain their love for one another even when they foresee the Thought Police torturing them to confess to everything else. When Winston professes his love for Big Brother after having emotionally betrayed Julia, it is the act that completes his conversion to fanatical behavior; it represents the triumph of the Party in getting inside him and affecting something central to his humanity. It has succeeded in controlling his emotions, something even more difficult than controlling his mind.

So for Orwell, to interfere with the processing of information, whether intellectually or emotionally, is to rob people of an important part of their humanity. To dehumanize in this sense does not mean turning people into machines; rather, it means turning them into processors bereft of critical faculties, as entities who do not autonomously construct themselves. To dehumanize means artificially to structure the intellectual, emotional, and sensual content of people's lives, to make that content uniform and responsive to some external power. Rather than a fully functional human, one is instead a passive receptor of information whose emotions and senses are molded and controlled from the outside. A fanatic is the primary manifestation of such a being. Orwell drives this point home in several ways, but the clearest comes toward the end of the book. He has O'Brien, in reforming Winston, deny the objectivity of history, matter, and logic and in so doing dredge up again obscurantist positions of the past that were or are peddled by fanatics who paint the world in their own subjectivist terms and force Winston to agree. There were no dinosaurs—their bones are inventions. Stars are nearby sparks of fire. The world is the center of the universe. The earth is only as old as are humans. To accept these canards is to accept passively another's understanding of the world.

Another basic conception Orwell associates with human nature throughout his work is that of corruption. The root of evil is not the desire for goods or the pursuit of power per se. Orwell is not opposed to desire, and sees the exercise of power as an important tool for obtaining the good life. Rather, as a kind of moralist, he roots evil in the transformation of a good thing into something harmful in its impact on others. Thus, corruption for Orwell entails the destruction of the common sense that lies behind morality. A rational person seeks to harmonize with his surroundings. A rational person sees the long-term benefits of acting in ways that take account the good of everyone else. A rational person recognizes the humanity he has in common with others and does not seek to rob them of the attributes that make them human. But, much as More argues that excessive wealth stimulates appetites and Neville argues that a benign environment will atrophy virtues, Orwell holds that excessive power and wealth breeds an intense desire to retain and expand one's holdings such that common sense and its accompanying common morality are discarded as hindrances. Their moderating influences are at odds with the satisfaction of the expanded appetite. Given his socialist background, it is initially surprising that Orwell adheres to the notion that power is corrupting. That is usually deemed a conventional, liberal position by socialists. But Orwell tends to equate power and wealth and is deeply suspicious of concentrations of either. As with more conservative commentators, he accepts the proposition that the possession of power erodes moral bearings, stimulates appetites, and unleashes harmful emotions. In this he depicts powerful people in the same way that he depicts wealthy people. That is not to say that he describes dictators and tyrants as slobbering monsters any more than he does the rich. Outwardly they appear to be tightly controlled, and indeed he imputes a certain discipline to such creatures, just as Plato credits discipline to the person whose dominant appetite is for money. But it is the discipline imposed by their inflated desires, not that of morality. Thus the image he borrows from London to describe the rule of the Party—that of a boot smashing a face—does not describe only capitalists in their quest for money in his understanding. It also describes the people who hold excessive amounts of power, including socialist dictators.

With this background in mind, we can see how the link between corruption and dystopia runs through fanaticism for Orwell. Fanaticism enables the corrupt behavior of the rich and powerful. By ceding their moral responsibilities to such people, fanatical citizens license their actions, allowing them continually to gather power and wealth until, brought up against the desires of other wealthy and powerful people, struggles erupt within governments and between states. Consumed with such struggles and unconcerned with the plight of the ordinary people who have fanatical belief in their program, leaders construct a society that is to their advantage, built to use ordinary citizens, and preserve and protect the power and wealth of elites.

To conclude, Orwell's humans are not entirely plastic. While he sees their potential to be programmed and dehumanized, as well as their potential for autonomous self-construction, it is in how they do things that they become changed more than what they are. Fanaticism is a way of being. His humans are also more coherent than Zamyatin's; Orwell does not argue that there are contradictions in their character. He does point to weaknesses, particularly the desire for certainty, which lead to unintended and unfortunate consequences. He is closer to Morris in his argument that we should consider stripping away some of the trappings of civilization (sophisticated communications, capitalism) in order to get at what is essentially human. But he does not draw humans as benignly as does Morris, and in his identification of weaknesses and corruption resembles Neville's understanding of the human condition, but without the latter's emphasis on virtues and the need for environmental challenges.

Applications

Despite the obvious influences Orwell absorbed from his readings of Zamyatin, London, Koestler, and others, he succeeds in creating a different type of dystopia. As noted in the introduction, he is not intent on delegitimizing the goals of progress and civilization, or in discussing how governments are the problematic perpetrators of civilizational violence against human nature. His is a criticism of the wrong-headed ways people approach the job of creating and sustaining civilization, and thus his dystopia is about the degeneration of government as an aid to the creation and maintenance of civilization as an expression of human nature. Yet, he is also squarely in the dystopian tradition in warning against current trends, specifically the fanatical devotion to a cause and the ways the powerful manipulate poverty, class, danger, and war to consolidate their power over the community. Further, while he emphasizes the lack of material security, his account hints at a utopia cast on its head. The names of Airstrip One's ministries (Love, Plenty, Truth) point to the promise of utopia (or at least good government) and suggesting More's interest in a government focused on the general welfare. He is clearly satirizing some concepts of utopia, but he is also satirizing and criticizing important elements of contemporary society that could not be changed except through radical means, and here and elsewhere points to the importance of material security that More privileges.

Orwell presents us with a clear proposition: that fanaticism, orthodoxy, and the quest for certainty are dangerous. We should consider this proposition carefully. Again, we may concede the point in broad terms, but then ask, so what? Don't we already know that they are?[12] The question then becomes, are these never good? I think that is a tougher proposition to defend. Orwell clearly sees them linked to a whole host of undesirable political, economic, and social developments, including the unchecked exercise of power, the stratification of society, and asceticism forced on the lower classes. Yet might not deep convictions, a desire to preserve a truth and find a solid place to stand be important and desirable things in at least some circumstances? Do strong convictions and adherence to a consistent philosophy inevitably, or even usually, lead to Big Brothers and Thought Police? Don't we need strong convictions to fight against tyranny and other evils? Indeed, doesn't Winston in his fight against the Party and the state imbibe in these, as Orwell has O'Brien note? If Orwell were to concede this point, he would have to revert to a more conventional stance, in which danger comes from certain types of groups. The project would then be to identify these groups. Orwell apparently thinks that the Soviet Union and Germany in the 1930s were controlled by people who manipulated fanatics and that Britain was tending in that direction. Was he correct? Was it fanaticism that created Nazi Germany, Stalin's Soviet Union, and the aspects of British government that Orwell despised, or was there something else that accounts for the developments he deplored? If he was correct, are there groups that now meet that standard? "Cults" are generally identified as such, but are there others? Have, for example, the core adherents of the two major parties in the United States given in to their

desire for certainty and become fanatics, thus freeing the leaders they admire
from accountability? What also of the followers of various talk radio hosts and
political television shows? Are they not fanatics? What also of various religious
groups who attack science, radical environmentalists and anti-globalizationalists,
and conspiracy theorists of all stripes? Are they, like the poor, always with us and
thus no special threat, or are their numbers increasing to toxic levels and their
leaders becoming dangerously influential and powerful?

One way of thinking about these questions is to assess the plausibility of
Orwell's dystopia and the type of fanatical behavior he portrays. Would it make
sense for people to devote themselves so strongly to such a dysfunctional and
unfulfilling state? It is true that Orwell accounts for important chunks of this
behavior by referencing the manipulation of thought and emotion that occurs
now, just as it did in the 1930s and 1940s. He also suggests that at least sometimes
fanaticism is feigned rather than real. But in all too many cases he does portray
citizens as Goodthinkers and Doublethinkers. Why would they take on such
attributes? Is it psychologically possible? Orwell's references to the dangers created
by wars and the state of constant mobilization are plausible contributors, and we
should recognize and take seriously the contemporary manipulation of conflicts
and the fears that accompany war as ways of controlling people. Many citizens
do automatically suspend their critical faculties when leaders argue that the state
is in danger, as demonstrated by contemporary studies of the "rally 'round the
flag" effect.[13] But ultimately, won't the majority of people, potentially fanatical
or even fully fanatical as they may be, tire of such a condition of mobilization?
Evidence for this is mixed: Cuba, the Soviet Union, and mainland China did
sustain such behavior for significant periods of time. However, such levels of
energetic devotion could not be indefinitely sustained. How far can governments
or other entities that exercise power push these instruments of control? Might
there be natural limits that either stop societies from entering the territory Orwell
explores, or at least makes their time in that territory relatively short?

Orwell does appear to recognize the limits of mobilization in his portrayal
of the Party's actions. Just as a well-scrubbed environment is said to reek of an
unclean mind, so the emphasis on spontaneous demonstration, parades, and
events betrays the Party's uneasiness with the level of commitment to be found
among ordinary citizens. It appears that while the desire for certainty leaves
people vulnerable to fanaticism, most people are not naturally fanatical, or
else are unable to sustain fanaticism indefinitely. Orwell assumes that the Two
Minute Hates, Hate Week, the Thought Police, telescreens, and thought control

must be in place to stimulate and cultivate manifestations of fanaticism just as, to use a religious metaphor that Orwell would undoubtedly approve, religious organizations use calendars of spiritual events to keep up the devotion of their followers. But this raises a question about the very heart of the story. If fanaticism must be manufactured over the long run, is it really as much of a danger as Orwell fears? First, can it be so manufactured for long periods of time? Second, if it can be manufactured, will constructed fanaticism bring the same benefits to rulers as the spontaneous and natural variety? And third, can a state sustain the expenditures of resources necessary to manufacture it?

Orwell may plausibly reply that a vast majority of people need not be natural fanatics in order for a dystopia like Airstrip One to be established. The actions of a critical mass may be sufficient to establish an all-powerful government. He could argue that constructed manifestations of fanaticism are useful to governments because they perform the required tasks of diverting people from critical thinking, exhausting them mentally and physically, and otherwise keeping them from holding government accountable, all the while the energy they retain is harnessed in the interests of the powerful few. To the question of whether fanaticism can be constructed, he would have to leave this to our assessment of the evidence available. He appears convinced that it had been created in Germany, the Soviet Union, and in England during World War II, and would attribute that success to the overall desire for certainty that is part of the human character. He would also point to contemporary developments associated with the early Cold War, 9/11, and terrorism to argue that the manipulation of war rhetoric has allowed elements within the US government over time to obtain vastly expanded powers over the actions and thoughts of citizens.

Another important question of contemporary relevance has to do with the degree of manipulation that Orwell depicts. Is it possible to manipulate large numbers of people in this way? Excluding the proles and the natural fanatics, a large proportion of the population must be emotionally and intellectually prodded to act in ways the Party and state require. Can this be done? Orwell hints that it is easier to do so with people who are more rather than less intelligent. The proles are not manipulated—they are merely fed the raw meat of sex and violence. But otherwise can people be manipulated into performing the intellectual gymnastics and emotional twists that Orwell describes? Or would the majority of people be even more cynical than Winston? As Orwell importantly notes, the use of people's desire for security in the form of the solidarity that almost naturally arises during times of war is an important weapon in this endeavor.

While we might take Orwell's proposition that almost everyone will be forced to exhibit fanatical behavior as an exaggeration, the evidence we have of leaders using war as a means of manipulating majorities into supporting policies may make his proposition more plausible than is comfortable. The same may also be said of those who (religiously) follow particular talk radio hosts, television personalities, and other leaders.

What Orwell appears to want from citizens is for them to use rationality and common sense rather than automatic adherence to some party line when confronting a political problem. We can use here a contemporary example to illustrate this point as well as to think about Orwell's response to an important political problem. There appears to be a straightforward connection between Orwell's concerns and contemporary government surveillance programs. The obvious fear is that such programs invade citizens' privacy and provide the basis for punishment of individuals without due process. Such programs would appear to violate Orwell's generally liberal regard for negative liberties. He would probably be concerned by the threats to privacy and free expression such practices pose, as well as fearful that they could be used as part of a larger attempt to impose orthodox beliefs regarding politics or national security. At the least, he would probably hold that they should be openly acknowledged and subject to strict oversight. He might well argue that unless absolutely necessary, they should be discarded lest they become associated with attempts to use war and national security as bludgeons by which to control politics and relegate ordinary citizens to a passive political role. He might also go so far as to view them as part of a troublesome trend by which elites use the state and technology to strengthen their hold on power and utilize the fear of surveillance and denunciation as tools to cow the population.

Such conclusions, however, are difficult to make on his behalf, and those who quickly and automatically invoke him in their attempts to associate his views with particular positions engage in the type of lazy thinking that Orwell also opposed. One cannot say that he would automatically condemn surveillance in strident terms. While a tory anarchist in his self-description, by the later stages of his life he was not a pacifist and would not automatically condemn a community or a government for engaging in activities associated with self-defense. He did, after all, provide the British security services at the beginning of the Cold War with the names of people whom he thought were national security risks. But more largely, to have himself invoked as an authority, as if characters and portions of *Nineteen Eighty-Four* were Biblical, and his work reduced to clichés, would probably lead him to view the perpetrators of such actions as fanatics, or at the least the kind of cranks he associated with those who seek the comfort of unquestioned orthodox beliefs. To confront complex situations with a clear head, to process information by using rationality as common sense and to avoid slogans, prefabricated talking points, and preselected analysis would be his prescription for dealing with this problem. He would probably not look favorably upon the automatic, simple-minded chanting of "Big Brother" in response to political events even when such chanting is used to criticize government policies.

This all leads us to the larger point. Orwell is ultimately concerned with the loss of individual autonomy. Such a loss can be voluntary, as with the fanatical (or simple-minded) acceptance of an ideology, religion, or set of talking points. Or it can be triggered or coerced by the actions of powerful individuals pursuing more wealth and power while playing with the human need for certainty. He points to the danger of the state (or the party, or a church, or a cult) imposing a way of life and, more importantly, a way of thinking on people both as a way of holding onto power and privilege and as an expression of a profound sense of being right. Orwell reiterates many of the deeper problems Jack London identified in terms of the convergence of power, interest, and self-righteousness, including the deep inequalities of wealth and power that are a side-effect of fanaticism. But he goes further in terms of what happens when this convergence occurs, pointing not only to inequality and general oppression, but also the deep desire of those in control to root out differences and impose uniformity and orthodoxy.

Accepting this view means thinking in two ways about politics and human relations in general. One way is to think critically about inequalities of power and of wealth and their effects. Both types of inequality, Orwell would argue, are the tools by which elites of all types seek to gain, maintain, and increase their control. Both types should be, as far as possible, eliminated. Parts of this analysis turn on its head some types of liberal analysis that holds the attempt artificially to create economic equality leads to harmful concentrations of political power, and that inequalities of wealth are much less sinister than concentrations of political power. While Orwell agrees with much liberal analysis, he parts company here. The skepticism liberals display toward political power should extend to everyone who holds power (whether it be state power, economic power, or the power of the media), he would argue, with particular attention paid to attempts to manipulate reasoning and emotion and to control language and information. He would note that those who exercise power based on their wealth are just as well placed to engage in such manipulation as those who exercise political power. We should constantly question those who attempt to gain or exploit any type of power differentials by warping rationality, spinning data, and imposing explanatory narratives, whether they base themselves in government organizations, large corporations, NGOs, radio or television, or their own personal fortune. In sum, he would argue that we should regard suspiciously concentrations of any type of power. We must scrutinize all attempts by individuals and organizations to garner power and resist those attempts that threaten the means by which we establish and keep our identity and autonomy.

Orwell would argue that these problems are just as much as with us now as they were in the 1940s. Economic inequality has grown, the power of the state has increased, and the techniques by which the control of thought is contrived—propaganda, the monopolization of news and sources of information, the twisting of information and the revision of history, the incessant incitements to patriotism produced by wars—are even more prevalent now thanks to television and the internet, and are exercised not only by the state, but also by private actors. One might argue against him that these problems have always been with us and we still function as thinking humans. There will always be inequalities of power and wealth and asymmetries of information. Anyone who creates and disseminates information controls it. Moreover, how do we eliminate inequalities of wealth and the means of controlling information without increasing the power of the state or other institutions? Confronting these dilemmas requires creative, constructive thinking and a belief in the efficacy of institutional design to solve problems. Orwell appears to believe that there are few practitioners of the first, and he himself had little of the second, which is why some commentators label his position a politics of despair. But must we agree?

Moving on to his view of human nature: accepting his understanding of human nature would entail a fundamentally rethinking of some current assumptions. Many people tend to think about autonomy in terms of the control of our material lives and bodily movements, as well as of expression. While Orwell would agree, he would have us go further than these negative understandings. We might be free to process information formally, but if the information and means of processing (language and rationality) are manipulated from the outside, are we really free? He would argue that we are not and, worse yet, that we do not realize that we lack freedom. In this regard, Orwell would argue that many people now are woefully ignorant of the effects information has on their ability to understand the world correctly. He would again point to radio talk show hosts, cable TV shows, televangelists, government propaganda organs, and public intellectuals and other talking heads whose general sloppiness of language and analysis damages the public's general capacity to think clearly. In response, one might reply that this is the price we pay for having negative liberties. One does not always like how those liberties are used, but the alternatives are worse. If we were more rigidly to control how information is provided, how could we be assured that those doing the regulating would not do a more thorough job of manipulating available information than those they regulate? And again, how are we to square the circle of concentrations of power and wealth? Decreasing the scope of government tends to empower the rich, while doing away with concentrations of wealth tends to empower governments. To condemn both is understandable, but what is the solution?

As we can see, it is not clear how Orwell's socialist principles and liberal understandings can be made coherent. His appreciation of the dangers of concentrated power and criticism of a communal life do not sit easily alongside his criticisms of liberal capitalism, market inequalities, and his desire to see through socialist economic reforms. If all power corrupts, how can the problems associated with the various types of concentrations of power be avoided? Orwell is probably pointing to an anarchistic and syndicalist solution, wherein control over resources is vested in those who work in related sectors of the economy rather than in the state or private organizations. But such a scheme has never been successfully practiced. Might Orwell really be revealing to us the insuperable problems we face in attempting to keep our autonomy? It might not totally be the case that he counsels despair, but it does appear that he is pointing to a contradiction in our political lives that may be as important as the contradiction Zamyatin locates in human nature.

A final note has to do with Orwell's general attitude toward fanaticism and orthodoxy. It is to fanaticism that Orwell attributes many other problems. Accepting this conclusion should make us think deeply about our commitment to causes and leaders. Orwell argues that deep devotion creates much more harm than any good that might arise. Such single-minded dedication is not the solution to problems. It is not conducive to a true morality. It is not good for us intellectually or emotionally. It is ultimately corrosive of our ability to live autonomously. We should approach any organization, leader, or cause that demands high levels of commitment with extreme skepticism, if not downright aversion. We cannot let ourselves get caught up in, and subsequently lost in, the notion that it is right, good, uplifting, or moral to only be part of something larger than ourselves. If we are persuaded by Orwell's argument, we must accept the dictum that remaining a genuine human means retaining the necessary critical distance from any community that allows us to live autonomously as an individual.

To follow Orwell also means seeing poverty, class distinctions, and war as the products of elite manipulation powerfully aided by the desire for certainty and the other attributes of fanaticism. These conditions, he would argue, are not natural or inevitable. Their continued existence is explained by human factors, including the interests of the rich and powerful in perpetuating them. He would probably point to the authoritarian character of many contemporary religious and political movements as well as ubiquitous calls for complete deference to the state as productive of important social, economic, and political problems. Orwell wants us to avoid these problems and would probably hold that we currently are not doing enough to confront and undermine fanatical organizations. We are on a slippery slope, he would argue. We are too naïve in accepting elites' claims to interpret the world, to define morality, and to exercise power, with potentially devastating future results.

Notes

1   Abbott Gleason, Jack Goldsmith, and Martha C. Nussbaum, eds. *On Nineteen Eighty-Four: Orwell and Our Future* (New York: Princeton University Press, 2005).
2   Jean Bethke Elshtain "The Relationship between Political Language and Political Reality," *PS: Political Science and Politics*, Vol. 18, no. 1 (Winter 1985).
3   Abbott Gleason, "'Totalitarianism' in 1984," *Russian Review*, Vol. 43, no. 2 (April 1984).
4   Jennifer Roback, "The Economic Thought of George Orwell," *The American Economic Review*, Vol. 75, no. 2, Papers and Proceedings of the Ninety-Seventh Annual Meeting of the American Economic Association (May 1985).
5   Erika Gottleib, "The Demonic World of Oceania: The Mystical Adulation of the 'Sacred' Leader" in *George Orwell's 1984* (edited and introduced by Harold Bloom), Bloom's Modern Critical Interpretations, updated edn (Infobase Publishing, 2007).
6   George Kateb, "The Road to 1984," *Political Science Quarterly*, Vol. 81, no. 4 (December 1966).
7   Judith Shklar, "*Nineteen Eighty-Four*: Should Political Theory Care?" *Political Theory*, Vol. 13, no. 1 (February 1985).

8   See W. J. West *The Larger Evils. Nineteen Eighty-Four: The Truth behind the Satire* (Edinburgh: Canongate Press, 1992).

9   See *Down and Out in Paris and London* as well as any of his early essays on tramping and the poor.

10   For a discussion of the broad resemblance between Morris and Orwell in terms of their attachment to a kind of romantic anarchism, see Anna Vaninskaya, "Janus-Faced Fictions: Socialism as Utopia and Dystopia in William Morris and George Orwell," *Utopian Studies*, Vol. 14, no. 2 (2003).

11   Here I depart from Gleason's understanding in "'Totalitarianism' in 1984."

12   This is very close to the position Shklar took in "*Nineteen Eighty-Four*: Should Political Theory Care?"

13   There is a massive amount of literature on this phenomenon. For an early and fundamental discussion, see Jong Lee, "Rallying around the Flag: Foreign Policy Events and Presidential Popularity," *Presidential Studies Quarterly*, Vol. 7, no. 4 (1977); see also William Baker and John Oneal, "Patriotism or Opinion Leadership? The Nature and Origins of the 'Rally 'round the Flag' Effect," *Journal of Conflict Resolution*, Vol. 45, no. 5 (2001).

8

Conclusion

We have encountered a variety of ways of describing the human condition, conceptualizing an improved state, creating a more just and productive economy, and understanding the good life. We have also seen the various ways a hellish existence may emerge from current conditions. Some of the prescriptions and warnings have been prescient. We certainly are more likely to provide some goods and services communally than before. A consumer lifestyle is now general throughout the population. We have also experienced the perils of concentrated power, manipulations of nationalism in the context of wars, and an overall loss of privacy due to technological advances. But we have not embraced any of the utopian schemes, nor has the world as a whole descended to a dystopian condition.

The fact that we cannot treat these stories as predictions does not rob them of their relevance. The questions they raise about human nature, the good life, the best and worst human institutions, the causes of disorder, the place of material goods and material security, privacy, and freedom all continue to be of supreme interest to reflections on our political, social, and economic lives. In summing up what we can gain from these stories, I will engage in three activities. First, I will discuss more completely the similarities and differences of the main messages of these stories. Second, I will attend more closely to discussions about how the conditions described in these stories are said to come about. Third, I will isolate and discuss some of the important common themes we find in these stories and how those themes are relevant for us today.

Thinking about utopias and dystopias

Utopia and *Isle of Pines*

These stories appear to point in very different directions and demand different things of government. More sees problems as addressable by our community as a whole, mostly through governmental structures. It is the community that should supply the material security and moral structure that makes a good life possible. In particular, the community should provide food, clothing, housing, healthcare, and employment to its members, as well as discipline and oversight rather than leaving people to attain these on their own through the market and purely private moral contemplation. More assumes the community can and should plan the economy because he believes that experience makes it possible for us to understand the world thoroughly. Can we muster enough knowledge to plan our lives so comprehensively? Policy tendencies over the past few decades have moved in the opposite direction, adopting the neoliberal argument that government involvement in economic affairs should be minimized to allow markets to increase productivity and provide the rewards necessary to take the risks that result in productive and innovative economic activities. So now the emphasis is on the classically Smithian argument: responsibility for making economic decisions should be scattered across millions of people in the context of the market if we want rational decisions and the greatest productivity and efficiency. Can this position still be supported given the recent economic problems we have experienced, which many largely attribute to the operations of neoliberal approaches? Are decisions made by millions of people, or does the presence of large corporations, powerful political and media elites, and wealthy individuals mean that decisions are made by the few, as in Utopia, but in an unaccountable fashion?

In terms of particular policies, More suggests that we focus too much on punishment and not enough on material support and general supervision as ways of keeping order. We would live in a better ordered and generally more content society if we were to adopt his paternalistic government. He would also argue that we have enslaved ourselves to an economic system that does not make the wealthy happy and which impoverishes the unfortunate. We would be happier if we gave up some of our economic and moral freedom in exchange for the certainty, security, and equality that he suggests constitutes the good life. He holds that we work too hard and do not pay sufficient attention to our intellectual lives. We would be happier, better persons if we further curtailed our work week and traded our never-ending quest for better clothing, gadgets, cars, and houses for more leisure, and thus move even further than European countries have in balancing leisure against purely material measures of living standards.

One suspects that Neville would urge us to reject such propositions. He would probably advocate a view broadly similar to that of many social and economic conservatives who argue that the discipline of life itself is the better schooler of people than are governments and other blunt instruments of the collective. He appears agnostic with regard to our ability to understand the world thoroughly enough to plan, and is opposed to the proposition that we can change our environment artificially to deactivate harmful human impulses. He does not see increased leisure and economic security necessarily as good things. He certainly does not see it as government's job to make our lives as painless and worry-free as possible. He sees evil as more deeply entrenched than does More and would want to persuade us of the need to buttress the political and social institutions that act as external sources of discipline and focus government on order, virtue, and the support of civilization rather than the attempt endlessly to expand the economy.

In all, Neville is confident that an environment without challenges is disastrous for humans. Disorder, decay, savagery, and the loss of the good life comes when certainty and comfort color our lives. We should avoid creating such an environment artificially and insofar as we do live in a place where the standards of living are high and work is easy, adjust our governments accordingly. Should we accept these propositions? The first appears perfectly in accord with the laissez-faire, free market liberalism that has colored our perceptions of the world for the past quarter century. It urges us to view our existence as a struggle that cannot and should not be finally won, even if we perceive progress in terms of civilization and the physical transformation of the world. The second proposition is more alien, representing a different contextual understanding of politics than is now accepted. We tend to think of good government per se, not one whose form is dependent upon the types of contexts with which Neville is obsessed. But does he have a point? Should we think about government in more nuanced terms, adjusting it to take into account general living conditions? Might the fact that the United States and the West are relatively wealthy indicate that we should have a government that focuses on virtue and discipline?

Neville's more general understanding of the effects of material wealth and leisure also appears to rub against the contemporary assumption that a good life means continual material progress and ease and is made up of increasingly individual forays into life unencumbered by overt forms of discipline. We do, even if implicitly, idealize the good life as a perpetual vacation. Are we persuaded by this story that we are wrong? Are we pursuing an Isle of Pines to our ultimate peril, or is Neville simply a priggish spoilsport?

Looking Backward and *News from Nowhere*

We have here two very different utopias. One is based on the premise that people are primarily consumers of goods and leisure, the other on the understanding that people are primarily creative beings. One is based on extending the organizations and methods of industrialization into the future, while the other suggests that we should largely return to a preindustrial idyll. One sees people as content to participate in labor armies for 25 years with the prospect of early retirement, while the other holds that humans are too restless and desirous of variety to acquiesce to such arrangements. One argues for equal shares of a pool of value created through industrial means while the other follows More in abolishing all holders of value. One sees the change to a utopian future in terms of a quick intellectual shift, while the other fears that the transition will be long and bloody.

These differences are interesting because both are written in response to the same contexts and identify, for the most part, the same problems. Both are bothered by current working conditions and unequal distributions of wealth. Both see market economics as deeply problematic. Both see most people living in modern society as deeply unhappy and unfulfilled. Both attempt to reduce politics to uncomplicated matters, Bellamy to coordination and economic calculations, Morris to coordination and conflict management. Both attempt to eliminate laws. Both are deeply indebted to More's *Utopia* for their understanding of the ways in which environments influence human behavior, though both also depart in important ways from More's understanding.

Likewise, both make problematic assumptions, particularly in terms of economics. Bellamy does not elaborate sufficiently on the nature of the technological advances he assumes. His extrapolation of the use of telephones is interesting and may be more relevant now than 50 years ago, but what of the other parts of his vision? Are labor and capital so fungible that they can be directed hither and yon with the ease which Bellamy describes? Would enough people be willing to take on dirty and difficult work for short hours when easier work may be available? Would noneconomic incentives really spur people to do their best over the long run, or does such a system share enough characteristics of mobilizational systems that we would be confident that inhabitants would burn out over an extended period of time?

Unlike Bellamy's utopia, Morris includes material creativity as an inescapable part of the good life. As creative beings, Morris's humans could not be happy in Bellamy's utopia. They would not see themselves fulfilled by expressing their personalities by constructing patterns of consumption. They would reject both the labor armies and the proposition that real life starts when retirement begins. People need to work in order to fulfill themselves, not in the regimented contexts of labor armies, but individually or in the contexts of free cooperatives. Labor in this sense is too important for humans to have it confined to one segment of life or to have such outside forces as the state control it. Morris also assumes that a predominantly nontechnological economy can support the gracious and leisured life that the denizens of his future enjoy. Is that possible? Can a handicrafts and agricultural economy do more than provide the bulk of a population with an existence that is barely above that of subsistence? Without a plethora of labor-saving devices, can everyone enjoy large amounts of leisure? And would people really be willing, in the interest of creative labor and contributions to the general welfare, voluntarily to take on dirty and heavy tasks? We might be skeptical that such tasks fit with the life of easy and free wandering that Morris outlines.

The questions and proposals these stories provide us are of the utmost interest. Are we really creative beings or consumers? Will people be happy with equal but sufficient shares of wealth, or even happier with few but beautifully wrought things? Is it better to live under a military-like discipline for a few decades of life and then live in retirement from middle age, or to live a free and easy life of a wanderer from one's childhood? Is industrialization necessary for us to live well or is it a curse? Are humans naturally sociable and amenable to work, or do they need a variety of stimulants to work hard? Do we need a government that controls a centralized economy, or a rudimentary form of cooperation that leaves economic affairs to small, self-sufficient communities? Are "progress" and "modernization" the ways forward or do they represent false steps that we must retract, retracing our way to an earlier, simpler, and economically less complex way of life?

As such we must take the measure of Bellamy and Morris. In answering the questions as they do, what are they? Are they as they saw themselves, visionaries who reveal to us the way forward and thus act as prophets of a better world? Or are they silly cranks who in their conceit discard common sense and prescribe changes that would bring us infinitely more harm than good?

We and *Nineteen Eighty-Four*

Both these stories see dystopia coming ironically through the supposedly benevolent actions of leaders and parties who promise us happiness and security. However, *We* has affinities with *Isle of Pines* in casting doubt on the attainment of utopia itself by questioning the process of attaining a radically better world. *Nineteen Eighty-Four* is not dubious of the proposition of civilization providing better life; rather, it casts doubt on our ability to see that task through without succumbing to fanaticism. At first glance, we would expect Zamyatin to be less animated by a fear of progress than Orwell given his more radical Bolshevik history. Orwell's self-admitted "tory anarchism" would seem to put him in more sympathy with condemnations of radical change. Yet this is not quite right. Zamyatin's criticism of utopia is more fundamental than Orwell's. Zamyatin challenges the notion of progress in the form of civilization itself—this is what Soviet officials rightly saw as subversive in his writings. To grant his premise is to admit that the very foundations of the Soviet project, insofar as they are implicated in the Western understanding of civilization, are wrong-headed. Orwell does not target progress, but the fanatical pursuit of progress or any other goal. Orwell can share in the larger dystopian dismissal of cranks and enthusiasts[1] and suspicions of promises of heaven on earth, but not reject the possibility that fundamental change, if soberly and carefully conducted, could be beneficial and desirable. However, by locating the root of fanaticism in an innate desire for certainty, security, and safety, he also indicates that the specter of dystopia will always threaten us.

There are also other fundamental differences between these stories. Zamyatin sees the desire for progress as destructive of humans when it is conceptualized in terms of security and the domination of Nature. The mechanization of humans that he satirizes is not animated solely by a fascination with machinery, but extends further. As his description of the future shows, the City is meant to isolate humans from Nature and demonstrate how humans have conquered our physical environment by way of science and civilization. The price to be paid in his mind is enormous, with the medical procedure that ends the novel summing up his position. As a transformational process, it consists of the application of technology in that it is a *medical* (as opposed to a spiritual or intellectual) process applied to humans with the intent of improving them. To "improve" here means to reduce humans by stripping them of the attributes that make them act in arbitrary and irrational ways. What is removed is imagination and with it importantly the desire to experience anything other than a sterile, regulated, and uniform environment.

Zamyatin confronts us with a stark choice. We can continue to pursue progress as the application of technology and civilization in general to our lives. We gain a vacuous kind of happiness as we attain greater and greater physical comfort and security. We lose freedom, variety, texture, and the capacity to use our imaginations. Or, we can back away from technology and civilization. By doing so, our lives will probably be shorter, less comfortable and much coarser. What we gain is what we lose in a technologically advanced society—freedom, emotion, physical sensations, imagination, and the need to apply our bodies and minds to the utmost in order to survive (a theme that again appears to echo Neville's point, though here the villain is civilization, whereas Neville sees the loss of civilization as the evil condition). Is this right? Is there a choice to be made between civilization and freedom, between reason and happiness? If so, we are making a fundamental mistake in putting our faith in the frontiers of science and the wonders of technology. We would be better served, as Morris also would have it, to consider other conceptions of the good life that more comprehensively explore our character as humans. We should scale back on our pursuit of technology and cease thinking of the good life as one in which we are increasingly apart from human and physical Nature. Or are Zamyatin and Morris wrongheaded in their understanding of the effects of science, technology, and civilization on humans? Might we be able to have some important measures of both security and freedom, and freedom and happiness? Alternatively, if Zamyatin is right which alternative would and should we choose? He seems to plump for freedom. Should we do the same?

Orwell's concern is different. He is more amenable than Zamyatin to thinking about progress in the form of the mechanization of life (though he displays a strong nostalgia for unspoiled natural vistas), but sees the quest for progress in that or any other form as sharing with other quests certain vital dangers, namely those posed by fanaticism and dogmatism that end in the forced mobilization of the population. Progress is like any political or religious cause, including patriotism, in that it can be elevated to unquestioned orthodoxy. *Nineteen Eighty-Four* therefore does not present us with the tragic choice that *We* inflicts on us. There is a choice made at the end of the novel—to continue fighting Big

Brother or to give in—but Orwell does not see this as an actual moral choice. It is rather a matter of how much emotional and physical abuse one can endure before yielding. Orwell's larger point is not ambiguous. We must not mindlessly pursue certainty or yearn for a prophet of truth. This does not rule out progress and condemn us to a primitive existence. It also does not mean, contrary to some interpretations, that we should not look to the community for economic security. The problem is not the state in itself. Orwell is equally suspicious of churches, parties, classes, corporations, and any other organization that seeks total power. None of these entities are in themselves evil, nor are any immune from abuse. Each can inflict great harm when those who control them claim total mastery of the truth and demand total obedience, that is, when they claim to be bigger than the individuals that constitute them.

The problem for Orwell (and where it appears he becomes an apostle of despair) is that he sees the progressive road importantly blocked by prophets of truth who take power. They have at their disposal an arsenal of hard and soft instruments of domination. Orwell would warn us not just against full-fledged dictators, but also the trends he sees leading to the takeover of government and society by less obvious purveyors of fanaticism. We should be suspicious of anyone who distorts the past and plays with language, whether they be socialist, conservative, liberal, fascist, religious, or atheist. We should closely question those who argue for the necessity of war and probe their purposes. We should jealously defend our freedoms against agencies that purport to help us while doing nothing to empower us. We should react with skepticism to the echo boxes created by public intellectuals who take on the roles of talk show hosts, preachers, television personalities, entertainers, politicians, and masters of social media. We should resist our mobilization by the state. We should ask ourselves if inequality (of both power and income) is necessary to the production of the material wealth that makes the good life possible. We must guard our privacy, our energy, our free time, and our sexuality against all those who would use them for their own ends and ultimately to enslave us to a cause. We should be suspicious of those who wish to enforce a morality of any kind. We should be wary of calls to patriotism and war and be particularly vigilant during times of conflict and emergency. We must take particular care of history, language, rationality, and common sense, for he argues that the core of humans is their ability autonomously to judge events. How can we be responsible citizens without being able to make independent judgments?[2]

What does this mean in practice? Superficially, it means not just guarding the civil liberties that are part of the liberal tradition, but also remaining skeptical of all centers of power, whether private or public, in their attempts to control public discourse. Yet as we have seen, this is not as easy as it appears. The past, as Orwell himself has Winston acknowledge, has always been malleable. It was not Stalin or Hitler who first rewrote history as a conqueror. There appears no way to prevent it from happening, just as there is no way to prevent governments, corporations, or pundits from interpreting news to further their interests and politicians from spinning events in their favor. The other particular threats he identifies are also difficult to counter. Constitutions are not always potent bulwarks against threats to negative freedoms. Are there ways of preventing elites from going to war and using war to keep themselves in power? Peace movements almost never get traction; most often they are pushed aside by the forces of patriotism and fear. Can we question the need for inequalities? Yes we can, but it remains to be seen if Orwell is right that inequalities can be removed. Can we prevent a few people from gathering a preponderance of power and wealth into their hands? We have votes, but they can be manipulated, miscounted, and discarded. Can we attempt to see through people who set themselves up as all-powerful fonts of truth? We can try ourselves, but will everybody want to do so?

More fundamentally, Orwell points to the emotional roots of the quest for certainty as the problem. If, as Orwell seems to hold, those roots are caught up with the hardwired desire for safety and protection and find a benign expression in the desire to belong to a community and set up a state, how can we escape the circumstances that breed and encourage fanaticism? It appears that the temptation will always be with us. It pervades everything—civilization, religion, socialism, liberalism, conservatism, the quest for economic growth, even the ideal of equality. All can ultimately be implicated. If so, even if Orwell does not present us with the tragic choice Zamyatin supplies, are we not still trapped in the picture of the future Orwell paints for us? Can we ever escape the urge to give in to the certainty and security that comes from vesting our judgment and identity with an all-powerful, all-knowing, and infallible leader?

Perhaps we are best served by paying special heed to Orwell's warning about orthodoxy. Skepticism is a healthy thing to breed if we do not allow it to take us over entirely. How to encourage skepticism? That is the problem. Skepticism is a difficult thing to teach, particularly if Orwell is right that we crave certainty. Furthermore, too much skepticism turns into a corrosive cynicism. We should want our fellow citizens to believe in something. Without some belief, we are left with nothing but a destructive nihilism. Everything falls apart; the center does not hold. Believing in something is what gives people a sense of themselves. So how can we balance skepticism with belief without straying into either cynicism or fanaticism? That appears to be the most important and difficult problem that Orwell highlights.

Origins, transformations, leadership, and environments

There is disagreement over the rise of utopias and dystopias. Some see one or the other emerging directly out of conventional society. Others see them coming about because of radical changes. In general, utopian and dystopian societies are said to arise in one of three ways. Either a founder (either real or fictional) is responsible for creating the society. Or there is a series of changes that occur over time that produce the new society. Or a cataclysm destroys the old society and a new one emerges. Below I survey these discussions and attempt to make sense of them in contemporary terms.

Founders and leaders

Utopia is the clearest example of the role of a founder and transformational leader. King Utopus is said to have created Utopia socially, politically, and even physically. In the realm of dystopias, the Party holds that Big Brother founded Airstrip One, but we know from Winston's memory that this was not the case. The Benefactor is also something of a founding figure for Zamyatin's dystopia and, as with Big Brother, continues in the role of extraordinary leader, ultimate decisionmaker (at least publicly), and the focus of community identity and solidarity.

   This discussion raises the question of faith in leaders, particularly those who are transformational and charismatic. Should we look for such leaders? Can individuals have the answers to the problems we face? Are there people so extraordinary that they can, and should, mold society for us? Western culture in general is ambivalent with regard to founders. Moses, Romulus, and Lycurgus are credited with playing large and positive roles in much thinking about politics, but Napoleon, Stalin, and Hitler are also held up as examples of the dangers of putting large powers in the hands of individuals. American culture is in one sense friendly toward the concept of the founder and other extraordinary leaders given the elevated stature the leaders of the Revolution are accorded. Yet many strains of political culture also resist the argument that human rationality is sufficient to grasp the complex workings of economics and society such that one person's plan should be accepted as a blueprint for change. Radical change is consigned to the past, with the Revolution designated, from both a practical and moral standpoint, with being sufficient for our purposes. To follow a leader who would transform our institutions and environment again is often seen as abandoning that legacy, turning our backs on our identity and risking disaster.

Discussions of founders and transformational leaders seek to place emphasis on the benign, or malign, influences of isolated geniuses. The good life or its opposite comes out of the minds of individuals who are either lauded or condemned. In the case of utopias, founders are the link between the problems of conventional society and the goodness of the better society. They are the means by which the perfect arises out of what is radically imperfect. In dystopian writings, the figure of the founder is condemned for his or her hubris or evil intent. To think that one can understand humans and have the audacity to change cherished institutions and traditions in the mold of one's own mind is to run against the collective learning process, conceptualized in Orwell's mind in the form of common sense. Or it is to play a grand trick on the rest of one's community by appearing to propose solutions to central problems while actually concentrating power and wealth in one's own hands.

Utopias and dystopias therefore display both sides of the question of faith in founders. Dystopias embrace an almost democratic distrust and disbelief in extraordinary leaders. They reject both the claim to extraordinary character they are said to embody and the faith necessary to allow them to mold society. For dystopians, the risk in believing in a founder is both too great and not well considered. Not only is the prospect of serious abuses of power in play, but also the very real possibility that a founder, even if benign, is seriously mistaken in his or her understanding of the world. Utopians tend to take the figure of founders more seriously. Utopias in general hold that the world, including the humans who inhabit it, can be understood comprehensively. Hence the concept that a person could do so is not alien to the utopian mentality. Perhaps more troubling is the faith some would place in such persons. Knowledge is not always accompanied by moral rectitude, as dystopians argue at great length. In the end, as we noted with regard to Orwell's skepticism, faith in an extraordinary leader means a suspension of disbelief, and it is up to us whether we are willing to make such a suspension and to what degree we should suspend our critical faculties.

Because even utopia cannot be perfect, and founders assuredly also cannot be, does that mean we discard both concepts? Or do we, in a flip of the old pragmatic saw, refuse to see the perfect as the enemy of the good and follow a potential founder despite the inevitable moral and intellectual blemishes we will detect?

Gradualism and environments

Gradualism marks *Looking Backward* in that while there is a break in thinking, the transition takes place over a period of time, it is the product of a general realization that itself is produced by a long-term economic process, and it is nonviolent. The degeneration that marks the community in the *Isle of Pines* is a gradual transformation, this time wrought by particular conditions. Orwell's Oceania is also the product of a series of events that gradually transform it from a liberal to a dystopian society. These events, particularly the ongoing wars, serve to recruit people into fanaticism. In focusing on gradualism, these authors point to the weight and direction of history, economic forces, environments, and the inability of humans as individuals to control human fate. The good life, or the dystopian life, is something that is difficult if not impossible to resist. There is no single tipping point, no single individual, or any particular condition we can target. If we are to resist, we must do so broadly and continuously rather than narrowly and sporadically. If we welcome the change, there is not much we can do to hasten the process.

Gradualism raises the question of the direction of history, whether on the large scale or in terms of a particular community. Is there a direction, and if there is, where will it take us? We might argue that both utopians and dystopians are too confident of their ability to read out the direction of history, even in the short term. While we may be able to explain events after the fact, there may be no coherent linkages of events and conditions that would allow us to predict what will happen. More important is reliance upon history to move us in a particular direction. There is as much faith deployed in utopian gradualism as there is in a utopian founding. Are we satisfied with leaving the resolutions of our problems to the impersonal forces of history? Conversely, are we so taken with the inevitability of tragedy that we are willing to give up on the prospect of any sort of progress?

Gradualism, as we see, also raises the issue of agency. What types of forces are responsible for changes and what can humans do to intervene in the course of events? Many strands of Western political cultural are voluntarist, embracing the notion that humans make and therefore can change their own history. It is not impersonal forces or tendencies, but human will and energy that determine the nature of our communities. Likewise, those cultural strands tend to discount the effects of environments on humans, holding that human nature remains the same no matter the contexts in which individuals or communities live, meaning that both those entities can rise above circumstances to construct themselves rather than being constructed from the outside. Indeed, such views must allow for such self-construction because they place moral responsibility on individuals and must assume that individuals possess autonomy in order to justify such placement.

Rejecting the potential of gradualism means abandoning the belief in the efficacy of history and environments to generate change. It would be with relief that we could turn to the judgment that dystopia does not inevitably creep up on us, but also equally a psychological blow to accept that history and environments do not act as does the classical conception of markets, leading us firmly to a better place through some social and political equivalent of an invisible hand.

Cataclysm

The societies portrayed in *News from Nowhere* and *We* are said to arise out of cataclysmic events. Both authors point to long-term, terrifying wars that serve to depopulate the region, if not the planet. This clears the ground of prior social and intellectual structures. For Morris, the war is an unfortunate but cleansing event that finally forces humans to focus on the correct level of civilization and economic development. For Zamyatin, conflict reinforces the human desire for security and pushes out the competing desire for freedom, leaving humans open to the dehumanizing effects of technology and unfettered rationalism.

In these stories, cataclysmic events act in the same ways as founders—bridging the seeming disconnect between conventional society and utopia or dystopia. But in cases of both utopia and dystopia, the message seems to be that the rise of such societies is not around the corner and are, in that sense, extraordinary. This seems a bit puzzling in the case of Zamyatin, for why warn against something that may never arise except for some unfortunate and rare series of events? Yet, perhaps Zamyatin does not buy the argument that a cataclysmic war has a low likelihood of occurring. Given his understanding of the innate desires for security and freedom, the conflict he sees residing within individuals may easily and inevitably externalize itself in the form of overt, physical conflicts.

For Morris, the puzzle is more resilient, as it does not appear that he wishes for a cataclysm, yet is unsure whether the needed changes can be made in its absence. There is also the possibility in his landscape that should a cataclysm occur, utopian changes would not.

Thinking a bit less largely, the concept of an extraordinary event raises the question of what we should do when a crisis occurs. One response is to take advantage of a crisis to enact necessary changes. But that course presumes we know which changes to enact; if we are mistaken, we create the very scenario we wish to avoid. Moreover, there is a need to guard against those who would take advantage of such circumstances to push forward agendas that would narrowly benefit themselves. Wars, emergencies, natural disasters, and similar events leave the population vulnerable to manipulation, calls for patriotic sacrifice, and nationalistic references of the lowest sort that equip leaders with the power to alter permanently power relationships in their favor. This is partly what Orwell appears to have warned against.

It is always difficult for us to foresee what will happen during crises, but perhaps it would be a good exercise to think through such events before they occur. As a community, what should we do? How do we, and should we, defend the norms (laws, rules, constitutional rights, and guarantees) that we deem so important during ordinary times? When leaders argue, with the force of events and conditions behind them, that certain actions must be taken for the community to survive, actions that violate those norms, what should we do? Perhaps what we need is a conversation that sets out what types of actions are acceptable, beyond which we agree that the community as we know it would not survive in its true form, given the violence such actions would inflict upon the nature of the community itself.

Returning to a larger understanding, if cataclysm is an extraordinary event, perhaps we should not worry about it. Whether for long-term good or ill, it probably will not occur. If it does occur, then the imperative is to see that good things follow rather than worse. Can good come of widespread tragedy? Is such a wiping clean of the slate conducive to radical reform, or will it merely plunge us further into an abyss by making us willing enablers of dystopian schemers? And if utopia would arrive on the heels of such a catastrophe, would we be capable of enjoying the good life, knowing that it comes with the price of a period of death, destruction, and unbearable misery? Even more to the point, is it moral to wish for or facilitate a cataclysm in the hope (or even the certainty) that a much better life would result for the survivors? What price are we willing to pay for utopia?

Themes

We can compare utopias and dystopias both among themselves and between the two genres in terms of the propositions they offer us. The utopias we have examined here provide us with the following propositions:

	Human nature	Problems	Good life	Key changes
Utopia	Hardwired and programmable; Act greedily when faced with scarcity or unequal distributions of wealth	Inequality, poverty, immorality Disorder	Material security, social solidarity, leisure	Planning, no private property or money, responsible government, training, simplicity
Looking Backward	Hardwired and programmable consumers respond to nonmaterial incentives	Inequality, poverty, conflict, psychological discomfort	Free, equal and secure consumption, leisure	Planning, no private property, equal, limited shares, mobilization of labor, nonmaterial incentives to work
News from Nowhere	Hardwired productive and social beings	Inequality, pollution, unsatisfying labor	Free productive labor	De-industrialization, de-urbanization, consensus politics on the small-scale simplicity

Similarly for dystopias, we find the following propositions:

	Humans	Problems	Manifestation	Resulting loss of humanity
Isle of Pines	Require challenges to develop discipline	Provision of all needs	Loss of civilization, culture, science, morality	Live like animals— unconstrained sex and violence
We	Torn by innate desires for freedom and security	Quest for security as conquest of inner and physical nature	Loss of imagination and emotions	Live like machines
Nineteen Eighty-Four	Process information and desire certainty	Quest for security in form of certainty	Loss of memory, rationality, language	Lose autonomy and live as fanatics

These propositions raise a substantial number of questions beyond those we have already addressed, particularly those pertaining to dystopias and the contrast between utopias and dystopias. First, what does it mean to live in a dystopian fashion? What is it that marks a radically bad way of life? Note that while utopias are characterized by material security, it is not necessarily the case that dystopias are characterized by the opposite. Only *Nineteen Eighty-Four* marks dystopia with widespread poverty. Rather, it is generally something deeper in humans that is portrayed as under threat—our ability to think, to reason, to live a civilized life, to experience all our emotions, or to live autonomously in terms of our bodies and minds.

Another question has to do with the larger point dystopias raise. Which is the worst life? Is it to lose our ability to reason independently or to lose our ability to experience the human condition? Is to live as a fanatic worse than living as a machine or as an animal? What would be the more horrible outcome, to lose our civilization and technology and live as do those on the Isle of Pines, or to lose our humanity because of civilization and technology and live in the One State? Or is it to live a life of poverty, squalor, and constant mobilization? I think many people would argue that life on the Isle of Pines would be preferable to the others. To lose civilization is probably better than losing control of our internal selves; moreover, life on the former island appears more generally pleasant than the lockstep society of the One State and the constant mobilization and poverty of Airstrip One. If this were the case, what does this say about ourselves? Do we really hanker after a permanent vacation no matter the loss of civilization, culture, and science it may entail?

What of the risks that attend trying to attain the utopian good life? Is it worth the effort to gain the peaceful inner self as portrayed by More, Bellamy, and Morris if we risk the colonized inner self as portrayed by Zamyatin and Orwell? Is the material security that More and Bellamy offer so valuable that we would accept the possibility that we will end up living as Neville or Zamyatin portray? Are we willing to make the major changes demanded by Morris, discarding our technology and moving backward to a prior way of life? Is the freedom to work with our hands and wander about worth that effort? Are we so afraid of living on the Isle of Pines that we are willing to risk finding ourselves under a Big Brother or a Benefactor? Risks are tricky things to calculate because there is risk in *not* attempting to engage in change and reform, as More and the other utopians would surely remind us. The project of thinking about and acting on utopia isn't dreaming about a fairy land of perfection; it is about working through and resolving contemporary problems which if left unresolved may soon engulf us, just as the dystopians suggest.

Of more immediate concern is the question of power. If utopia is importantly about the correct use of power and dystopia about its abuse, what is the correct use and what is the worst abuse? Morris and to some degree More speak of decentralizing power; Bellamy centralizes political and economic power while separating them from material gains and social status. Are these prescriptions useful? Does power by itself corrupt, or must it be accompanied by other factors before it becomes dangerous? Meanwhile, the dystopians differ in the ways in which people with power abuse it, finding that they will concentrate on different targets. Orwell and Zamyatin identify freedoms as targets, but also go deeper to hold that power will attack rationality, emotions, memory, and imagination. Neville, the outlier, sees the disintegration of power as a problem. Which of these is the more persuasive? If we wish to avoid the loss of autonomy and the good life, which type of attack should we fear most, both in terms of the loss of something central and in terms of which kind of attack would be most conducive to an agent's capacity to control and abuse us? Or is it the loss of power and the disintegration of the state and the breakdown of society, which Neville identifies, that should give us most reason for concern?

In addition to the connections raised by the preceding questions and the question of origins, there are also a number of larger connections in these stories that serve to unite internally parts of the utopian and dystopian genres. These connections sometimes also cut across genres. These produce useful questions for our consideration, not only because these are intrinsically interesting commonalities, but also because their reoccurrence across stories signals that they are topics that commonly resonate among people who are rethinking politics.

The past as a model for a better future

As we noted, not all utopias are future-oriented. Both *Utopia* and *News from Nowhere*, as well as *We*, find in the past important clues to a better life. Have we lost something essential in constantly moving forward through social innovations and improved technology? As we become more urbanized, individuated, and technologically sophisticated, do we become less human or perhaps more pertinently, less happy? Are the more communally oriented social forms of the past more conducive to providing the good life for everyone? These questions are also raised in *Nineteen Eighty-Four*.

Moreover, there is a general theme of history that runs through some of these stories, though not always consistently. Orwell is consumed with the need to preserve history as an objective record of the past, as is, to some degree, Zamyatin. For them history, memory, and the past provide important resources for the full development of humanity. Bellamy also appears to have history in mind, as his utopians are aware of history as the old days, just as are some of the inhabitants of Morris's future, particularly Ellen. What role should history play? Is it a storehouse of data, relevant to understanding the human condition? Does it contain useful practices and structures that have been lost and we should attempt to regain? Or is it a dead hand that stifles innovation and would condemn us to repeat our mistakes should we be so foolish as to consult it?

The place of greed and money

In general, the utopian stories argue that while material security is important, greed does not deeply characterize humans. Greed is either something that is stimulated by outside forces (More, Bellamy), or is an artificial accretion (Morris). Several conclusions can be drawn from this assumption if we were to accept it. People do not need lots of material goods, though material security is important. People will not need money as a rationing device. People do not need money as a spur to hard work. We might not need the productive power of capitalism and industrialization and, therefore, also need not pay the price of those systems, including inequalities, pollution, boom and bust cycles, the need to export goods, and the need to accumulate capital.

Is this the case? Can we assume that people are not naturally greedy and can be satisfied with fewer goods that are either beautiful, as Morris argues, or utilitarian, as More holds? Will people be content with an equal but limited portion of credit they can use in a variety of ways, as Bellamy argues? We tend to assume that humans are natural consumers and would be deeply unhappy without a high and ever-increasing standard of living. If that is wrong, as these authors hold, then other possibilities arise. We can make people happy in ways other than by providing them with goods. Work may be a greater source of happiness than we think, as might leisure. Security may be more highly prized than we realize. A limited amount of choice among goods and lifestyles may be sufficient. Inner peace and the ability to deal with the tragedies of life may be more important. The freedom to choose our work and wander about freely may make us happier. But if these authors are wrong, then their prescriptions would backfire spectacularly. Rather than seeing a life with fewer goods, an emphasis on material security and the creativity of labor as good and fulfilling, humans may see it as dystopian.

Crime as a sickness

Conceptualizing crime is important. *Looking Backward* and to some degree *News from Nowhere* point to organic causes of unsocial behavior and to the paradigm of medicine and cures as the answer. Can we profitably use this paradigm? Are people who ignore or disregard laws and social norms "ill" in some recognizable fashion? Will the use of this paradigm lead to a less violent and happier society, or will it end with the situation depicted in *We* and *Nineteen Eighty-Four*, where the state uses this definition of disorder to reach inside the minds of its citizens to impose a strict conformity?

More is different, in that he attributes crime mostly to social factors, but also cannot escape the conclusion that some people will be disorderly because they lack the will to be orderly. This does not undermine his main argument that crime can be radically reduced by changing social circumstances, but it does not lead him to the medical paradigm. Is this right? More would argue that the large number of people we imprison is a sign that we have largely failed to fulfill our social responsibilities. Is this right? Is crime really more a measure of social rather than individual dysfunctionality?

Note also that *Isle of Pines* attributes crime to particular factors that are not necessarily widely accepted. Neville argues that humans lack self-control and are easily led to abuse otherwise good things. A focused state, culture, civilization, and/or external challenges are necessary to rein them in. Orwell sees the powerful and rich, those who abuse the poor and the powerless, as the real criminals and not those who must steal or otherwise flout conventional rules to survive.

The powers of government

It is not just the dystopias that raise the topic of power. *News from Nowhere* also condemns the growing power of governments, while *Utopia* does the same in terms of central and irresponsible governments. However, in other ways *Utopia* as well as *Looking Backward* invest more powers with and divert more responsibilities to governmental structures than is now the case.

These contradictory messages urge us to think about power in more nuanced terms—power over *what* appears to be the more pertinent question than *how much* power. One aspect of such a question has to do with the state's participation in social construction. To what degree should the state be in the business of social construction? If a significant portion of the population, by being socially constructed, become more settled and exhibit more self-control, should we accept such a mission on the part of the state? To what extent should we require people to be constructed by the state as an outside force? We force people to be orderly; to which other goals can we rightly use collective instruments of force and punishment, and to what degree is it useful and morally defensible to connect social construction with order?

Likewise, there is a strong, though more conventional, contrast between *Isle of Pines* and *News from Nowhere* in terms of social construction. Where the latter assumes so many resources in people that government becomes small-scale exercises in local coordination, the former sees people as so empty that government must play a strong role alongside culture and physical environment to keep people in line. Do we really need a strong state to help check the ravening forces of human appetites, or do states merely perpetuate themselves by their exercises of authority?

The elimination of politics

Utopia, Looking Backward, and *News from Nowhere* look forward to the transformation of politics into a technical science. Factions and fundamental policy differences among citizens will disappear, in part because differences of interest will also vanish and in part because reason and pragmatism will prevail. Thus the nature of organizational work will change alongside economic changes. This is clearest in *Looking Backward* and *News from Nowhere.* It is also the case that politics will be eliminated in several of these understandings because organizational work will be done by specialists and experts. Of course, the argument that rule by experts will be benign also depends on the proposition that differences of interests will be eliminated, leaving behind only common interests and a common good that can be grasped and furthered best by people who possess relevant knowledge. The ultimate model here is Plato's *Republic.*

The dystopian stories cast doubt on this proposition. *Nineteen Eighty-Four* makes this argument the most directly by creating masterful "expert" figures who are said to rule benignly in the common interest, but who really exercise power in the interests of the narrow ruling elite. Its message is that we should view with suspicion those who pose as experts, messiahs, or any other type of person who makes a claim to a higher understanding and knowledge. It also cautions us against claims that politics can be eliminated in the name of technical knowledge or a higher spirit. Both, Orwell would argue, are cloaks for the exercise of the most brutal form of power politics, for we can never rid ourselves of the issues that informs politics.

The role of technology and industrialization

Does technology serve us well? Is it our servant or our master? Does it, as *News from Nowhere* argues, poison us and spoil the natural landscape that provides us aesthetic stimulation and resources necessary for our bodily health? If all work was performed with the aid of machines, would this be good? Morris thinks not. Work is what fulfills humans.

We views the danger differently. Zamyatin does not argue that technology spoils the natural environment, but that it cuts us off from that environment. We are not sick because of technology; we become tools because of technology. Zamyatin is also much less optimistic about possible solutions to the problem. Where Morris sees the elimination of most technology as revealing a better way of life complete with fulfilling work, culture, and aesthetic value, Zamyatin predicts that such a move backward would result in a much rougher and physically dangerous way of life. We cannot be fully human and live the life of carefree labor and sophistication of which Morris dreams.

Bellamy and Neville view technology much more benignly than do Morris or Zamyatin. Both see technology as increasing productivity and making possible a better material life. Here the watchword is the careful use of technology. All believe humans can, if cognizant of the need, remain masters of technology and would view the attempt to strip humans of technology based on the dangers it represents as a simple-minded and perverse response to the challenge and potential of technological innovation. Bellamy is probably the more enthusiastic, as his future society depends upon increased mechanization, while Neville sees the use of technology to order society and Nature as a sign of progress and civilization.

Can we do without some of our technology? Given that technology is also associated with energy consumption and pollution, is it a good thing to move constantly forward on the technological front? Given the increasingly unhealthy because sedentary condition of modern humans, should we be seeking yet more labor-saving devices? Should government fund technological innovation, or should it be more active in seeking ways of living that are less dependent upon technology? Or is technology the way out of many of our problems, including those dealing with energy and the environment?

The virtues of simplicity

Two of the utopias discussed here, *Utopia* and *News from Nowhere,* reject the view that utopia implies mindless consumption. While each is insistent that the good life described provides a sufficiency of material goods, they do not emphasize the quantity of goods. *Utopia* leads the way in insisting on the plainness of goods and the simplicity of the lives people follow. That does not mean that there is not a kind of richness described there, most notably in the form of culture and even in the quality of goods, but there is absent the complications of modern life and the push for increasingly higher standards of living built around the accumulation of material things. Richness of life is attained by stripping it of superfluous concerns and of the attempt to clutter it with too much material debris. The others also speak of high-quality goods, the need to look for the good life in more than material possessions, and the relief that comes from living a less complicated life.

Looking Backward along with *Nineteen Eighty-Four* provides the counterarguments. The first does define the good life in terms of a high standard of living, though even it insists on limits. Everyone cannot have the best and most of everything. Yet the emphasis is on everyone living a moderately affluent life, a life that importantly includes consumption as well as leisure. Orwell meanwhile criticizes the concept of state-sponsored asceticism (even if he himself had ascetic tendencies). To leave citizens in conditions in which they do not always have enough goods, or high-quality goods, not only robs them of the opportunity to live the good life, but also limits their intellectual horizons, exhausts them physically and leaves them vulnerable for recruitment into state-sponsored fanaticism. The cult of simplicity is really a way for political elites to keep ordinary citizens under their pampered heel.

In which direction should we turn? The central aim of modern economics, as well as of the modern state, has been the quest for an ever-increasing standard of living. Economies must continually expand and popular consumption must underpin that expansion. As we increasingly approach the limits of the natural resources we have available to us, can we afford to retain this understanding? If not, we face several tasks. One is to redefine the concept of the good life to de-emphasize standards of living and material goods in general. This may entail the substitution of any number of other goods: culture, security, communal solidarity, the joy of creative work, leisure, choice, and inner development are put forward in these works as possibilities. This substitution may be more difficult than it appears. It may not be the case that our hardwired desire for goods can be shut off, controlled, or otherwise neutralized in the ways that More describes. We may find evidence of this in the epidemic of obesity to be found in highly developed states. Despite a general sufficiency of food, human instincts, and psychology remain rooted in the primitive state in which the next meal is in doubt and the dictum that caloric intake is to be maximized reigns supreme. The same very well may be true of material goods and standards of living in general.

The second task would be to reconfigure government. One of the projects of current governments is to build strength through the acquisition of those factors that result in the creation of material goods in the form of capital, raw materials, and human resources. Members of governments have incentives to do this because the more materially prosperous the nation, the more power they wield. Can we reprogram leaders to avoid such measures or create environments, as Bellamy and More describe, that will remove such incentives? Or are we stuck with the reality that leaders will always find advantage in promising a better material life in the short term, even if we were to understand rationally that such a life is harmful to us in the long run?

The advantages of small scales

Both utopian and the dystopian stories can agree here. Utopia and the society described in *News from Nowhere* are built on the small scale, not only because utopian techniques seem to work better on such a scale, but also because the small appeals to them as a better way of life. For More and to some degree Morris, the good life has importantly to do with interactions among familiar people who build bonds of trust and goodwill among themselves. The benefits of the small scale for these authors also entails the ability to do without the organizational structures necessary to coordinate and manage large groups. For Morris, removing such structures lifts a burden from society not only in terms of costs, but also for relationships. Bureaucracies and large organizations must be fed to survive. They have their own separate and functionally necessary culture. That culture emphasizes objective routines that treat everyone in a manner suited to the best interests of bureaucracies. And they reach into ordinary society to complicate ordinary face-to-face relationships. More and Morris would reject such routines as detracting from the good life.

We and *Nineteen Eighty-Four* identify the same theme from the opposite direction. In these dystopias, large societies simultaneously atomize families and dominate individuals. They substitute the individuated face-to-face relationships enjoyed by members of utopias with a forced devotion to the state and uniformly flattened and utilitarian relationships with everyone else. Large-scale societies here breed fear and ultimately dehumanize their citizens through their size, the necessary ways they must structure life in order to function and by the imperial takeover of inner lives.

Having gone down the road of urbanization and nationalism, it may not be possible to pull back to the small-scale living that utopians desire. Moreover, increases in population make the large scale increasingly necessary and the free space to decentralize increasingly scarce. The attempt to implement a small-scale solution may lead us to absurdities. Yet it is undoubtedly true that we pay a steep price in time, relationships, contact with Nature, pollution, and probably overall health for our large-scale civilization. Is there some way of capturing the benefits of small-scale living even within the confines of the large communities and structures that seem an inevitable part of modernity?

Closing thoughts

We began with the proposition that we should understand our own foundational assumptions in order to confront current events and the increasing obsolescence of current ways of thinking. These stories present us with a wealth of ideas by which to probe our assumptions and go about rethinking what we want from society, economics, and government. In particular, they point to clusters of questions that should be part of every person's self-reflection:

What are humans? Are they mostly hardwired or programmable? What is their hardwiring? Will they change behavior through changes in environments, or must they be trained differently to change? Can we eliminate greed, jealousy, competition, envy, violence, and negative emotions? Or should we work around them? Is the attempt to eliminate them dangerous? To what ends should we go to eliminate disorder? How far have we already gone? In general, should we construct citizens or allow them to construct themselves?

What kinds of political institutions should we create? Should we decentralize power? Should we centralize planning powers in official hands? What types of powers in general should we give community or the government? Are certain goals or policies dangerous? What leads to abuses of power?

What kind of economic system should we embrace? Should we retain or rid ourselves of money? What types of incentives to work hard are effective? Is industrialization good or bad? Should we embrace egalitarian principles in terms of the distribution of goods? Should everyone be forced to work? Should we value leisure as much as we do the creation of material goods? Is material security a good thing for individuals or for societies?

What are the sources of disorder? Are people naturally disorderly, or are they disorderly because their environment disorders them, or forces them to be disorderly to survive? Does property create disorder? How should we deal with disorder and does the fact that we now punish a significant portion of our population for being disorderly in accepted terms indicate that something is wrong with contemporary society?

What is the nature of the good life? Does it lie in choice or certainty? Do we need lots of material goods to live a good life? Might a simple life also be a good life for everyone? Is attention to the inside or the outside of our persons more important? Is the good life solitary and individual or is it communal? Is civilization part of the good life, or as an artificial way of being does it detract from the good life? Are different stages of civilization more conducive to a good life than are others? Is material security an essential part of the good life, or is it a threat to the good life?

Finally, what constitutes the bad life we wish to avoid? What should we fear most? Is it violence and the breakdown of order? Is it material scarcity and the prospect of a pinched and impoverished existence? Is it a tyranny that binds us so that we have no freedom of choice or movement? Is it a society and government that controls our inner as well as outer lives? Is it the loss of social solidarity? Is it the loss of civilization? Is it too much civilization, or too much industrialization?

My hope is that the preceding discussions can sharpen our attention to these questions and make them appear less academic and abstract. That is the point of these stories. They converse with us with regard to important matters of political philosophy by trying to bring to life the operation of institutions and the lives, actions, hopes, and fears of people. They may be fictitious and the places they describe "nowhere," but they bring to us very real concerns and questions that pertain to us here and now.

Notes

1 As he demonstrates in a rant against contemporary English radicals in the second half of *The Road to Wigan Pier*.

2 For those who have read "Politics and the English Language," this is Orwell's point. He is not just a grammar fanatic or an expositor of clear writing. He thinks that simple, elegant writing reflects and promotes common sense and rationality. We should view with suspicion those who would clutter the language with difficult words and complex compositions, for it is likely that they are attempting to distort language to gain power.

Bibliography and Further Reading

Aginsk, F. "Zamyatin's Novel *We*, in the Context of Works and Ideas of the Proletkult," *Canadian-American Slavic Studies*, 45:3–4 (2011), pp. 367–389.

Aldridge, A. "Polygamy in Early Fiction: Henry Neville and Denis Veiras," *PMLA*, 65:4 (June 1950), pp. 464–472.

Amey, M. "Living under the Bell Jar: Surveillance and Resistance in Yevgeny Zamyatin's *We*," *Critical Survey*, 17:1 (2005), pp. 22–39.

Appelbaum, R. *Literature and Utopian Politics in Seventeenth-Century England*. New York: Cambridge University Press (April 8, 2002).

Auerbach, J. "'The Nation Organized': Utopian Impotence in Edward Bellamy's Looking Backward," *American Literary History*, 6:1 (Spring 1994), pp. 24–47.

Baker, W. and J. Oneal. "Patriotism or Opinion Leadership? The Nature and Origins of the 'Rally 'round the Flag' Effect," *Journal of Conflict Resolution*, 45:5 (2001), pp. 661–687.

Baker-Smith, D. *More's Utopia*. Toronto: University of Toronto Press, 2000.

—. "Reading Utopia," in G. M. Logan (ed.), *The Cambridge Companion to Thomas More*. Cambridge: Cambridge University Press, 2011, pp. 141–167.

Beilharz, P. "Looking Back: Marx and Bellamy," *The European Legacy*, 9:5 (2004), pp. 597–604.

Bevington, D. "The Dialogue in 'Utopia': Two Sides to the Question," *Studies in Philology*, 58:3 (July 1961), pp. 496–509.

Bloomfield, P. *William Morris*. London: A. Barker Ltd, 1978(1934).

Boesky, A. *Founding Fictions: Utopias in Early Modern England*. Athens: University of Georgia Press, 1996.

—. "Nation, Miscegenation: Membering Utopia in Henry Neville's *The Isle of Pines*," *Texas Studies in Literature*, 37:2 (1995), pp. 165–184.

Borenstein, E. "The Plural Self: Zamjatin's *We* and the Logic of Synecdoche," *The Slavic and East European Journal*, 40:4 (Winter 1996), pp. 667–683.

Bostaph, S. "Deepening the Irony of *Utopia*: An Economic Perspective," *History of Political Economy* 42:2 (2010), pp. 361–382.

Bowker, G. *Inside George Orwell: A Biography*. New York: Palgrave Macmillan, 2003.

Bradshaw, B. "More on Utopia," *The Historical Journal*, 2:1 (1981) pp. 1–27.

Bruce, S. "*Introduction*," in S. Bruce, ed., *Three Early Modern Utopias*. New York: Oxford University Press, 1999, pp. ix–xlii.

Carden, P. "Utopia and Anti-utopia: Aleksei Gastev and Evgeny Zamyatin," *Russian Review*, 46:1 (January 1987), pp. 1–18.

Chang, H. "Zamyatin's *We*: A Reassessment," *Philosophy, Literature and History* (May 2003), pp. 233–250.

Claeys, G. "Industrialism and Hedonism in Orwell's Literary and Political Development," *Albion: A Quarterly Journal Concerned with British Studies*, 18:2 (Summer 1986), pp. 219–245.

—. "News from Somewhere: Enhanced Sociability and the Composite Definition of Utopia and Dystopia," *History*, 98 (2013), pp. 145–173.

Cooke, B. *Human Nature in Utopia: Zamyatin's We. Studies in Literature and Theory*. Evanston: Northwestern University Press, 2002.

Cotton, W. "Five-fold Crisis in Utopia: A Foreshadow of Major Modern Utopian Narrative Strategies," *Utopian Studies*, 14:2 (2003), pp. 41–67.

Davis, J. *Utopia and the Ideal Society: A Study of English Utopian Writing, 1516–1700*. New York: Cambridge University Press, 1983.

Davis, M. "Remaking the Nation through Brotherhood in the Utopian Fiction of William Dean Howells and Edward Bellamy," *Contemporary Justice Review*, 8:2 (June 2005), pp. 177–192.

Delveaux, M. " 'O Me! O Me! How I Love the Earth': William Morris's News from Nowhere and the Birth of Sustainable Society," *Contemporary Justice Review*, 8:2 (June 2005), pp. 131–146.

Drinkwater, J. *William Morris A Critical Study*. London: M. Secker, 1912.

Elshtain, J. B. "The Relationship between Political Language and Political Reality," *PS: Political Science and Politics*, 18:1 (Winter 1985), pp. 20–26.

Elton, G. R. *England under the Tudors*. New York: Routledge, 3rd edn, 1991.

Engerman, T. "Hytholoday's Utopia and More's England: An Interpretation of Thomas More's Utopia," *The Journal of Politics*, 44:1 (February 1982), pp. 131–149.

Ferrara, M. "A Religion of Solidarity: *Looking Backward* as a Rational Utopia," *Renascence*, 59:2 (2007), pp. 83–92.

Forbes, A. "The Literary Quest for Utopia, 1880–1900," *Social Forces*, 6:2 (December 1927), pp. 179–189.

Frye, N. *Anatomy of Criticism: Four Essays*. New York: Atheneum, 1966.

Fukuyama, F. *The Origins of Political Order: From Prehuman Times to the French Revolution*. New York: Farrar, Straus and Giroux, 2012.

Gleason, A. " 'Totalitarianism' in 1984," *Russian Review*, 43:2 (April 1984), pp. 145–159.

Gleason, A., J. Goldsmith, and M. Nussbaum, eds. *On Nineteen Eighty-Four: Orwell and Our Future*. New York: Princeton University Press, 2005.

Gottleib, E. "The Demonic World of Oceania: The Mystical Adulation of the 'Sacred' Leader," in *George Orwell's 1984* (edited and introduced by Harold Bloom), Bloom's Modern Critical Interpretations, updated edn, Infobase Publishing, 2007, pp. 51–70.

Hexter, J. *More's "Utopia": The Biography of an Idea*. Princeton, NJ: Princeton University Press, 1952; reprinted, New York: Harper Torchbooks, 1965.

Hill, C. *The World Turned upside Down: Radical Ideas During the English Revolution.* London: Penguin, 1984.

Hirschmann, A. *The Rhetoric of Reaction: Perversity, Futility, Jeopardy.* Cambridge, MA: The Belknap Press of Harvard University Press, 1991.

Hoisington, S. and L. Imbery. "Zamjatin's Modernist Palette: Colors and Their Function in *We,*" *The Slavic and East European Journal,* 36:2 (Summer 1992), pp. 159–171.

Holzman, M. "Anarchism and Utopia: William Morris's News from Nowhere," *ELH,* 51:3 (Autumn 1984), pp. 589–603.

Hutchings, W. "Structure and Design in a Soviet Dystopia: HG Wells, Constructivism, and Yevgeny Zamyatin's *We,*" *Journal of Modern Literature,* 9:1 (1981), pp. 81–102.

Kateb, G. "The Road to 1984," *Political Science Quarterly,* 81:4 (December 1966), pp. 564–580.

—. *Utopia and Its Enemies.* New York: Schocken, 1972.

Kern, G., ed. *Zamyatin's We. A Collection of Critical Essays.* Ann Arbor, MI: Ardis, 1988.

Kinna, R. "William Morris: Art, Work, and Leisure," *Journal of the History of Ideas,* 61:3 (July 2000), pp. 493–512.

Kumar, K. *Utopia and Anti-utopia in Modern Times.* Oxford and New York: Blackwell, 1987 .

Lee, J. "Rallying around the Flag: Foreign Policy Events and Presidential Popularity," *Presidential Studies Quarterly,* 7:4 (1977), pp. 252–256.

Leslie, M. *Renaissance Utopias and the Problem of History.* Ithaca, NY: Cornell University Press, 1998.

Levi, A. "Edward Bellamy: Utopian," *Ethics,* 55:2 (January 1945), pp. 131–144.

Levitas, R. *The Concept of Utopia.* Oxford and New York: Peter Lang, 2010.

Lewis, R. "*News from Nowhere:* Arcadia or Utopia?" *The Journal of the William Morris Society,* VII:2, 1987, pp. 15–25.

Lipow, A. *Authoritarian Socialism in America: Edward Bellamy and the Nationalist Movement.* Berkeley: University of California Press, 1982.

Lloyd, T. "The Politics of William Morris's 'News from Nowhere'," *Albion: A Quarterly Journal Concerned with British Studies,* 9:3 (Autumn 1977), pp. 273–287.

Logan, G., *The Meaning of More's "Utopia."* Princeton, NJ: Princeton University Press, 1983.

Logan, G., ed., *The Cambridge Companion to Thomas More.* Cambridge: Cambridge University Press, 2011.

Mahlberg, G. "Authors Losing Control: The European Transformations of Henry Neville's *The Isle of Pines* (1668)," *Book History,* 15 (2012), pp. 1–25.

—. "The Critical Reception of the *Isle of Pines,*" *Utopian Studies,* 17:1 (2006), pp. 133–142.

—. *Henry Neville and English Republican Culture in the Seventeenth Century: Dreaming of Another Game.* Manchester and New York: Manchester University Press, 2009.

—. "Historical and Political Contexts of the *Isle of Pines*," *Utopian Studies*, 17:1 (2006), pp. 111–129.

—. "An Island with Potential: Henry Neville's *The Isle of Pines* (1668)," in J. C. Davis and Miguel A. Ramiro (eds), *Utopian Moments: Reading Utopian Texts* London: Bloomsbury Academic, 2012, pp. 60–66

—. "The Publishing History of the *Isle of Pines*," *Utopian Studies*, 17:1 (2006), pp. 93–98.

Mann, N. "Eros and Community in the Fiction of William Morris," *Nineteenth-Century Fiction*, 34:3 (December 1979), pp. 302–325.

Manuel, F. E. and F. P. Manuel. *Utopian Thought in the Western World*. New York: Belknap Press, 1979.

McCarthy, F. *William Morris: A Life for Our Time*. London: Faber and Faber, 1994.

Meier, P. *William Morris: The Marxist Dreamer*. Sussex, England: Harvester Press, 1978.

Meyers, J. *Orwell: Wintry Conscience of a Generation*. New York: W.W. Norton, 2001.

Morgan, A. *Nowhere Was Somewhere: How History Makes Utopias and How Utopias Make History*. Chapel Hill: University of North Carolina Press, 1946.

Morton, L. *The English Utopia*. London: Lawrence and Wishart, 1952.

Mumford, L. *The Story of Utopias*. New York: Viking Press, 1962.

Nakano, Y. "On the History of the Novel *We*, 1937–1952: Zamiatin's *We* and the Chekhov Publishing House," *Canadian-American Slavic Studies*, 45:3–4 (2011) pp. 441–446.

Nelson, E. "Utopia through Italian Eyes: Thomas More and the Critics of Civic Humanism," *Renaissance Quarterly*, 59:4 (Winter 2006), pp. 1029–1057.

Nendza, J. "Political Idealism in More's Utopia," *The Review of Politics*, 46 (1984), pp. 428–451.

Nordstrom, J. "*Looking Backward's* Utopian Sequels: 'Fictional Dialogues' in Gilded-Age America," *Utopian Studies*, 18:2 (2007), pp. 193–221.

Olander, J., E. Rabkin, and M.Greenberg. *No Place Else: Explorations in Utopian and Dystopian Fiction*. Carbondale, IL: Southern Illinois University Press, 1983.

Patai, D., ed. *Looking Backward, 1988—1888: Essays on Edward Bellamy*. Amherst: University of Massachusetts Press, 1988.

Prettyman, G. "Gilded Age Utopias of Incorporation," *Utopia Studies*, 12:1 (2001), pp. 19–40.

Randall, N. "Introduction," *We*. New York: The Modern Library Classics, 2006.

Richards, T. "Archive and Utopia," *Representations*, 37, Special Issue: *Imperial Fantasies and Postcolonial Histories* (Winter 1992), pp. 104–135.

Roback, J. "The Economic Thought of George Orwell," *The American Economic Review*, 75:2, Papers and Proceedings of the Ninety-seventh Annual Meeting of the American Economic Association (May 1985), pp. 127–132.

Roddin, J., ed. *The Cambridge Companion to George Orwell*. New York: Cambridge University Press, 2007.

Sargent, L. "Is There Only One Utopian Tradition?" *Journal of the History of Ideas*, 43:4 (October–December 1982), pp. 681–689.

—. "A Note on the Other Side of Human Nature in the Utopian Novel," *Political Theory*, 3:1 (February 1975), pp. 88–97.

Scheckter, J. *The Isle of Pines, 1668: Henry Neville's Uncertain Utopia.* Farnham, Surrey, England and Burlington, VT: Ashgate, 2011.

Schiffman, J. "Edward Bellamy's Altruistic Man," *American Quarterly*, 6:3 (Autumn 1954), pp. 195–209.

Shklar, J. "*Nineteen Eighty-Four*: Should Political Theory Care?" *Political Theory*, 13:1 (February 1985), pp. 5–18.

Sibley, M. "Apology for Utopia: II: Utopia and Politics," *The Journal of Politics*, 2:2 (May 1940), pp. 165–188.

—. "Utopian Thought and Technology," *American Journal of Political Science*, 17:2 (May 1973), pp. 255–281.

Simms, V. "A Reconsideration of Orwell's 1984: The Moral Implications of Despair," *Ethics*, 84:4 (July 1974), pp. 292–306.

Skinner, Q. "Sir Thomas More's *Utopia* and the Language of Renaissance Humanism," in A. Pagden (ed.), *The Languages of Political Theory in Early Modern Europe.* New York: Cambridge University Press, 1990, pp. 123–158.

—. "Thomas More's Utopia and the Virtue of True Nobility," in Skinner, *Visions of Politics, Volume 2, Renaissance Virtues.* New York: Cambridge University Press, 2002.

Slusser, G. "Descartes Meets Edgar Rice Burroughs: Beating the Rationalist Equations in Zamiatin's *We*," *Canadian-American Slavic Studies*, 45:3–4 (2011), pp. 307–328.

Stefani, S. "The Unified State and the Unified Mind: Social and Moral Utopia in Zamiatin's *We* and Plato's *Republic*," *Canadian-American Slavic Studies*, 45:3–4 (2011), pp. 263–288.

Stillman, P. "Monarchy, Disorder, and Politics in *The Isle of Pines*," *Utopian Studies*,17:1 (2006), pp. 147–175.

Surtz, E. "Epicurus in Utopia," *ELH*, 16:2 (June 1949), pp. 89–103.

Taylor, T. *Orwell: The Life.* New York: Holt, 2004.

Thomas, J. *Alternative America: Henry George, Edward Bellamy, Henry Demarest Lloyd and the Adversary Tradition.* Cambridge, MA: Harvard University Press, 1983.

Thompson, E. P. *William Morris: Romantic to Revolutionary.* New York: Pantheon, 1977.

Towers, T. "The Insomnia of Julian West," *American Literature*, 47:1 (March 1975), pp. 52–63.

Trevor-Roper, H. "The Intellectual World of Sir Thomas More," *The American Scholar*, 48:1 (Winter 1979), pp. 19–32.

Vaninskaya, A. "Janus-Faced Fictions: Socialism as Utopia and Dystopia in William Morris and George Orwell," *Utopian Studies*, 14:2 (2003), pp. 83–98.

Waithe, M. "The Laws of Hospitality: Liberty, Generosity, and the Limits of Dissent in William Morris's *The Tables Turned* and *News from Nowhere,*" *The Yearbook of English Studies*, 36:2 (2006), pp. 212–229.

Watkinson, R. "The Obstinate Refusers: Work in *News from Nowhere,*" in S. Coleman and P. O'Sullivan, eds., *William Morris & News from Nowhere: A Vision for our Time*. Bideford, Devon: Green Books, 1990, pp. 91–120.

Weber, H. "Charles II, George Pines, and Mr. Dorimant: The Politics of Sexual Power in Restoration England," *Criticism*, 32:2 (Spring 1990), pp. 193–219.

West, W. J. *The Larger Evils. Nineteen Eighty-four: The Truth behind the Satire*. Edinburgh: Canongate Press, 1992.

Wiseman, S. J. "Pamphlet Plays in the Civil War News Market: Genre, Politics, and Context," *Prose Studies*, 21:2 (1998), pp. 66–83.

Index

CPSIA information can be obtained
at www.ICGtesting.com
Printed in the USA
LVHW080604130819
627465LV00008B/58/P